"In those times of darkness and despair, there were good people too. Their tale must also be remembered."

— Elie Wiesel

I wish to thank Elie Wiesel, University Professor and Andrew Mellon Professor in the Humanities, for his interest in the manuscript; and for graciously sending the above response regarding the yet unknown genocide of the Ukrainian people.

Dedication

This book is dedicated to the memory of my parents, Vasily and Nionila Sakevych, with the hope that there will be some increased awareness that those two good and honest, simple and unknown Ukranians were real people who lived and thrived and contributed until their world was crushed by totalitarian forces; and to the memory of their three children, Natalia, Gabriel, and Grisha, whose lives were taken by those same forces.

One Woman
Five Lives
Five Countries

By
Eugenia Sakevych Dallas

To Phyllis :
It is a pleasure to meet you.
With Best to you always
Eugenia Dallas
10—14—04

One Woman: Five Lives; Five Countries
© 1998 Eugenia Dallas

Second Printing August 2001

International Standard Book Number: 0-88100-107-4

Library of Congress Card Catalog Number: 98-67925

Cover painting by:
K.O. Trutovsky "Girl with Sheaves"

Contents

COUNTRY FIVE: Scotland and Life as a Pampered Wife

BACK TO COUNTRY FOUR: The United States of America and Life at Home

Preface

For most of my life, much of my life I did not want to remember. Certainly, I had no thought or desire to write about it.

In the late 1980s, however, as events in the Soviet Union caught the world's attention, I began remembering times, places, and events.

The Russian Revolution, a creator of World Communism, led to unknown Genocide 1932-1933, in Ukraine, a story that was never fully told.

1918 Ukraine becomes a Democratic Sovereign Independent Republic until 1921.

Rural Ukraine was a good place to live in the mid-1920s.

About ten million Ukrainians died in 1932-1933, starved in an act of genocide ordered by Joseph Stalin to break the back of the stubbornly patriotic Ukrainians.

Three million were sent to Siberia; few returned. Six to seven million Ukrainians were killed in World War II.

Other millions died. Those who lived were forever scarred. (Please see Ukraine: Notes on a Nation at the back of this book for a more detailed history, and suggestions for further reading.)

Events in my life were tied to those realities.

As I was remembering, I was also thinking. The world is little aware of those losses-or even that Ukraine is a nation. (Perhaps we Ukrainians have been too accepting, too adaptable, to make our suffering known.) I began wanting to put faces on some of that time, to provide a picture of my parents and of my sister and two brothers whose lives were ended, and of my life that was driven into lives in other countries.

I knew I needed to write about those early years, but, always, I had wanted a beautiful life. I wanted to forget misery. For decades, I tried to bury most memories of my first nineteen years. When my personal despair or despair for my people—so mixed I couldn't separate the two—made me feel like an invalid, I simply pushed the memories deeper and moved on.

In 1990, when I started writing, I found the process painful. Some parts eventually had to be dragged out of me. (An hour of answering questions made my head ache; two hours exhausted me.) I was, however, compelled to write the book, and, I must add that along with the great and continuing pain of remembering came some relief, some acceptance.

The strongest impressions and visualizations of the past came easily. More information came with a little coaxing. Establishing one event brought recall of other events. My 1966 visit with two older brothers I had not seen for thirty years had confirmed, corrected, and added to my memory. Reading various historical works clarified impressions—as did talking with others who had similar experiences. Repeated questions about what I had written prompted many "Oh, yes, of course" remembrances.

Perhaps it was because of attention given to genocide attempted in other countries that I was able to write some parts. Perhaps it was because of attention given in the 1990s to sexual abuse that I was able to write other parts.

As I was writing, there were times when the parts of my life seemed connected; at other times, my life seemed disjointed. Some stranger appeared and sent me or took me to the next phase of my life as if I had no plan, no direction—even though I thought I was acting on some understanding of my situation.

All of the parts did, however, proceed from the same early events. One set of circumstances put me in position for the next. Thus, I could not stop my narrative when I was sent out of Ukraine, or when the war ended, or when I found a career or when I was relocated to the United States. I had to continue the sequence—to show that life does go on, that one does, indeed, travel some course and that, with freedom, a good life is possible.

It is appropriate at this time for me to acknowledge and thank editor L. P. Boston for his skill and patience in putting my life story into clear sequence for publication. For this I am most appreciative.

I have been encouraged by some expressions of interest in my story. An early version was published in Ukraine. Articles appeared in Ukrainian newspapers. In California, I was interviewed for a possible film script and a television program. Friends naturally were interested. Now, I hope that readers who find their way to the book will also find some interest in these pages.

Ukrainian Holocaust (1932 – 1933)

Peaceful, hard working, happy, gregarious people,
With their golden fields of wheat
Blue skies, Ukraine my country,
Breadbasket of Europe.

Suddenly black clouds of terror
From the neighbor to the North.
Darkness blew over the green hills
The peaceful golden steps of Ukraine.

Bullets riddle my country, They took my freedom, my land
And brutally turned us into a colony

Run by hostile ruthless outsiders

By Force they made us give them
All our food to the last morsel.
In return they gave us prisons in Siberia
And Genocide in Ukraine.

Countless Numbers of Children
With protruding frightened eyes, outstretched little hands
Pleading for food, crying.
Some of us survived - **Orphans Forever**

The free world was silent!

Written by Eugenia Dallas for Nov. 1998 Commemoration of Ukrainian Genocide.

Our Hopelessness, Bewilderment,
Gave way to panic.
We sunk deep into resignation,
Mental apathy, stupor, and despair.

The Communist Terror, their sadism
Made us pay dearly with our lives.
Extermination by slow starvation
Was done quietly, so that no one in the world
Would hear or know about it.

We Must Pledge to Preserve,
Memories of Ukrainian Genocide
To ensure that the world,
Does not repeat the past.

Today and Always - we must not forget the pain
That was inflicted upon Ukraine.
Today and Always, we must remember our
Obligations and responsibilities
Toward our loved ones, who perished so unjustly?
Today and Always, Their memories must be kept alive forever.

The Russian Revolution, a creator of World Communism, led to unknown Genocide 1932-1933 in Ukraine, a story that was never fully told.

Country One: Ukraine and Life With My Parents

Chapter One
Kamjana Balka and Pervomaysk 1925(?)–1931

Officially, I do not exist. I was born; it was the duty of the village priest to record births. He did not record mine. In the Ukrainian tradition of finding joy in events, my parents made a grand celebration of my birth because I was a girl, and in my family and in the village there weren't as many girls as boys. Perhaps the priest celebrated a little too much and forgot his duty.

My parents, the ones who would have known my birth date, were lost to me when I was five or six years old. Any family record that might have existed was lost when we were forced out of our house without any possessions. When I was nine or ten years old, I was in the care of two of my brothers. They agreed that I was born in late summer but disagreed on the year, one thinking I was born in 1925 and the other thinking 1926. They settled on 1925, then chose 24 August as day and month.

The place of my birth was certain: Kamjana Balka, a small village north of Odessa in the wheat plains of southern Ukraine.[1]

It is definite I was christened Eugenia, the youngest of six children born to Vasily and Nionila Sakevych. The oldest of the children was a son named Jasha. The second child was a daughter named Natalia. The third, fourth, and fifth were boys named Gabriel, Grisha, and Mykola. Jasha was about twenty years older than I, and the others were born two or three years apart. Mykola was probably ten years old when I

1

was born.

Our father grew up in that same village. His father was born in the 1840s and lived in a village that was the property of a count. Like most villagers in those days, grandfather was in servitude to the count. (Such servitude—slavery—was abolished in 1861. My brother Mykola called our grandfather a serf.)

As a young man, our grandfather drove a wagon, transporting water to the fields. As he drove, grandfather often fell asleep, probably because he was visiting a girl the night before, but it didn't matter because the horse knew where to go. It did, however, matter to the count, who hit grandfather with a whip whenever he caught him asleep. One day my grandfather was hurt and angered enough that he grabbed the whip and hit the count. In those days instead of sending people to prison, the nobility sent them to the army for harsh duty, and my grandfather was sentenced to twenty-five years of service. The army, however, was good for grandfather, and when he returned, he was a well-to-do man. He married a young, beautiful widow with two children, and together they had three more children, one of whom was my father.

My mother and father, like their parents before them, were farmers. The land was all they knew. The land was in their blood. They owned their land; they would not be in servitude as my grandfather was. It was, indeed, their pride and joy that they were self-sufficient landowners. The Ukrainian word to describe them has been translated as "peasant," but they were not peasants in the Western sense of the word. They were farmers. My father had much land and hired workers, which, in that area, made him wealthy. By any national standard, we weren't wealthy landowners.

Life in my little part of rural Ukraine—at least, through the eyes of a child—still had some certainty and tranquillity in the 1920s (even though the Russian Revolutions of 1917 and 1918 and the Bolshevik's seizing of power in Ukraine in 1922 produced great upheaval then and later). Through my child's eyes and in memory, my parents and their farm were perfect. I cannot find a way to avoid idyllic descriptions.

My father was a handsome, stocky man with classic features. Physically, he looked like the last czar of the Russian Empire and wore his beard short and neat like the czar's, which was the style in those days. Father was kind, mild, and gentle, but also strong. He was calm, controlled in his actions, and always ready to help anyone in need. My father loved to talk. He discussed all matters with his sons, gently teaching them from his life's experiences. Neighbors often wanted to talk to him; they wanted to know what he knew, to know what he thought. Almost always there was laughter sprinkled through his conversations. (I think I inherited some of his characteristics.)

My mother was a more emotional person but at the same time a healthy minded person. She was perfectly organized and definitely in charge of her home and her children. She knew how to do all jobs and never stopped working. She was always cleaning, sewing, cooking, milking cows, working in garden and orchards (and fields when necessary), and preparing food for storage. Still, she made time for me. I can visualize my mother: ash blonde hair, green eyes, slim and tall—long skirts, the local fashion at that time, making her look taller. (I inherited some of her physical characteristics and traits.)

I had a child's absolute and total trust in my father, and a child's complete and wonderfully warm and satisfying attachment to my mother.

Mother, I'm sure, was especially attached to me. First, I was a girl. She already had four boys but only one girl. Her sisters and brothers had almost all boys in their families. Second, it had been a long time since she had a baby in the house. I was also spoiled by my four big brothers and big sister. I had sweets from everyone. My brothers tossed me into the air as if I were a ball and then caught me. One brother made me climb trees and then jump into his arms. He was sure I would become an acrobat.

I have clear memories of my earliest years, but they lack order. I recall scenes and events in isolation, each one like a painting—a faded painting. I cannot connect events with each other or with whatever else occurred during that time. Or I remember composites: all harvests become *the* harvest; all picnics by the river become *the* picnic.

I can still see my childhood home. My father built our house from the ground up. It was a big house, made of stone with a tin roof, a sign of wealth in those days. There were separate rooms for cooking and sleeping—not just one room the way many houses were. My mother had her idea of what a European house should be, and she wanted large windows. Large windows weren't practical because of the severe winters, but my mother prevailed. To stay warm, we children slept side by side in a big wooden bed. No one in that area at that time had indoor plumbing or electricity. Kerosene lamps gave us light.

In the kitchen was a large tiled oven, which provided heat for the house. There, my mother baked big loaves of bread and did all the other cooking for her large family. She made it my job to taste-test her work. I doubt I actually rendered judgments that changed preparation of food, but I felt important. Mother talked to me all day long and treated me like a little grown-up. She included me in her jobs and did things just for me. In all my later years, what I missed most was the feeling I had when my mother and I shared private and special times. When I thought I was actually helping her cook, it was a time of deep contentment. When she cut and sewed dresses for my dolls, it was a time of excitement and delight.

There were large barns and a grain silo behind the house, and vegetable gardens and fruit orchards on the sides.

There were places for all kinds of domestic animals and for storing all kinds of provisions. We had horses, ponies, cows, pigs, goats, chickens, ducks, geese, rabbits. We had wheat, potatoes, cabbage, beets, greens of different kinds, carrots, onions, beans, apples, pears, cherries, plums. It is hard to think of any domestic animal or kind of food we didn't have. Like our neighbors, we had a well from which we drew good water, and, of course, there was an outdoor toilet.

My mother dried some fruit and made preserves from others. For storing perishable food, we had a cooling room dug deeply into the earthen floor of one of the barns close to the house. Farm families, of course, produced every item they ate. Enough meat and vegetables and fruit had to be prepared for harsh winters when the snow was often five to seven feet deep. My parents, who persistently did what they knew best how to do, always had plenty of everything.

Behind the house—on at least one occasion—was a pile of straw, and when someone removed it, hundreds of gray mice ran out, not knowing which way to escape. There were families of big and small mice. I loved the babies.

Our back yard went all the way to a river sprinkled with huge stones. Our village, Kamjana Balka, took its name from those rocks. I remember going down to the river for picnics and for night fishing. And I remember my mother's cooking the fresh catch.

My father's fields were outside the village—a long walk or short wagon ride from the house. When my mother worked in the fields with my father, they took me with them. To keep me safe, they put me on a haystack or in a wagon full of hay. At threshing time, three horses pulled a huge roller around and around in a circle, separating grains of wheat from the stalks. One day, I left my safe place and started to run to my father. My path was in the path of the horses, and I would likely have been killed had not my father seen me in time. His quick movement and my realization of the danger I was in

5

scared me so much that a picture of the scene is still vividly in my mind.

Another time, I cried out so loudly that all adults raced toward me, assuming I was in great danger. Someone rescued me from a grasshopper which, I insisted, bit my finger. The adults may have thought a grasshopper posed no danger, but in my sight that creature was enormous and frighteningly ugly.

As a toddler, I wanted to help. I followed hired girls who were perhaps ten or twelve years old. (I was always around older children and adults.) I followed the girls to a pasture of geese, and they gave me a little stick like the bigger ones they carried. I felt proud I was part of the hard-working family.

Our house was always bustling with people, especially during harvest time. Families took turns helping each other gather their crops. Cooperation and mutual help were simply a way of life. When it was our turn to harvest, my mother cooked meat and kasha and made great kettles of borscht to feed everyone. Even though harvesting is backbreaking work, there were singing and laughing in the fields. In the evenings people were too tired to dance, but they never stopped singing. All that activity was exciting for me. My father would put me to bed and tell me, "Genia, we have to rest so we can build up fat and strength for winter." Satisfied with his words, I always went to sleep quite obediently.

There was a celebration after the harvest. Sometimes there was a dance for young people—my sister and brothers and others their age. After my oldest brothers left home, there were gatherings of their friends when any of them came home for a visit. Everyone in the village seemed at times to be in our house. We Ukrainians could turn any occasion into a social gathering for eating, drinking, laughing, talking, singing, dancing.

Winter was a favorite time of the year for social gatherings and for other reasons, too. Happily enduring deep snow and severe cold was part of our tradition. We liked winter. With no planting or harvesting, outside work was limited to maintaining buildings and equipment and caring for the animals, which didn't take all day. We had time to rest, to play, to read, to be with family and friends. Villagers who wanted to rest or read or sew or build or repair or clean special things could have the time they wanted. Those who wanted to socialize could easily join others of the same mind.

Houses were not far apart, and going to neighbors' houses, which was frequent year around, was easy. My older brothers went sledding around the village with their girlfriends. Of course, I wanted to go with them, but teenagers and young adults couldn't be bothered with a child. They did take me along sometimes when they went Christmas caroling from house to house. My brothers had excellent voices, especially Gabriel. Winter was wonderful.

There were special programs at church at Christmas time. I liked the music very much. The music at Easter was also wonderful. At Easter, it was customary to decorate the whole house with fresh greenery, and mother made Easter eggs and baskets of food which we took to church for blessing. We didn't go to church only for special occasions. Religion and the church were important traditions in the lives of Ukrainian farmers, and I can well remember mother's getting me ready to go to church.

Weddings at the church were major events in our village, and when my sister Natalia was married, our family made the occasion a big celebration. I had a part in the wedding. When the priest asked Natalia and her husband to walk around the altar, I went with them. The best man held golden crowns above the heads of the bride and groom as we walked. I have never forgotten those golden crowns with their sparkling gemstones. There was a church full of people looming above me with the priest at the center. I have some memory I did something else, maybe with flowers. The church was filled with flowers. There was singing and playing of music. Music continued after the wedding, and there was much talking. Despite hazy details, the impression remains bright. Everything was beautiful.

Special occasions and ordinary days alike provided joyful moments and much laughter. We were simple, down-to-earth, realistic people who worked hard and were happy. That is the way I would describe our life. That is the background for the fragments of childhood I recall.

One of my earliest and clearest memories is of being sick when I was no more than two years old. I was lying on a high wooden bed next to the oven that heated the whole house. I can remember opening my eyes as if I was coming out of a coma. I saw a room full of people, some sitting quietly as in prayer, some talking softly. I think every woman in the village was there in a circle around my bed. My mother was standing over me, looking ten feet tall and preoccupied while applying cold towels to my sweating body. I must have gone in and out of consciousness many times for the impression to be so strong. How long it took me to recover I do not know, but looking back and trying to put all pieces of information together, I have become sure it was rheumatic fever, which left me with a heart murmur.

One of my most enduring memories—one that still causes my eyes to mist—is of being in a sleigh. My father held the reins, and my mother cuddled me in her big coat and rug of furs. I don't know where we were going, but it was early morning. Pink reflections of the horizon promised a frosty day. The snow sparkled like tiny diamonds. Strong white horses struggled with their footing on the slippery, icy carpet, and the sleigh slid smoothly—so smoothly I went to sleep. For some reason, the sleigh stopped, and I peeked out to look at the sparkling snow and the powerful horses. After a minute or two, the sleigh started and went in a different direction. I wondered, "How is it that parents know which way to go?"

The frosty air became colder as we moved, and I retreated to the warmth of mother's arms and layers of furs. I was happy. I had comfort and security. I was surrounded by my parents' steady love.

To match that winter memory, I remember the middle of a warm day when I slipped out or was let out to run around the house. Pleasant rain was falling. Washed and soaked by the warm drizzle, my satisfied body retreated to the open door of the house. My mother was watching over me—as always.

I remember another kind of rain. One of my brothers, Gabriel, a teenager and a likable, kind, and good person, and I were walking somewhere in my parents' fields. Suddenly, the sky darkened, and out of nowhere came a stormy rain that lasted at least twenty or thirty minutes. It was as if giant buckets of water were being poured from above to water the plants. As the rain began to fall, thunder rolled across the sky. My brother started to run, his big hand wrapped tightly around my little hand. I was almost flying, my legs hardly touching the ground. Gabriel was tall and long-legged, and with his strong, long steps we must have looked like jumping gazelles.

I don't know why I remember awakening so often. Perhaps it was simply that I took many naps. Perhaps it was that I awoke to good things. One early morning I awoke in the trolley wagon and saw my brother Gabriel and my father walking behind the wagon. We were in the familiar fields of Kamjana Balka. Everything was calm and tranquil. The horses were walking slowly. The two men were as usual absorbed in their conversation. Mischievous as I was, I took the reins in my hands and made the horses run. My father and brother, thinking I was asleep, were sharply surprised and started to run to catch the horses. I thought the whole scene was fun. I laughed and was happy. At first, father was not happy. Then he laughed, too. He and Gabriel were relieved I was not hurt and handled the horses well.

I can visualize my father on that day. I can see him

laughing. I can see his beard and mustache. And I remember sometimes he got soup on his mustache, which made me laugh and say, "Your mouth is crooked," or, "Your mustache is leaking."

One little misadventure did not produce any laughter. I was about four years old, and I had a great desire to visit my sister. I knew well enough how to get to the neighboring village where Natalia and her husband lived, but I wanted someone with me, so I persuaded two girls of about six or eight years of age to walk with me. Somehow, I used my imagination to get others to do what I wanted to do. I invented fanciful stories that caught the attention of other children, stories of going places I had never seen even in pictures, stories of doing impossible things such as flying, stories of wonderful events that would soon occur. On that day, the girls were willing to go, and we started walking. They were much taller than I, and I began having trouble keeping their pace. Of course, I couldn't quit; I had to continue.

Unhappily, I failed to tell my mother about going, and she was frantically searching for me. There were no telephones or cars to make her search easier. When she finally found me, she scolded, "Don't do that anymore. You're too smart for your age." Mother was angry but elated and relieved to find me, and I was relieved I did not have to keep pace with the larger girls any longer. I might have been satisfied with myself for being able to get older girls to do my bidding, but I became ashamed and upset that I caused my mother such concern. Later, she was gentler as she explained to me the reasons that she had to know where I was at all times, and I could feel that our special relation was restored. My misery was relieved. But I never forgot that lesson. The strength of mother's admonishment was permanently recorded in my brain.

That experience didn't make me feel any less loved or any less safe and comfortable. We were still a happy family. But some short time later things began to change. Slowly, I became aware that our house was not as happy, not as comforting as it had been. Nor was the village as happy.

Our family also got smaller. Natalia was married and living in the other village. Gabriel left, probably in the summer of 1928, to enroll in a military academy. A year later, Grisha went to Kiev to study art. Soon after that, Jasha was either recruited or conscripted to go to the Urals to work in a mine. Only Mykola and I were left at home.

Our house was still a place of activity. Many people—relatives and friends—appeared to talk with my father. Villagers seemed to expect him to have answers, to tell them whether rumors were true. Over and over, someone said, "The Bolsheviks are coming. We will have troubles. We will lose our land."

Of course, I did not understand what was being said. The subject was not familiar, and the words were unknown. A child can, however, sense fear and desperation. There was a big meeting at my aunt's house one time, and there was none of the laughter always heard when our people got together. If I understood nothing until that day, that grim lack of laughter made me understand that my parents—and other families—were troubled.

In the next few years, I gained some understanding of *Bolshevik* and *collectivization*, of *kulak* and *enemy of the people*. The Bolsheviks, the Communists, were coming down from the north to make collectivized farming the new order; members of the Party were there to educate us, the ignorant *kulaks*. To us, *kulak* was a Russian word that labeled poor farmers as wealthy landowners.

Collectivization, we were told, was the system that would make individual farms part of big regional farms, supposedly owned—somehow—by all the people. The big farms would be far more productive and would make life better for everyone. Anybody who selfishly wanted to own his own land, a *kulak*, was, therefore, an enemy of the people.

Ukrainian farmers, however, had that strong sense of owning and working their own land, of being strictly independent, of being in no way or manner dependent on some member of the nobility or other landowner. They were the people whose ancestors had gained their freedom from the serfdom of the past; they were *the people*. To the farmers, it was the revolution that secured their land, and the Bolsheviks, of all people, should want farmers to keep the land. To the Bolsheviks, however, such people and such ideas had to be crushed if their idea of communal order was to succeed.

The more villagers talked about all those things, the more I sensed in my child's way that the certainty and tranquillity which shored and shaped my first few years were disappearing. Without understanding what was happening, I had the feeling that all adults would disappear and children would be left all alone.

Then, the Communists did arrive. They had meetings and more meetings that every farmer had to attend, and they told the villagers over and over that they would be better off in a collective and asked farmers to sign papers putting their farms into a collective. At first, Party leaders said that the villagers had time to think about signing. The farmers delayed, trying to find ways to hold onto their property. They told themselves, "We're hard-working people. We didn't do anything wrong. Surely the commisars will come to their senses. All of this will stop." But, of course, it didn't stop. More and more commisars arrived, and different groups of commisars went to all houses again and again. All the commisars had guns, and the militia had more and bigger guns. One of the Communist Party functionaries who was sent from the city kept a big revolver stuck in his belt so everyone could see it and walked around as if it were his job to shoot anyone who didn't do what he said to do.

My father would not buckle under, and he was one of the first arrested, to be accused of being an enemy of the people, a bourgeois land owner. In the winter of 1929-1930, he was arrested and taken away from us in the middle of the night. The next morning it was obvious something was wrong. My mother had sadness on her face I had never seen. She was still strong and gave me comfort. But my father was gone. The man who had my absolute trust, who was always the measure of strength, was no longer there.

The commisars usually made arrests at night so others wouldn't see their neighbors being taken away. And they arrested the strongest farmers first. Villagers woke up and learned that the farmers they looked up to were gone. With their leaders gone, they found it harder to resist. Some signed over their farms to the State. Others refused and were also arrested. Some were arrested for crossing the Party functionaries, who were always irritated by the independence of farmers. To achieve their goal of destroying private enterprise in Ukraine, the commisars used any method available, and their methods were often brutal.

The Party people who appeared in Kamjana Balka were from distant places. They didn't know farmers or farming. Party members from Russia, Georgia, Armenia, or Belarus were sent to Ukraine; Ukrainians were sent to those countries. Russians were sent everywhere. (That method was also applied to youth workers from every part of the former Russian Empire; they were organized, mobilized, and sent to countries far from their own.) That system meant great numbers of people didn't know what was happening in their home countries, and also that the Bolshevik functionaries and Party militia had no attachment to the people they policed.

People were frustrated and angry because what the Party people were doing made no sense. The people were also afraid and desperate because they were being badly treated and losing what they had worked for. But there was nothing they could do. A few farmers left without knowing where they would go or what they would do; they simply wanted to get away. Perhaps we were naive for staying; perhaps we should have gone west with the first signs of trouble. Some time after the forced collectivization started, the village became a prison: it was forbidden for the farmers to appear in any village but their own. They were unarmed, disorganized, and leaderless. They could be and would be crushed mercilessly. The happy, hard-working, friendly, self-sufficient gregarious people would find themselves starving, bewildered, and helpless.

The motto of the Communist Party was "Us Against Them." The commisars were masters of manipulation. They turned brother against brother, children against parents. Children were trained at school to spy; they were told to tell their teachers what was being said at home "for the good of your country." Neighbors who were formerly close were suddenly cut off from each other.

My father came back from prison after several months, maybe a year. That was not usual. Maybe he was being held locally in an attempt to break him so he would join the collective and be a lesson to others. When he returned, he was different, quiet. He didn't laugh, and he didn't work around the farm at all. In an unclear image, I see him as appearing ill. Today, I would say he was spiritually broken. He must not have been politically broken because in late 1930 or early 1931, he was once more arrested. I never saw him again.

During the next eight or ten years, I heard my brothers remark on many occasions it was a cruel twist of fate that our grandfather had struggled against being a serf to Russian landowners so his son could be free, so we could become a part of the people, and his son, our father, was to be called an enemy of the people and sent to a Siberian prison.

My mother remained strong for her children, but assaults on our family continued. We didn't know at the time father was in Siberia to do hard labor, and we had no information about Jasha except he was in the mines of the Urals.

Natalia's husband was going through the same kind of treatment my father experienced. Gabriel was at the military academy but was facing expulsion because his parents were farmers, "enemies of the people." Grisha, at the university in Kiev, saw trouble ahead. Sometime in 1930 or 1931—maybe before my father returned after being arrested, maybe after my father was arrested the second time—Grisha wanted to get my brother Mykola into an orphanage, which could be the only assurance Mykola would not starve. That my mother agreed was surely a sign of desperation. Mykola would have been a teenager by then, and Grisha got him to Kiev and taught him the way to present himself to be taken as an orphan.

Not long after my father was sent away, the commisars appeared again in numbers: militia and others. Apparently, they wanted our house for their use. They chased us out with rifles and took every single thing we owned. I stood out front and watched them take our last grain of food. All of our animals were led away by horse and wagon. My mother argued with the militiamen. She begged them to leave food for her family, but they shouted her down, then ignored us completely. We got to keep one cow, at least for the time being. That was supposed to show the humane nature of the Party.

I felt sorry for the animals, especially the small ones, but men with rifles herded them all away except that lonely cow. It was terribly upsetting to see our animals leaving and being treated cruelly. Tears were starting, and I looked to my mother. She was controlling herself, so I did, too. If she had cried even one tear, I would have fallen apart.

My mother was left defenseless. She took our cow and me, and we fled—in the spring or summer of 1931. From Kamjana Balka, we moved about twenty kilometers to Pervomaysk. There we lived in a small brick house with a tin roof. I don't know whose house it was or how we got it. The militia had taken our money. On our arrival, all our neighbors knew who we were and where we came from. They might not have seen me because I was hiding in my mother's skirt.

We had not one seed of food when we arrived. Our main food came from our cow. My mother managed to get some items in the village, maybe bread or flour or vegetables, probably in exchange for milk. Some people shared what they had, at least for a while. Eventually, we started eating weeds and even tried to make soup from nettles.

It was strange not having the big family and being the only child with my mother. I can clearly see mother and me at different times and places. I repeatedly asked the same questions about my father: "Where is he? Why isn't he here? When is he coming? How will he find us?"

Mother kept giving me the same answers: "The authorities took him away. But he's done nothing wrong. As soon as the authorities realize that, he'll come back. And he knows we're here."

I also asked about my brothers, especially Gabriel and Grisha. They were the ones who gave attention to me.

My memories of Pervomaysk are mixed. In some ways, I was an ordinary child. I know I played (usually alone), I visited neighbors, and people were nice to me. Perhaps that was the normal adaptability or resilience of children. In other ways, I was a terrified child, fearful of everything and everybody. The unfamiliar place created an emotionally terrifying atmosphere.

I do remember that I cried several times in Pervomaysk. Once, we were at some building, and mother had to go to some other place. I cried, wanting to go with her. She said, "I cannot take you." She explained that she was trying to get some papers to my brother and that she had to walk too far for me to walk all the way. I could not comprehend that I couldn't walk with her and continued to cry desperately to go with her. She talked to me until I was calm. That may have been the last time I cried child's tears. I realized in some unstated way I couldn't be a child any longer.

16

Later, I would learn mother was trying to help Gabriel stay in the military academy. She wanted to get documents to him to prove that we were no longer farmers, that we no longer had any property, that we had nothing. I could understand wanting to help Gabriel. He was good to me, so I watched mother walk away.

After mother left, I started walking the other way. I saw someone stoning a dog. The dog had bitten an old woman, and her son and others were throwing rocks from a nearby roof. The dog was chained and could not run away. I felt sorry for the dog and wanted to unchain him, but the people were too threatening. Sadly, I walked myself home.

I remember wandering the streets of Pervomaysk. It was much bigger than our village. I went many places alone. That was part of the normal life in Ukraine at that time. We feared the militia, but there was none of the fear of the 1990s about children walking by themselves in the street. As small as I was, I stopped and talked to all kinds of people without any hesitation. And they liked me. I guess I still had a smile to give.

I remember our neighbor up the hill, a kind old lady. She made me feel welcome, and we were getting to be friends. One day, when I went to see her, I saw her son had just hanged himself. Other members of the family had all disappeared. There had been a father and brothers and sisters; then the last son— not yet twenty—had to take the place of all of them, and he couldn't do it.

He was hanging outside, and his mother, a tiny woman, was inside desperately crying. I went to her and stood there talking for a long, long time. I don't know what I could possibly have said. A child of five or six years? Talking to a woman who had just lost the last member of her family?

My mother got a letter from Gabriel, telling her he showed his superiors the documents she sent but the documents didn't help. The officers only saw Gabriel's father had owned a farm, which must make Gabriel also an enemy of the people and subject to expulsion—unless he renounced his heritage and denounced his family. Gabriel expected to be formally expelled from the academy whenever his case went through all the channels. He was then twenty-three years old with no certainty about what would happen to him. My mother cried as she read the letter. She wasn't one to cry very long, however. She still had to survive for herself and for me. I think I inherited that trait from her.

We were in Pervomaysk until some time in the fall of 1931, only a few months. There was actually a good harvest, but Party commissioners and functionaries took all the food from the farmers. Stalin's militiamen guarded grain silos and stuffed their faces while peasants began starving. And we were among them.

The *Kolchoz* (collective farms) were in charge of the harvest, but they were not doing a good job. After the workers left, wheat and potatoes could be found in the fields. The State showed no interest in the unharvested produce, which would only rot and soon be covered with frost and snow. My mother went to the fields and collected in her apron some of the leftover grain and potatoes, went home happy, and made some soup for us. She had found a way to feed us.

When mother went again to the fields, she took me with her. It was like being on our own farm again. I was happy. I was carefree. As long as I was near my mother, I had no problem. I ran, jumped, and dug out some abandoned potatoes or picked up wheat stalks, proudly contributing to our survival.

Our neighbors, a Communist family, apparently observed us scavenging in the fields, for the militia came in the middle of the night. Four or five militiamen surrounded our house and watched us. At dawn, rifles in their hands, they moved toward us. As soon as they started moving, my mother handed me a small bundle wrapped in a small rug, and said,

"Throw this in the bushes." One militiaman let me out of the house. He didn't even look at me. I went behind our house to the outhouse. Another militiaman followed me. I got scared but threw the package into some bushes and kept walking. I don't know what was in that bundle or what happened to it. I was not asked about it, and I don't remember that anyone else ever mentioned it. Perhaps there was a paper that showed my father's ownership of the land or papers about the family—maybe my birth date—or other information I would treasure today. Many times across the years I visualized watching something valuable disappear before my eyes—sinking in water or disappearing in flames.

With their rifles pointed in our faces, the commisars marched us out of the house and robbed us again. That's the way they operated, pushed people into a corner and terrorized them. Our cow, whatever rotten food we had, my mother's wedding ring, they took it all. We had nothing left.

Then they watched us for days. We stayed behind closed doors, not even allowed to fetch water. Finally, my mother was officially arrested for collecting the frozen stalks of grain. A fat commisar accused her proudly. "You were taking the people's food. Stealing from the State." She was taken away.

My sister Natalia was there at that time, and I remember her being with us in the house. I can't remember her being there when mother and I went to the fields or when we were prisoners of the militia. When she arrived, I don't know, but she was there. Her husband was not. Maybe he had been arrested.

It was morning when mother was arrested. She was officially charged with stealing from the State and sentenced to three years of hard labor in Baikal, Siberia. I can see her sitting on the porch of one of the village houses that was converted to militia headquarters. I can feel her looking at me. She didn't cry. She just stared, and I read her mind, read her eyes—such pain. She looked at me as though she would never see me again. She sensed it. I wanted to stay with her, but the militiaman said to Natalia, "You take her." Natalia led me away, and I never saw my mother again. I didn't cry; I was becoming accustomed to having what I loved taken away from me. In later years, I would cry. If Natalia hadn't taken me by the hand and pulled me away from our mother, I would've gone to prison, too.

Before being shipped off to the prisons of Central Asia, my mother was held in a local prison in the Odessa region of Ukraine. She managed to write to Natalia that she had no food. We didn't either, but my sister got hold of some beets and mailed them to her. Beets sent by mail. Who knows whether my mother ever received them. Mail was probably intercepted because she wrote again there was no food in that prison at all. We didn't know until later that local jails and prisons didn't feed prisoners, that what food they got was supplied by family or neighbors. Eventually, the NKVD (The Peoples' Commissariat of Internal Affairs) shipped my mother to Central Asia. She never came back. Every time I see beets, I remember my mother.[2]

When my mother was arrested and sent away, I was five or six years old. I had in my memory fragments and impressions and experiences of a secure and joyful life on our family farm. And I had in my memory painful scenes and experiences of insecurity and fear. The forces that produced the change were part of the painful memories. I still didn't know the meaning of "enemy of the people," but I knew that was what my father and mother were called. My brothers were called the same thing. Even I was labeled "enemy of the people." But I knew the difference between truth and what the commisars and militiamen were calling us. As a small child, I knew the difference.

Country One: Ukraine and Life Without My Parents

Chapter Two
Kyiv 1931–1936

My father and mother were gone. Perhaps I had child-like faith they would be back. Maybe I did understand in some way that, like our neighbors, they would not be seen again.

There was no hope for our survival in Pervomaysk. Grisha, who was attending the university in Kyiv, thought it would be easier to find work and food there, so Natalia and her husband, Pavlusha, took me to Kyiv in the fall or winter of 1931.

The distance was over 400 kilometers or 250 miles, a trip we must have made by train, for there was no other way we could have gone. It would seem I'd remember that trip, for I had never travelled or ridden a train before. Probably we rode the train at night, and I slept. At some time we were there. In a few minutes, I saw far more people rushing along streets than there were in our whole village. The tall buildings one after another were like something from a fairy tale. I was never afraid of anything, just curious. The city seemed unreal and fascinating to me. The place we were to live, however, was sadly real. We had one corner of a kitchen in someone's home. Even in the kitchen, it was icy cold. We all slept in one bed, huddled together to stay warm.

Some things were entirely new to me. Instead of the kerosene lamps we had on the farm, an electric light hung from the ceiling. Water came from a faucet—not from a well. I don't remember anything else about that place or the neighborhood. We were there only a month or two.

We had no food and no way of getting any. Natalia went into the woods and collected herbs, mushrooms, and other plants, which she boiled and we ate as if it was soup. Pavlusha and Natalia took turns going out to look for food or work. One was always gone. Neither had any preparation for non-farm jobs, and there were far too many people for too few jobs. But the worst part of looking was that former land-owning farmers were despised and unwanted by those who controlled businesses in the city. It was not yet illegal to hire farmers in the city, but a law wasn't needed.

From that first house, we moved to the Pecherska Lavra monastery. The monks who had run it were Ukrainian Orthodox. Many of them had been killed by Communists, a lucky few got away, and the monastery was left empty. The Bolsheviks decided Pecherska Lavra would be good for hous-ing people in need. Probably because Grisha always knew what was happening and how to do things, we were granted permission to stay. We got one big room with two beds, a table, and a *plyta,* a large tiled oven. Those ovens were quite efficient; we could cook on one side and be warm while we slept on the other—that is, we could if we had any food or wood. Most of the time we had neither. Fortunately, spring was arriving, so we were no longer freezing at night. There was a toilet in another part of the building, the first indoor toilet I ever saw. To get our infrequent baths, we went to public bathhouses many blocks away.

Pavlusha did not give up trying to find some kind of job and was finally hired in another part of town as a shoe repair assistant. He had to leave very early to walk to his job and did not get back until very late. I seldom saw him. His pay was so small he managed to buy for us only bread—when it was available.

Still, we were lucky to have any money, especially because Natalia became ill. Sick as she was, with almost no food and no one who knew about illnesses to take care of her, she just lay there without any emotion. Someone said she had a kidney problem. If she hadn't been ill, she could have cooked soup from nettles; she had learned where to find them and how to handle them.

I tried to find bread crumbs on the shelves where in the past bread had been stored. On the shelf I found a towel in which bread crumbs had become stuck. I picked off every crumb.

With nothing I could do at home, I sometimes wandered outside the monastery gate. One day I saw a store with long lines of people hoping to get that precious half-loaf of bread per person. The city dwellers were allotted certain small amounts of food, but country people did not get any rations. I stood there, watching. Coming out of the store was a kind lady with a whole loaf and an extra little piece, together probably weighing no more than one kilogram (maybe two pounds). She glanced at me. I looked at the bread she held tightly to her body. She sensed my deep hunger and, with a beautiful smile, gave a precious little piece to the child with the sad eyes. She had a soul of understanding and the compassion to help. I never saw that lady again, but her smile remains always in my dreams. I practically inhaled that piece of bread without moving from the spot.

It must have been the way I looked, a starved, skinny child with a big belly, for people took pity on me. Ukrainian people were always compassionate and willing to share. Maybe I was begging. I don't know. Another person tore off a piece of her loaf and took a few steps toward me to give me something. And then one more. I went home with my bread pieces and tried to feed my sister, but she made almost no response.

The bread lines were always long. The end was never in sight. One day, an elderly man, after standing in line for hours, finally received his half-loaf of bread. He grabbed it, biting and swallowing fast. He fell down on the spot and died.

He would never feel hunger again. I was told later an empty stomach could not take in food fast and would swell up. People did die from eating too fast after having nothing to eat for long periods of time, but there were so many people dead in the street nobody paid attention. Each morning, before daylight so people wouldn't see, horse drawn wagons went through the streets and carted dead people away.[3]

People died because their bodies were weak from hunger. I knew one little boy my age who was blind from starvation. His parents, brothers, sisters, aunts, uncles—the whole family—were already dead from Stalin's starvation.

In those times, when thoughts of food affected all my thinking, I once envied a boy because his leg was broken. Near the monastery was a sandy hill, and several of us children were sliding down that hill when the boy lost control and broke a leg. Nearby was a Bolshevik kindergarten attended by Bolshevik children from the neighborhood. They had food. Right away, a teacher from the kindergarten ran to help. She had some soup and began feeding it to the boy. He was lying there in pain, waiting for medical attention, and eating soup. I did envy him. I wanted that soup. I looked with starving eyes on each spoonful moving to his mouth. I was wishing I'd broken my leg. Then, I would be eating soup.

Natalia, adding to her illness, contracted malaria. For that, a doctor came, prescribed medication, and sent me to a pharmacy over a mile away. I didn't feel well either and on my way home broke into a sweat. Soon, I was cold and shivering, then alternately hot and cold and in pain. I sobbed all the way home. I don't know how I paid for the medicine, how I got home, or what happened when I did, but I had malaria, too. No one seemed to notice. [4]

Pavlusha tried to get Natalia admitted to a hospital, but he was refused. As Natalia got sicker, there was an attempt to get me admitted to an orphanage so I would have food, but officials found out I had an older sister and rejected

24

me.

Our oldest brother, Jasha, arrived in Kyiv. He had finished his time in the Urals and had a wife, Marussia, and a baby boy, Kolia. That was probably in the summer of 1932, for I'm sure we hadn't spent a second winter in Kyiv. I was never sure why Jasha was in the Urals. I didn't think he was a prisoner, but if he had gone voluntarily, he would have had some food ration in Kiev or some kind of support from the state—and he had neither. With no money and no job, Jasha couldn't find a place of his own, so we all lived in the same big room.

Natalia got sicker. She just lay there, half conscious, staring. She was still young, around twenty-six. Finally, Pavlusha got permission for her to be admitted to a hospital. Some kind of emergency crew came to take her away, two men, I think. I didn't see whether they were in a truck or a wagon; I was told to stay inside. That was the last time I saw her, for relatives were not allowed to visit patients in a hospital. A few days later, Natalia died.

Natalia was buried at a cemetery in Kyiv. Before the casket was closed, Marussia told me to kiss Natalia's cheek, which I did. There was no cross, no stone, nothing to identify her by name.

I did not cry when my mother was taken away because she was so strong she made me strong. Natalia, in effect, became my mother and was good to me, but Natalia had been sick for months, and I was never clinging to her skirt as I was with my mother. I don't remember whether I cried for the loss of Natalia. I know I was deeply sad. My father was taken away, then my mother, next my sister—the people I loved taken from me one by one. I don't think my child-mind was able to make any sense of those losses, but I was probably beginning to believe that was the way life is.

Pavlusha left the room to us and found a place to stay near his work. I was in a new family. Even though I barely remembered Jasha, I could easily see him—twenty years older than I—as my father. I didn't see Marussia as my mother. My little nephew, Kolia, who was under two years of age, became a baby brother, and, at about age seven, I became his baby-sitter.

Marussia was not like anyone I'd ever known. To narrate that period of my life, I have to tell about Marussia even if I get other things out of order. She was orphaned at an early age and was brought up in an old tradition, which she carried on. She was taught, for example, to wrap newborn babies in cloth like mummies for the first three months of their lives to make the legs and bodies of the tiny creatures grow straight. The constant crying of wrapped babies was simply endured. (In a grim joke, it could be said the practice prepared babies for a lifetime of suffering.) Marussia was also taught to work hard and to be immaculately clean in everything. She cooked and kept our home always very tidy.

Although Marussia married a Ukrainian, she detested Ukraine. She told me not to speak Ukrainian, that it was a peasant language. I had to speak Russian with her.

Beyond not liking Ukrainian people in general, Marussia particularly didn't like me. At the time, I didn't understand the reason but came to think it was because she suffered a lot with my brother. Jasha was quite handsome, and there were always women around him. Today, I can understand her pain. When she was angry with Jasha, she drank too much vodka and then beat me. She saw Jasha in me, and I became the substitute object of Marussia's rage.

The beatings took their toll. I had trouble concentrating at school. I started wetting my bed, and Marussia made me sleep in my urine. No matter how hard I tried to wake up in time, I could not. My bed was a little mattress on the floor. The mattress was thin, and when it was wet, it was cold, but lying on the wet mattress was my punishment. I started having the same nightmare over and over. I was falling into a tunnel, a hole, which had no end. I just continued falling and falling. In daytime, I became jumpy. I always knew I was in trouble with her or soon would be and would be punished physically. Once she was so angry she threw a knife at me; I still have a scar on the back of my head.

It stuck in my memory that Marussia gave little Kolia a piece of bread with butter if he was obedient and sat on the little pot instead of soiling his clothes. Maybe it was natural for a mother to reward her baby and to punish another child.

The more Marussia beat me, the more I missed my mother. At school I stared at the teacher and thought about mother. I missed her terribly. And I missed my father. I wasn't absorbing a thing any of the teachers said. I didn't say anything to Jasha or to anyone else. A child was raised to respect all older people, and that meant not bothering them with childish concerns. My brother was having enough problems trying to find work and food. He couldn't be aware something was wrong or take time to do anything about it. Marussia was simple, not educated, not cultured, and I'm sure she had no awareness of the effect her beatings had.

I must say, though, when I had scarlet fever, Marussia was kind to me. She put me in a real bed and changed the sheets to keep the wounds clean. And once, when the snow was heavy, and because my galoshes were tattered and torn, Marussia was waiting for me after school with a little sled and dragged me home through deep piles of melting snow. One day, Marussia sat down with me and asked me to read with her. She could barely read herself, and I know I couldn't. I was both impressed and frightened she was paying attention to me, sitting next to me while I struggled to read. But all the time I lived with Marussia, I was nervous.

When Jasha was away, Marussia enjoyed vodka. After the official famine was ended, probably in 1935, Marussia invited a neighbor lady to have a drink and dinner in our room. The larger the dinner, the more vodka. I have no idea how she bought vodka all the time whether we had food or not.

Jasha began looking for work as soon as he arrived, but he had the same problem Natalia's husband had. He knew only farming and hard labor, and no one in Kyiv wanted to hire a farmer's son.

Marussia found odd jobs and managed to feed all of us in the beginning. No matter how much she drank, she never stopped working. One time, Marussia brought home little packages of all kinds of food. She had been gone for a few days. Kolia was missing his mama, and we were both hungry. We cried ourselves to sleep those nights. Then Marussia returned with all that food. She put the packages down in front of Kolia and me, then slowly unwrapped each one. We were ecstatic. Everything looked wonderfully delicious. We hadn't seen so much food in years. I didn't know what to take first, but when I started, if Marussia hadn't stopped me, I would have gotten sick from eating too much.

Somehow, I got the idea Marussia was working briefly in a restaurant for the military or high-ranking Communists. It was simply impossible for me to imagine that so much food, so many different things, could be available to some people all the time.

Finally, Jasha got some kind of work at a university in Kiev but not the one Grisha was attending. We moved from the monastery to a university room that was 12 x 14 feet with an upright stove in the wall. With Jasha working, we could afford a good supply of potatoes. That is what we lived on. I was lucky. There, I was clean and warm, and I had food every day.

One time Jasha and Marussia went somewhere and on their way out of the house told me to cook the potatoes. I didn't know how to prepare food. The oven was large, taller than I was. I overcooked the potatoes and burned a hole in our pot. When Jasha and Marussia got back, Marussia whipped me. I felt horrible, unwanted, like a weed, in everyone's way.

A fragment I remember from that time was walking along railroad tracks on my way to see Natalia's husband. I heard people screaming, "The train is coming!" I leapt out of the way, and a train roared by. Maybe I was thinking so hard I didn't hear the train. Maybe I had my hat pulled down over my ears.

I was walking by the tracks another time when a young soldier accosted me. He was guarding cattle cars, and the area was deserted. I sensed he had bad thoughts, and when he turned his head to see whether anybody was in sight, I ran away. Today, I assume he intended to rape me. At the time, I was probably seven, maybe eight, but perhaps I had already developed survival instincts.

Gabriel came to visit us. He was in his uniform: a light leather jacket, navy trousers. and high boots—a tall, handsome, and presentable young man who wanted to be a cavalry officer. I can see him standing at the door even now. I remembered Gabriel most clearly from the farm, and I remembered mother was sad when she got a letter from him about his school. I didn't understand fully the letter or Gabriel's explanation there in Kyiv. What I do remember is he said "no" to the authorities at the military academy. Today, I understand the military authorities demanded he renounce his heritage and denounce his parents or be expelled from the academy. Gabriel could have stayed at the school if he had called his parents enemies of the people, and he wouldn't do it.

Gabriel was with us just a few days. I was sorry he didn't stay. The dull and drab place we lived was brighter while he was there. I don't think he knew where he was going or what he would do. Maybe he had to go back to the military academy to be told what to do. And maybe even if he had denounced our parents, he would still have been given a bad discharge.

Because Grisha was already in Kyiv, he and Gabriel must have spent some time together either at our place or somewhere else. If Grisha had to be at the university all day, he might have been at our place after I was asleep. I'm sure he had kept contact with Natalia.

As already indicated, my early school experiences were not good. Even if Natalia had lived and I didn't have Marussia, I would still have been hungry and cold and would still have suffered from separation from my mother. But I did go to school—actually to several schools in Kyiv. I entered the first grade probably in September 1932 somewhere near the monastery. We probably moved to the university house while I was still in the first grade. And I must have been in the first grade when Marussia set me down to read with her. My only memories of being in the classroom were of having the teachers call my name and not knowing what to say.

I'm sure I started the second grade while we lived at the university house. I remember on my way to the school, which was about two miles from our room, I walked around a cookie factory which filled the air with sweet smells.

At that school everyone knew right away who I was, the daughter of a farmer. There were others like me, but there were also children of Communists, who had already learned to call us enemies of the state or other names and to push or hit us. We got worse treatment if we tried to protect ourselves—at least I did until I learned to grab and twist their fingers. Soon, they left me alone, and I realized I could stand for myself. But I didn't do well in class.

In spite of being singled out, I somehow managed to make friends with different kinds of children. I remember one girl, neat and pretty, whose mother always picked her up from school and gave her a kiss as they went home. I'd cry because I didn't have that. Some of those friends invited me to their houses. I went every time I was asked and stayed as long as possible. I never wanted to go back to my own place. Their houses were nicer, and mean Marussia wasn't there.

It was probably when I was in the second grade but at

another school that Marussia picked me up after school one day. I think it was at that time because I was wearing some old, torn adult shoes Marussia found in a loft area above our room at the university—probably left behind by students. Because the shoes were torn, my feet got wet when the snow melted. When the weather was dry, my feet were warm.

Classrooms were crowded. Seats made for two pupils—with the promise of a better life under Communism—held four pupils. I once caught lice from another child but didn't tell Marussia for fear I would be punished. I poured kerosene on my hair, which was the usual way to kill lice. Every spring, Marussia took metal beds outside and burned them with newspapers to kill the blood-drinking insects.

While I was in the second grade, we moved to Velyka Vasylkivska Street where we shared one big room with a professor at the university. Jasha divided the room into thirds, one-third for the professor and the remaining two-thirds for us. The kitchen was my room. The bed was on soft springs. Kolia and I jumped on the bed like a trampoline. When I lay down to sleep, it was like a hammock. There were a few happy moments in that place.

I was transferred to a new school, which was much like the other. Again, I just looked at the teachers and thought about being back on the farm with my loving family and food and clothes and no hunger or cold or punishment. There was one teacher I admired, a kind man who treated all children the same.

In those first two years, there was never any excitement about learning. I was living in memory or imagination while in the classroom, glad to be out of Marussia's sight. Otherwise I didn't want to be at school. At the end of second grade, I still couldn't read. I would have to be in second grade again the next year.

The next year was better. I made some progress in learning to read, and I was enrolled in ballet class. Maybe it was because I liked the physical demands of ballet that I felt better about sitting down with a book. I especially liked wearing the little ballet costumes and performing in programs. I felt better about the way I walked and quit trying to slump down so I wouldn't be seen. Of course, ballet made me even hungrier, and even though the official famine was over and Marussia always had something for us to eat, food was scarce and choices limited.

People who worked for Bolsheviks had plenty of food and a good variety. The Communist Party people, high-ranking people, lived well. They had special stores, restaurants, and privileges which were kept secret from the world that thought everybody in USSR was equal. Those who worked for the state—teachers, for example—were given some rations. It was often said a full stomach does not understand an empty one, so I guess the privileged ones didn't feel the misery of the millions.

Children of my class didn't get much attention. I wandered around the monastery and the other houses alone with little or no supervision. I played with other children like me. Today, I might wonder how I could have played with conditions as they were, but I guess children play no matter what the circumstance.

My class, the *kulaks*, the peasants, had no food rations and no connection to anybody who already lived in the city. And nobody wanted any connection with us. There were two different peoples in Ukraine at that time, two different worlds.

There were also two languages. The poor people, the people I came in contact with, spoke Ukrainian. The people who had connections spoke Russian. It was fashionable to speak Russian, and Russian only. People who got some place in life spoke Russian. Russian was spoken in school and in all public places. All business was conducted in Russian. People who spoke Ukrainian were laughed at. At home, I tried to speak Ukrainian to Jasha, but Marussia would allow only Russian. Naturally, I absorbed Russian, and it was not long before I began to forget the language of my parents.

We did hear that farmers were starving. We knew we didn't have adequate food, but we didn't understand how farmers couldn't feed themselves. Producing food was what they did. In time, we understood Communists were directing the famine. While they were forcing collectivization, they were taking away all the food.

By going to Kyiv when we did, we avoided seeing the final destruction of Kamjana Balka. We had seen the beginning of the brutalization of villagers. We knew some villagers disappeared and some, like our parents, arrested. If someone resisted, they were instantly shot. Almost all villagers lost their property. Many lost their lives.

Grisha and the other students at his university, strongly aware of what was being done to the Ukrainian people, started a protest movement. In 1933, some three thousand students, including Grisha, were arrested in a massive and crushing sweep, then sentenced to three years' imprisonment. They were sent north of Leningrad (by two lakes, Ladoga and Onega) to build a canal as a gift for Stalin. Prison life was brutal for the students: miserable housing, poor food, and long hours of hard labor. They worked all day and at night got a piece of bread and dirty water soup. Many died. A few years later, when Grisha and I were the only two members of the family who were together, he told me, with great pain, about the agony and anger he and other students felt when they saw a proud and happy Ukraine being destroyed.

Grisha told me about other attempts to protest the system and the starvation, but protesters didn't have enough power to produce any effect. So many people had been moved out of their home regions there was no base. Connections between parts of the country were broken. Any revolt or sign of a revolt was quickly, massively, and savagely put down by

Communist forces.

In Kyiv, things were bad, but we were better off than the farmers and better off than Grisha. As long as we didn't call attention to ourselves or cross the path of a Party official, we could go about our daily routines.

I kept going to school. And I continued to displease Marussia, often without knowing what I'd done. Once, I got in trouble with Marussia because of a girl who lived across the street. Tamara was a tomboy, a rough girl, who was two years older but still in the same class with her younger sister who was my age. The two sisters decided to go home early from school one day. Marussia saw them in the street and asked where I was. Tamara lied and said, "Genia went with the boys to the forest." The truth was our whole class, with the teacher, went to the forest. Our class was taking that kind of trip often. Marussia told Jasha I was doing things with boys. I had, at best, a vague idea what she meant. Jasha, without asking me anything, took off his belt and beat me all over my body so badly I fainted. I never could tell Jasha what happened.

Events in the years of 1934 and 1935 are difficult to recall in a clear order. Mykola reached the age limit for staying in the orphanage during that time and got some kind of job and a place to stay. He found us, probably through the Bureau of Addresses, and he visited once in a while, but I don't remember seeing him more than two or three times. Somehow, there was never the closeness with Mykola there was with Gabriel and Grisha. We knew Grisha had been arrested but were not certain where Gabriel was.

Then, early in 1935, Gabriel returned to Kyiv. Jasha made him a little partitioned room, four feet by six feet, with no windows. It was nice for me to have Gabriel there. He was still just as kind to me as ever. He was thin, and he looked tired, but that was the appearance we expected everybody to have.

Soon after Gabriel arrived, I had a bad cold, and he presented me with two tangerines. To get tangerines in times like those, Gabriel performed a miracle. I couldn't comprehend I was looking at tangerines and they were for me. They might as well have been ten-carat diamonds. I just stared. My little nephew, Kolia, had no such problem and grabbed them from me. Gabriel said, "No, Kolia; they're for Genia." That was the first time since I reached Kyiv that someone stood up for me. Something just for me. Gabriel's action probably did more for my health and well-being than the fruit did, but, oh, I do still savor those tangerines.

Gabriel had a cold and then another cold, and I couldn't get him any tangerines. What was realized in time was that Gabriel was developing tuberculosis. With all of us crammed into that tiny space, we would see Gabriel dying slowly right before our eyes. It was next to impossible for a farmer to be admitted to a hospital, and, at home, without proper medical care and not enough food, he could only become sicker. In the 1930s there was no suitable medication for tuberculosis, certainly not in USSR.

A few months after Gabriel arrived, Grisha returned from prison. When Grisha saw Gabriel, he insisted Gabriel be taken to a hospital immediately. Grisha and Jasha went around begging for help, trying to get Gabriel under a doctor's care, but Gabriel's tuberculosis was so advanced no one would do anything. Grisha was a determined and persistent person and kept trying anyway. He also started searching for our parents. He went to many offices in Kyiv, and he wrote many letters.

One day when Gabriel was feeling well enough to do some walking, we went to a museum. I don't know whether Jasha went or not, but I know that Mykola was there because I have a clear image of him and his feet. Before we entered the museum, Mykola had to take off his galoshes, which he wore to keep his shoes from falling apart. His socks were no better; they were full of holes. Our old ability to laugh came back.

We enjoyed the museum. Afterward, we passed someone selling carrots. My brothers had enough money to buy a few, which we ate as though they were candies. And we laughed some more. I treasure that day we were together.

That was the first time I was ever in a museum. Without realizing it, I was getting some education by being in Kyiv. A year or two earlier, I saw my first circus, which was beautiful fantasy for me. I also saw my first picture show. It was a Charlie Chaplin film, "Modern Times," the Communists played to show the bad things about capitalism. Maybe I saw it in one of the propaganda classes that were to prepare us to join Pioneers of the Communist Party. I rode a bus a few times. I saw buses and trams along main streets, and on occasion, I saw an automobile.

At night, Jasha, Grisha, and Gabriel and maybe Mykola talked about Ukraine and USSR and the world. Grisha was the one who was most enraged by all he saw around him. He tried to continue a personal war against communism. I didn't understand much of what they said, but I forced myself to stay awake. It was a good and comforting feeling to sit and listen to them. It made me remember the talks they had with father. Once in a while, Grisha or Gabriel said something to me, maybe about what my future would be, maybe about the old life on the farm. Gabriel was a dear man and reminded me of things such as our being caught in a rainstorm, or my making the horses run. Those nights gave me great pleasure. I keep my memory of them with my memories of my parents and life on the farm.

Jasha was the only one working, and with two more people to feed, there was not enough money to buy bread and potatoes, our main food. Gabriel, especially, needed more food and more kinds of food, but we could get nothing. Gabriel got worse. To add to his problem, he also got worms in his stomach.

When Gabriel stopped opening his eyes, Jasha, Grisha,

and a friend took Gabriel to a hospital that took him in. There he died after a while, alone, in quarantine. The doctors opened Gabriel's head and did all kinds of things. When a person went to the hospital, that person became State property. When we got his body for burial, there were cuts and stitches everywhere. We buried him next to Natalia. After the war, Mykola put a cross on each grave.

My dearest brother, Gabriel, died not long after his twenty-fifth birthday. First Natalia, then Gabriel: two deaths in three years. Gabriel looked like my mother, and I loved that man. He was always kind and steady. He always paid attention to me. His thoughtful affection I treasure always.

Within six years, I had lost my parents, a sister, and a brother. I also gained another nephew, Ura, second son of Jasha and Marussia.

Grisha's many letters and other efforts to track down where exactly our parents were in Central Asia yielded from NKVD two cryptic documents which stated only that our parents were shipped by rail to the Baikal region of Central Asia (Siberia) by order of the Odessa NKVD. Those two torn, yellowed government forms—and fading memories—were all I was left with. Years later, I gave the documents to the Historic Museum in Bound Brook, New Jersey.

Not long after Gabriel died, the adults began talking about me, the remaining child. I don't know what Jasha and Grisha said to each other or what Marussia said to either of them. Grisha told me enough for me to understand he thought I was being mistreated. I don't know whether Grisha argued to take me away from Marussia (or away from Marussia and Jasha) or whether Marussia (or Marussia and Jasha) asked Grisha to take me away, but Marussia, with her two sons, certainly didn't want or need another mouth to feed. I was ten or eleven years old by then, had been exposed to tuberculosis, and needed more food—if not better treatment. I do know Grisha had to leave Kyiv and it was decided I'd go with him.

The place selected was Belaja Czerkov, a smaller city about a three-hour ride south of Kyiv, and in late summer 1936 we went there.

THE FORGOTTEN

THE 1933 MAN-MADE FAMINE IN UKRAINE

1933—1983
A Commemorative Exhibit

GENOCIDE

The Ukrainian Institute of America
2 East 79th Street, New York, N.Y. 10021
212/288-8660

38

Chapter Three
Belaja Czerkov and Other Places 1936 - 1940

Because Grisha had been a political prisoner, he always had to go to the police station to register. He was not supposed to stay in any big city at all and not in any other place more than six months without permission from the police. How he managed to stay in **Kyiv** for several months, I don't know. He and I moved from house to house and from town to town much more often than is indicated here. It will seem from reading the following pages that we lived in Belaja Czerkov about two years. We were in the Belaja Czerkov area that long, but I cannot remember all the little towns we lived in—sometimes only a month or two—or the exact sequence of going out of and back into Belaja Czerkov, and even if I could, it would be confusing to write.[5]

Grisha did register in Belaja Czerkov and got us a room with a lady who had children and who cooked cherry preserves and cherry liquor all summer. She let me taste the preserves, which were so good I managed to be in sight whenever I smelled cooking cherries. Our room was much like the rooms in **Kyiv**: bedroom, kitchen, everything in one with a toilet on another side of the house and a public bathhouse elsewhere.

Grisha immediately began looking for work. Mostly, he found temporary jobs. Communist Party functionaries liked to show their loyalty by displaying portraits of leaders, so Grisha got some jobs painting dry brush portraits of Lenin or

Marx. Sometimes he worked as a laborer—anything he could do to survive.

While Grisha worked or hunted for work, I wandered in the neighborhood. I befriended a lady who had some rabbits, and she let me play in her yard. I heard people say that during the famine she ate her husband. Maybe I was playing with a completely insane, grief-stricken woman, but she was nice to me. At ten or eleven years old, what did I know? It wasn't until much later I heard about cannibalism during the famine. People were eating dead relatives so the rest of the family could survive. I'm glad my mother and sister protected me from that knowledge.

In my wanderings I discovered big stones in the River Rus, which was very close, big stones like the ones I remembered from Kamjana Balka. I could go there and pretend I was back home.

One time, Grisha hid a man in a loft above our room and didn't tell me. When I happened to see the man, I was surprised, but he was so terrified to be seen that I can still see his face. I didn't ask questions. Grisha had taught me not to talk to anybody about things at home. The man disappeared quietly. Hiding a political refugee from the Communists was something that Grisha would do even though it was risky. We could have all been arrested.

Grisha was still in his twenties, a handsome young artist in his prime. Women seemed to swarm around him. I had the feeling that I was in the way—of the women, if not of Grisha. One such girlfriend was an older widow who taught at the local orphanage. She let Grisha and me move into her cottage with her, but because she already had two children of her own, there wasn't enough room for me. That woman, seeing the struggle Grisha had to feed and support me, suggested that Grisha get me into the orphanage where she taught. Grisha changed my name from Eugenia Sakevych to Eugenia Savich and coached me on the way to present myself. Then, he had me walk to the local police station, sit on the steps, and wait until someone found me.

I was taken inside and interrogated for a long time. Although the police were mostly nice, it was still tiring and at times terrifying. I had to keep lying. "I have no relatives. I have no one." A couple of times, I slipped on questions about where I was from. Grisha told me to say one thing, but my accent bespoke another.

The police called a woman who escorted me to a small house nearby. I was quarantined for one week. They were waiting to see whether I was healthy enough to be put into the local orphanage, which was a curious act because the house they stuck me in was infested with lice. Of course, in that part of the world, lice, worms, cockroaches, and other creatures infested buildings. After enduring attacks by lice for the week, I was admitted to the orphanage where Grisha's girlfriend taught. I was proud of myself for having survived that ordeal.

Grisha's girlfriend arranged clandestine visits between Grisha and me. The meetings were risky, for if the director of the orphanage discovered Grisha was my brother, I would be expelled, and Grisha would go to prison.

A new school year was beginning, and I was enrolled. I stayed at the orphanage until Grisha and his lady friend broke up. She probably wanted to marry, and I'm pretty sure he was with her only on my behalf. He endured a lot so I would get basic care.

We moved to another part of town and rented a small room on Zamkova Street. Grisha was getting different freelance art jobs. Grisha made new friends; he always had friends. We went to quite a few picnics by the River Rus, which was breathtaking. Boys dived off big rocks into the current. Everyone managed to provide some kind of food, which was cooked over campfires. Somebody played accordion, and we sang late into the night.

One time, I went out in a rowboat with a bunch of

other children. There were beautiful water lilies all around our boat. When the "captain" of our boat, a twelve-year-old boy, saw how much I liked the lilies, he ordered the others to collect them for me. I sat there like a prima donna as everyone scrambled to lay lilies at my feet. They collected so many I feared we would sink. I was impressed that the boy liked me. After all, he was older and taller than the rest of us. That was my first flirtation.

There was much earthy joking at those gatherings. I can remember one example. A woman was complaining she wanted to make *vareniky* (dumplings) but had no board to roll her dough on. Her husband said, "You can roll it on my big round belly."

I guess I began feeling more confident and relaxed among those people, for one day, I thought about the children of Grisha's friend who taught at the orphanage and went to see them. The thought didn't occur to me that going anywhere near that orphanage was stupid and dangerous. The director would surely be looking for a child who ran away from his orphanage. Sure enough, the director spotted me talking with some children. I guess I heard him because all at once I saw him rushing toward me, and then he was grabbing me. Fear swept over me. I twisted and pulled with all the strength I had. I was so wiry I slipped out of his grasp and ran. Fortunately, I was also fast. As I ran, I could hear him shouting at me to stop. When I could tell he was far behind me and probably out of breath, I glanced back and saw I was safe. At that moment, my stupidity, my thoughtlessness, hit me. My survival instinct and skills would be defeated by mistakes like that.

We moved again, and Grisha pretended to be a student at a local university. He sent me to the university kitchen to get meals for us. The food was put into two aluminum pots that sat one on top the other with a lid on the top one. I carried the pots home in a big leather bag. The motion of carrying caused food to spill into the bag. After many trips, there must have been at least an inch of grease lining the bottom. It wasn't appealing, but we didn't care; we were happy to be getting cooked food.

I started another new school. Once again, my ability to adapt and make friends quickly was put to the test. I guess I had some ability naturally and developed some more. I was already accustomed to meeting new people all the time. Sometimes I met children who didn't move from one rented room to another, children of parents who were highly ranked officials and had houses. That way of living was, by then, strange to me.

In that period, I remember playing with a little girl who showed me her uncle's fine stone house. In my imagination, it was the kind of house rich people occupied during the Czar's time. My friend, with her mother and eight other children, lived in a small house on the same grounds. At New Year's, my new friend took me to her uncle's house to see a beautiful Christmas tree, a tree that made such an impression on me I can visualize it today as easily and clearly as if it was last Christmas. It reached the ceiling and was completely covered with apples and oranges. I couldn't believe all that food was being used for decoration. I suppose it didn't occur to my friend I was perpetually hungry and saw that fruit as food first and as food last and as objects of beauty only in passing. And it probably didn't occur to her to offer me something. (I don't think she was perversely showing what powerful people could possess.) Oh, but I was powerfully tempted to grab at least an apple. It certainly didn't occur to me to ask for one because Eastern people never asked for anything that wasn't offered. In fact, it was not polite to accept what was offered until it had been offered two or three times. In my dazed disbelief, I tried to act as if everyone had a spruce tree with fruit on it.

Her uncle, a high-ranking officer in the Red Army, sat still for hours, staring and looking sad. Stalin had started a series of purges within the Soviet army, and the uncle feared the NKVD would come and take him away, so he waited. Hitler, I learned later, developed a propaganda campaign against Soviet army officers. Stalin fell for the trick and in 1936 began arresting and killing many of his smartest, most loyal men, accusing them of collaborating with Hitler's spies. If anyone tried to complain or write about what was happening, the NKVD simply wiped that person off the face of the earth. My friend's uncle was scared—and with good reason, for eventually, he was taken away by the NKVD.

In that period, dedicated Bolsheviks were breaking under the strain, sometimes wandering the streets with crazed looks on their faces, talking to themselves, repeating things over and over, mumbling about communism or Stalin. They had adopted ideals that were crumbling; the people they idolized and worked for turned out to be monsters. Converts saw what was happening in Ukraine; they saw the sad condition of the country. Maybe they had killed or brutalized someone. Maybe they were the ones who arrested my parents; maybe they were the ones who took all my mother had, every last grain of food. They had shown no pity and had become pitiable. I didn't see many of them, but the sight of the ones I did see stayed with me.

Grisha had warned me the purges were beginning. He said whenever members of the Bolshevik cadre showed what Stalin would call weaknesses, they had to be eliminated. If anyone was a target, everyone had to be nervous. We had to be even less visible.

Sometimes Grisha was getting enough work to keep him busy for several days, and we could buy more food than usual. Sometimes there was no work. We continued to move frequently, sometimes because Grisha thought we could afford a better place, sometimes because we had to go to a cheaper place, often because Grisha was required to keep moving. Once, when Grisha was working every day, we were renting a room from a husband and wife who had a two-bedroom apartment. We walked through the kitchen to our room. I was eleven or twelve years old and going to school, so I had time after school to go to the university to get our meals and still have some time at home before Grisha arrived. I was quiet because the husband worked at night and was sleeping when I got home. The wife worked during the day and was not there.

One day, when I got home, the husband was awake and waiting for me. He said something, then grabbed me and threw me onto the bed. Fear had enabled me to break away from the director of the orphanage, but this man was much stronger, and I could not escape from him. He weighed more than twice as much as I did and crushed me under him. I was terrified he intended to kill me so I tried to fight but could do no more than scratch his face. He raped me, and I didn't know what was happening. I was frantic; I was hurting terribly. He was telling me to get out and keep my mouth shut, but I was too stunned and dazed to distinguish words. I was surely in shock.

My brain stopped working the rest of the day and night. I don't know whether Grisha noticed anything or asked me any questions. I don't know whether I slept or couldn't sleep, cried or couldn't cry. I only know I felt bad in ways I had not felt before.

In the following days, I was like a terrified rabbit trying to escape a hungry wolf. The thought that the man would attack me again dominated any other thought I might have had. I avoided him for a few days, but one day, when I was sure he was asleep, he appeared in front of me. He didn't grab me. He spoke with kindness, but any hope I had I would get away disappeared. His kindness stopped when I tried to go around him. I started to cry, which did not help. He began telling me he would throw us into the street if I didn't collaborate with him in our secrecy. That frightened me because it

45

could be difficult to find a room and Grisha had looked a long time to find that one. The man told me to keep quiet and everything would be all right. I tried to ask him why he was doing that to me. He said I must be grateful to live there, that nothing is free. I tried to tell him that my brother paid for the room, that we did not live free. He didn't hear me. He did the same thing he did the first time.

The man started to threaten me more and more. He told me he could put Grisha again in prison. Maybe he was bluffing me, but I was so terribly scared I did believe him. I was afraid to tell Grisha. I felt as if it was my fault, that it was on my account my brother had to rent rooms. I knew no one else I could tell. My mother was the one person I could have talked with. If I tried to delay returning home till Grisha arrived, the man scolded me and threatened to tell Grisha I was wandering someplace I shouldn't be.

Today, I might say I should immediately have told Grisha, but that man's forcing himself on me was terrifying for a girl who was not prepared in any way for such an experience, who did not even know the meaning of "monthly period."

At that traumatic, confused time in my life, I didn't know what was right or wrong. Maybe everyday life was supposed to be that way. I knew I felt dirty physically because of that man, that I was humiliated and sick to my stomach because of his forcing me into sex. I started to have atrocious pain in my abdomen. I suffered emotionally and physically because I didn't know what to do or how to change my situation—so I did nothing.[6]

The stress did manifest itself. To buy food from stores, it was necessary to stand in a long line for bread, then go to another line for other items. Waiting in those long lines, I fainted frequently. I had fainted before and thought that was something that happened—maybe because of hunger. One time when I fainted, a woman started talking to me. Even though I did not say much to her, she told me to go to a doctor. She was sure something more than hunger was wrong with me, and I was thinking she knew what she was saying.

Before I did anything about seeing a doctor, we moved. I didn't know why my brother found a room in another part of town. I was afraid he knew something was wrong and I'd get him into trouble, but nothing seemed to happen.[7]

Fortunately for me, at that time, other and better things began to happen. Grisha met and began dating a beautiful, tall, red-haired Jewish girl named Sarah, who offered to use her connections to help him erase his past political record, wipe it clean, so he wouldn't have to keep running. She wanted to marry Grisha and move to a big city like Kyiv where they could start anew. Sarah spent much time with us, and we went to her home, also. Her mother, father, sisters, and brothers were good to me. One of her brothers, Srul, a shy, pleasant man of twenty-two, was the one who introduced Sarah and Grisha. Srul enjoyed explaining things to me; I not only appreciated learning, but also enjoyed having someone give me some attention. Sarah's whole family was entirely loving. At the time, I did not recognize how desperately I wanted to be a part of a real family once again, but I did absorb all the affection and attention directed toward me.

Grisha's attraction to women and for women meant he would be meeting other women and his romance with Sarah could come to an end. Once, when Grisha had to go to Kyiv, on the train he met Claudia, a blonde Russian beauty from Kursk. She had just completed a degree in agriculture and was on her way to apply for work on a collective farm as a zootechnics-expert or business economist. That time it was Grisha who fell in love. He did not let Claudia get away from him; he convinced her to go with him to our little room. They soon got married, which meant I would never see Sarah or Srul again. It was sad for me to give up my attachment to a family. But maybe losing families was the way of life.

We left the Belaja Czerkov area and traveled to a small town where Claudia got a job. Grisha was working often there, so I didn't see them much. I spent some time with a Polish girl who lived nearby. We frequently went swimming together. She was chubby and a good swimmer. I was skinny, always cold, and not a good swimmer. Her parents had all kinds of birds and gave me a baby peacock and a baby white turkey in a little cage. Those were the first animals I had touched or tended since the militia took away all the animals on our farm. I was delighted to have them even if Grisha and Claudia were not.

Claudia often had to travel, and Grisha was getting jobs that kept him away from home, so it was arranged I would live with Claudia's parents in Kursk, Russia, which was about three hundred miles (480 kilometers) east of Kyiv, but no more than one hundred miles (160 kilometers) into Russia. Grisha got me some clothes, and Claudia wrote the directions to her parents' house. Grisha put me and my birds, which I'd had for about one month, on a train, and, at age twelve, I was on my way to Russia. I would get there before time to start school in September 1937.

It was the first time I rode a train by myself, and it was my first time to leave Ukraine. I sat alone, clutching my cage with my two birds. Other passengers were pleasant and chatty. They all spoke Russian. I wanted them to leave me alone, but I also wanted to have some contact, to be included in some way. People asked me all kinds of questions, and I guess I answered more than I wanted to. Of course, they asked where I was going, but they also asked what I would do if Claudia's parents didn't want me. I assured them confidently Claudia's parents wanted me very much. I don't know where my strength came from, but—usually—I held my own.

At one stop a man, big and strong, got on the train and immediately started asking people where and to whom they were going. My instinct told me, "That man is dishonest." I held my cage more tightly after he asked me what was in it.

That evening people prepared for sleeping. The benches along the walls that were used for sitting during the day were used as one level of beds at night. Attached to the walls were two more levels of beds that could be pulled down for sleeping. Across the aisle from me, the man on the second bed level removed his shoes and placed them close to his body on the wall side. He put his coat in his suitcase and placed his suitcase under his head. Other people made similar preparations.

In a while, the train was pitch black, and people were asleep. The quiet was broken when someone screamed he'd been robbed. People began fumbling in the dark for their luggage. The man who had taken off his shoes and coat said all his belongings had disappeared. The big man who was so interested in everyone had also disappeared. No one remembered any stops of the train, so it was assumed that the man jumped from the train with his new belongings. Passengers were on edge the rest of the trip.

I arrived at Kursk, got my directions, and in an hour or two walked to my new home. Claudia's parents welcomed me. They were a kind, sweet couple, probably about sixty years of age. They had a nice, comfortable little house, and I was given a tiny bedroom that was created by a division of the dining room and living room. I was happy I had a home. I was well off.

Only one problem arose: I was not allowed to keep my birds in the house. There was, however, a place for them in the back yard in a wooden shack. The birds were free to roam the garden. It was late August or September. They inherited the garden, which seemed to make them happy; there was plenty of food to pick up from the earth. When severe frost came, however, it was the end of my poor birds. I did not cry. I was used to death. I kept quiet and kept my sadness to myself.

The school was about one and one-half miles from my new home. When it was time to register, I approached some teachers and started speaking Ukrainian, which they did not understand. I don't know why I spoke Ukrainian; maybe I was nervous and wanted the security of my native language. I was asked for a diploma from fourth grade. I had no diploma or any other papers.

I was sent to the director of the school, who began asking questions about my school history. Once again, I started speaking Ukrainian and was quickly told to speak Russian. When the director asked about grades, at first, I told him honestly what my grades were. He still did not understand me because I was visualizing grades in Ukrainian terms. Trying to put the grades into Russian terms, I saw it would be easy to elevate my grades, so, in a flash, I had higher grades. With my newly invented grades, I was accepted.

I was a new pupil in a school with a stable enrollment, and I was from a far country. I expected to be rejected, to be called an enemy of the people, but everyone seemed eager to talk to me. I never was the object of so much attention. I wasn't rejected at all; indeed, I became quite popular.

To my surprise, I started to study hard. I lived up to my lie. My grades improved, and by the end of the year were excellent. My Russian became fluent. I even picked up the Kursk dialect, which stayed with me for many years. It is said that a child, like a sponge, absorbs everything quickly, and I certainly did.

My home life made the difference. I was most happy and appreciative of my new parents-grandparents. They fed me enough to keep me from being always hungry. They gave me security, stability, and tranquillity: I could leave for school and return daily to the same home. I could concentrate in school and study at home. It was a pity it was only for one year.

I completed fifth grade, and late in the summer, Grisha and Claudia came for an extended visit. Suddenly we were like two families in a small wooden house. Grisha and Claudia slept in the living-dining room. Her parents had their little kitchen room. We had cooked potatoes and smoked fish every day. Everybody sat at the table and ate and talked.

Grisha and Claudia talked with her parents about me. Because of their age, Claudia's parents didn't want to take care of me indefinitely. I don't think they minded having me there that year. They always made me feel welcome, and I helped in the kitchen and the garden and did whatever they told me to do. The decision was finally made that Grisha and Claudia would take me back with them to Ukraine. I was sad to leave. The year had been good for me. The bad experiences of the years before didn't haunt me. Physically and emotionally, I was much stronger, much better.

Claudia got a job on a farm near Kryvyy Rih, so we moved there. Kryvyy Rih was a city in the same region as Pervomaysk and Kamjana Balka, which reawakened many memories. We got a large room with a separate kitchen. I remember Claudia's washing my back in that kitchen. She was kind to me but never close. I think her life with Grisha was difficult. Because of his former imprisonment, he suffered changes of mood and frequently got quite emotional. Taking care of me became an added burden for Claudia, and I was put into an orphanage again.

As soon as I heard the word "orphanage," the old feelings of insecurity came back. I could only think: "I'm in everybody's way; nobody wants me." Marussia didn't want me. Claudia didn't want me. Jasha and Grisha kept me out of duty. Claudia's parents really didn't want me either. There was no place I belonged. I began saying to myself and at some time to others, "I was born to suffer." Later, I would know Grisha loved me and going to an orphanage was for my own good, but I couldn't think that then.

It was late autumn when I went to the orphanage. Snow had already fallen. My orphanage home and school were in the country not far from Kryvyy Rih. There were about 400 children—girls and boys—all of whose parents were against communism, families who had had property in the country or the city.

There were so many beds in each room there was almost no space to walk. Our mattresses were of straw. Every so often the straw was thrown out and the mattress refilled with new straw. When that house cleaning was done, the yard was piled with mountains of straw.

There was a library, where I could read in peace, and many classes were offered. I studied algebra, French, German, and literature. I loved literature and loved to recite poems of Ukrainian poets Taras Shevchenko and Lesia Ukrainka. I even wrote some of my own poems, sad reflections about frozen rivers, ice breaking up and floating away, destination unknown. The writing helped me deal with some of my pain from the past and the present. I missed Grisha; we had no contact whatsoever.

A kind teacher sent one of my poems to a local newspaper, which published the poem. The teacher made a big fuss over me. She became a real ally and encouraged me to sketch and write. She even got me my own room to work in. I tried to continue writing, but my output was erratic. One day I could write freely; the next day, I had no interest, no desire to write. I lost concentration. I was depressed and eventually stopped writing entirely.

We also took ideology classes in which we were taught that communism was wonderful and the USSR was the greatest country in the world. We were shown pictures of American labor strikes and told all Americans were miserable wretches. One of the girls raised her hand and asked, "If they're so miserable, why do their clothes look better than ours?" She was told to be quiet.

They tried to teach me Taras Shevchenko, poet laureate of Ukraine, was an ardent Communist. They were brainwashing us and slowly succeeding. Other ideology classes included caricatures of Germans as pigs and lessons in how stupid and inferior Ukrainians were compared to Russians. In spite of myself, I began accepting some of those attitudes. I stopped speaking Ukrainian.

Ukrainian books were not used at the orphanage school—even though we were in Ukraine. Ukrainian books were, however, available. The orphanage director, a caring man, understood our background and the families we came from. He cared about Ukrainian culture and books. Secretly, he was supportive of me and other farmers' children who had no parents.

We also attended a shooting class. We studied the rifle: the way to take it apart, put it back together, and shoot. The rifles and the shooting always upset me. I was reminded of the militias which surrounded my home and took my parents away. When I realized no one noticed whether I was there or not, I stopped going.

Because I'd been exposed to tuberculosis, the director took me and another child to see a doctor. We left early in the morning on a sled. On our way back from the doctor's clinic, we went by the director's house where his mother lived. She welcomed us and served us a nice meal. We ate every morsel offered. She gave us what she had with love. Her sad face said she understood our plight. It helped to know there were people like her.

The director saw to it that the basic needs of every child were met. He was fair with us and the staff—too fair. He was removed, arrested in the night, because he cared for the children and for the future of Ukraine. Like all caring people, he was probably reported to authorities for working against the State. Employees who didn't care about orphans were stealing blatantly enough for the orphans to know it. Maybe the director tried to stop the stealing; maybe some of the workers just didn't like him.

A laundry woman, who worked hard washing our clothes by hand, appeared to be the one to work against the director. She had some small children and no husband. She started to give speeches, rude and humiliating speeches, criticizing other workers, honest and dishonest alike, with the director a main target. The speeches were empty, hot air, but other employees became afraid of her. She had learned the tricks of the Party well; she had found the way to make a better life for herself. She became a boss of other workers, and when our caring director disappeared, she became the director. Soon after that, we were eating oatmeal three times a day. We had soup made with oatmeal, then a second dish of thick oatmeal.

In the summer, orphans and teachers moved to a camp on the Sea of Azov where we went swimming every day. We lived in long shacks that had no windows. That summer is mostly a blank except a nine-year-old boy drowned. The story spread through the orphans that it was the director's son.

That fall, Grisha let me know he was in **Dnepropetrovsk** and told me how to find him. The following spring—in 1940, at age fourteen—I finished the seventh grade. The girls were given two dresses and four rubles, and the boys were given something comparable. We were driven in a truck to a nearby town and told, "Good-bye; you are free, finished; you're on your own." I don't know what happened to the other children. Some probably went to the technicum (trade school) where they would sleep in tiny rooms with five or six others and learn a trade. Some of them would be sleeping outside or in train stations. I was lucky I could go to Grisha. Kryvyy Rih was a sad place; I was not sorry to leave it. None of the girls I knew said much about leaving. We had left too many places without knowing what was next.

When we got out of the truck, we were in front of a bazaar. An accordion player was making music for dancing bears. We didn't know about shopping in the modern sense, but we had freedom and money in our pockets, and we wanted to see everything that was for sale and to experience moving among people. We spread out and that's when a Gypsy woman spotted a cluster of us girls. She could see we were naive and started telling us, "Give me one ruble, and I'll tell you your fortune." She talked on and on, inventing my life as she went, "You will be all right. You are going to go many places and meet very important people. Give me another ruble and I will tell you more." In one sinking moment, I realized three of my four rubles were gone, and I needed those four rubles for train fare and food. The Gypsy told the other girls their fortunes, too, but they walked away after giving her one ruble.

I started to think she had cheated me. The woman was walking away rapidly. I ran after her and told her, "You give me my money back." The Gypsy looked at me and said she'd already told me my fortune and couldn't give my money back. I said, "I'm going to call the militia." She saw I was about to shout or scream and gave me back my money. I was lucky that time and learned one more lesson by making a mistake.

We wandered around the bazaar and stopped to eat *pirozki* (a kind of dumpling) and drink *kvass* (a sour fruit drink). After an hour or two at the bazaar, I went to the train station. Just as there had been no good-byes when we left the orphanage, there weren't any good-byes when we left each other.

I got on a train to **Dnepropetrovsk** where Grisha and Claudia lived. The compartments had the benches that folded out for sleeping, but that night I couldn't sleep.

Country One: Ukraine and Life Without My Parents

Chapter Four
Dnepropetrovsk and Simferopol 1940–1942

Dnepropetrovsk was a large city in eastern Ukraine, but I found Grisha and Claudia without difficulty. They were renting one tiny room from another family. Grisha was surviving that time by painting Party propaganda slogans, which, given his hatred of communism, was torture for him. But that was the way he bought food. Claudia was working in an office. They had had no children during the two years I was in the orphanage.

Grisha and Claudia didn't seem happy anymore. Grisha, of course, still had to check in with the local police and keep moving, which meant Claudia hadn't been able to advance in her field.

I started looking for a job and found a good opportunity to be a nurse. I was all right until I had to look at blood and got sick. From then on, I was sick to my stomach all the time I was at the hospital, so I was told to leave. I couldn't get a job, and the only classes I could get were art. If I could draw portraits, maybe I could get work.

While I was studying art—in the fall of 1940, a few months after I reached **Dnepropetrovsk**—Claudia's parents got ill, and she left us to go stay with them in Kursk. We never saw her again.

Soon after that, Grisha's health started failing. Claudia's leaving was surely part of the reason but not all. Grisha did

suffer that brutal arrest and the three years of harsh imprisonment for protesting Stalin's starvations. If doing hard labor
and getting little food wasn't enough to break body and spirit,
he still had the stress and strain of repeated moving, regular
reporting to police, and constant struggling to eat. I watched,
terrified, as my only protector in the world got sicker and
sicker. At fifteen, I could surely have survived alone, but I did
not have the feeling I could.

With Claudia gone, Grisha and I usually ate at a cheap
student cafe. He was often ill or had no interest in going places.
There were no more picnics or gatherings at river's side. Also,
winter was approaching, so we sat in our room for long hours.
If Grisha had anything to read, he read. At times, he and I
talked about our home and parents and family. Often Grisha
explained to me what was happening in our country and in the
world. Many times, he did not feel like talking and sat quietly
or slept.

I became friends with one girl, Svetlana, in art class.
Her parents were Ukrainians, but they were in the Party and
quite well off. They had a huge apartment with two big rooms.
I asked Svetlana to ask her mother if I could wash floors for
them in exchange for a place to sleep and breakfast. They
took me in, and I was quite comfortable.

The mother and father fought all the time because the
mother was obsessed with her child and had no time for the
husband. I think she actually hated him. I'd never experienced
anything like that. Not even Marussia was against Jasha because of her children. My parents never argued. The family
arguments I had heard had to do with food and work and
survival. I didn't know what to make of people who had food
and comfort being unpleasant to each other and making the
whole house unpleasant.

In spite of her parents, I became attached to Svetlana
during that time. She was kind and clever. And with her, I saw
what her mother's concern could mean. When Svetlana got

her period, her mother helped her, cared for her. That, too, was unknown for me. When I was in Kyiv in the first or second grade, I saw mothers who were nice to their children, but I hadn't seen someone caring for a girl in the way Svetlana's mother did.

Svetlana's mother was not unkind to me, but I'm sure I was there only because she wanted to do everything Svetlana wanted. I was given radishes with salt and bread for breakfast, and I ate and ate and ate. I didn't know when to stop—couldn't stop. Svetlana's mother was not happy I ate so much and began giving me less food. I became aware she was aware of how much I was eating, but I still didn't know how to stop myself.

Svetlana and I continued to go to the art class. On some days I did good work. On other days, I couldn't. I was worried, distracted, emotional. I didn't have the confidence to try anything difficult and never thought of doing anything personal. Doing the portraits of Lermontov and other famous Russians in a class setting was safe. Soon it was time for Grisha to move again, and I left the class. The interlude of stability at Svetlana's house was nice, but conditioned as I was to instability, I probably couldn't have stayed there much longer anyway.

Grisha got more work painting communistic propaganda slogans. Every business had to show it was part of the revolution or risk trouble, so things such as "Our Hero Lenin" were on large signs on buildings and walls all around town. I began helping with the work, maybe painting a little bit, running errands, cleaning, and other such things. Grisha sometimes gave me money. A few people he worked for paid me to do some little job. I treated myself to one luxury, a small cross on a chain, but most of the money I saved.

At one factory, I talked with the factory manager and must have told him I didn't have any parents because he took me to meet some wealthy friends of his, a Party general and his wife who had no children of their own and wanted to adopt. During the winter of 1940–41, the couple invited me to their home a few times and fed me quite well.

They were hoping I'd convince Grisha to let them adopt me. Grisha refused to hear of it and forbade me to see them again. I went to their house one last time to tell them I couldn't stay. The husband and wife got angry. They were expecting us to jump at an offer from people who were so well-placed. They saw me looking at all the foods laid out on their table but didn't offer me anything. As hungry as I was all the time, it was torture to leave, but Grisha knew what was best. I wondered what I would've done on my own.[8]

All the while, conditions in **Dnepropetrovsk** became worse and worse. Government organized gangs harassed people on the streets, hitting and kicking them, spitting on them. Anyone who looked even slightly different was grabbed off the sidewalk and called "fascist" or "spy." There was no way to protest. Before a person could say anything, that person was in jail, and even for one with a clean record, it took weeks to clear the record and name.

One time Grisha and I were walking in the street, and we saw hoodlums beat a frail old man right in front of us. As Grisha and I tried to walk past that gang, one of them pointed to Grisha and yelled, "He's a spy." I smiled sweetly at the gang members, and they let us go. Such government intimidation created terrible fear that controlled the masses.

In the spring of 1941, everyone was concerned with the war in Europe. Grisha, who read papers and listened to radio reports and other people, was talking about Germany's moves toward the east—Poland, Bulgaria, Rumania, and so on. Grisha was saying the nonaggression pact Germany and USSR signed in 1939 didn't mean anything to the Nazis and they would keep going east right into USSR. And he was right.[9]

In June 1941, the German army invaded USSR to take

the granaries of Ukraine. Panic hit the people of Dnepropetrovsk, but at the same time, they kept their daily routines. People standing in line for food talked about how soon the Germans would arrive and whether to stay or flee to some unknown place. Many around us were already leaving. Old Jews knew they had to evacuate. Many Soviet people fled to Asia. The propaganda at the time was that anyone who didn't evacuate was sympathetic to the Germans.

Dnepropetrovsk was a large enough target that in September or October there were some air raids. Horrible, loud sirens would go off, and we'd run to basements. There was no such thing as a bomb shelter in Ukraine. If bombs ever hit one of those buildings, everyone inside was likely to die.

Grisha had been saying, "We must leave, but where to go?" He didn't want to evacuate deep into Asia or to any place under Communist rule. We didn't care who controlled the country as long as it wasn't the Communists. So we decided on Crimea, hoping to escape from there to the West.

Grisha got us on a night train to Simferopol, Crimea, the southernmost part of Ukraine that extended into the Black Sea. Grisha had an address of someone he knew. That was in late August or early September 1941. Sometime in September, Germans got to Kyiv, and a month later, they took Odessa.

The place we were looking for in Simferopol was a big, beautiful stone house, which, before the revolution, belonged to some wealthy merchants. In 1918, after the revolution, many families moved into that house. Several Jewish families were staying there when we arrived. The house featured big windows and an impressive entrance, which required going up a few steps and across a terrace. We got a room assigned to a lady who was away but expected to return. We had a window looking out on the terrace. Everybody used the one big kitchen.

With the strain of getting out of Dnepropetrovsk, Grisha's health got worse. I had hoarded a few rubles, which enabled me to buy some food from peasants. A neighbor three houses away had a cow, and I bought some milk. In the turmoil of the times, we were able to scavenge some food people left behind when they fled. When Grisha was well enough, he found work. We made it through the winter of 1941, but Grisha found no way for us to go west.

Even though Grisha was getting still sicker, he did meet some famous artists that winter. At Easter, he and I visited a group of artists. The mother and father who lived there had three little eggs—great treasures at that time—for their children. It was rare to see happy faces on children, but those children showed so much delight I'm sure the rest of us forgot our own hunger. And I suspect none of us allowed ourselves to think of the past when any social gathering would have been occasion for tables loaded with food of every kind.

We were able to visit another friend of Grisha's, a famous older gentleman who painted pictures of horses. Beautiful paintings. He was selling enough work to survive. Grisha met several other Ukrainians who had gone to Crimea just ahead of the Germans, but going around to visit people was dangerous.

Somehow, Grisha always knew people—tradespeople, artists, musicians. One of his friends said I had the size and appearance to be a part of the chorus in a theatre production. I had no experience as a singer or dancer, but that didn't seem to matter; I was told I could learn. Amazingly to me, I soon had a job in a small theatre which was staging the Ukrainian opera, *Zaporozhets Za Dunayem*. I didn't know a theatre was even in operation, but at fifteen and a half years old, I was part of a production.

The head of our theatre company, the local diva, was a beautiful lady with a beautiful voice. She took me under her wing, which was flattering. She said I had a good mezzo-soprano voice and gave me valuable lessons in singing. Often, she told me, "You have everything it takes to be a good actress. Study singing. Put a note in front of your face to remind you the only thing you have to do in life is practice, practice, and practice some more." But it was wartime. Who could think about a career in acting or singing?

While we were in rehearsal, the Germans began a spring offensive into Crimea. One morning, I was awakened early by the sounds of guns. I looked out the window and saw dead Soviet soldiers and horses lying on the river bank. German soldiers were entering the city. The disorganized Soviets, who had one rifle for every five soldiers, were fleeing in trucks, on foot, by horses.[10]

A day after the Soviet soldiers were gone, German soldiers appeared at our house and ordered everyone into the courtyard to see who was living here. About fifteen families appeared—very few men among them. I was scared, but compared to the way Soviet soldiers shoved and pushed and made people wait and wait, the Germans were well-organized. They lined everyone up and counted. We were then told to stay close to our own apartments and everything would be all right—if we caused no problems, we would be left alone. There would be a six p.m. curfew.

Two little Russian men ran out, shouting to us, "Someone's hiding in the loft! Come look!" None of us moved. The two men were surely guerrilla fighters left behind by the Soviet Army, trying to lure their own Soviet civilians into ambush situations. According to them, all of us left behind in Crimea were Nazi collaborators. As we learned later, every time guerrillas killed one German soldier, fifty innocent civilians close by were rounded up and shot. The Soviet men apparently were not concerned about that.

The night before the government changed hands, a wealthy Jewish man and a high official in the Communist Party, asked Grisha to help pack his belongings. Grisha helped, and the man quietly disappeared that very night. Many people headed for the coast and left by boat.

The Germans made all Ukrainian Jews wear the Star of David and Gypsies some other sign. Slowly, the Germans arrested Jews and Gypsies, and they were never seen again. Many were shot. I saw Germans putting Jewish people inside a fenced area. Grisha had a Jewish friend being held there and tried to get him out by telling the German soldiers his friend was not Jewish. The soldiers warned Grisha to get away or he would be put inside, also. The Gypsies had lived in shacks so close together that cooking odors from one shack spread to all. Soon, Gypsy shacks and mud sidewalks were empty.

When the Soviet troops fled Crimea, they poisoned food supplies so Germans would not get any food; they had no thought of feeding their own people. I went with a group to an abandoned marmalade factory where we opened barrels of jelly. Poison was visible on top, but people scooped it away and ate the marmalade. I took some home for Grisha, which he ate, but it made me sick.

We were stuck there in Crimea, with German soldiers all around us. Grisha and I had no experience or information we could use to plan any action. We survived, day to day, mostly on milk from our neighbor's cow. And life went on.

Rehearsals for the opera continued, and opening night arrived. Considering the conditions, we thought the opening went well. Our theatre was small and filled with people every night, many of them German soldiers. Grisha attended performances and was proud of me. After each show, I ran home because of curfew. I don't remember whether I had some kind of permit. I do remember I had a lovely Ukrainian costume and the experience was wonderful for me—I had never known such excitement, glamour, and make-believe. I even received some small payment, which was like a bonus, and it kept Grisha and me going.

The opera closed after a few weeks, and we still had the same questions about what to do—or try to do. Perhaps there was nothing we could do. Grisha held to the hope that somehow we would get to the West. Being sent back into the depths of Russia, into the USSR, was to him the worst fate imaginable. Even after the Germans occupied Crimea, he was looking for a way out. Each day, he said that if he felt better the next day, he would try to get to a port to see what shipping was continuing. If we had been in Sevastopol instead of Simferopol, that might have been possible, but the fifty miles might as well have been five hundred. There was no way for him to get there even if he had been well.

One day not long after the opera closed, I was not feeling good myself, perhaps owing to malnutrition and exhaustion, and was lying down. Grisha, who was much sicker than I, asked me to go get us some food. It was getting close to 6:00 p.m., and the second I stepped out of the house, a German soldier stopped me and started talking. Even though I had studied German, I wasn't proficient, certainly not good enough to understand dialects. I understood almost nothing he was saying, but it was clear he intended to talk until curfew time. I tried to say I needed to go only three doors away to get milk for my sick brother, but he kept talking and checking his watch. I was too terrified to walk away.

At six o'clock, he smiled and said he had to arrest me because I was out past curfew. He politely took me to the *Comandatur*. I didn't know what was worse, rude soldiers or polite ones. I didn't know what to think about that foreigner, that occupier, who was arresting me and smiling. At the *Comandatur*, soldiers asked a few questions, put me in prison, and left me there. I told them I had a sick brother. They didn't care.

I spent a week or more in that prison—a huge basement room with almost no light. The air was stale, and the room was filled with Soviet people of both sexes and all ages. We slept on a concrete floor with no blankets or pillows. Our food was some kind of watery, dirty, barley soup. Some prisoners had lice and various diseases. I tried to avoid exposure to the worst of problems.

Every once in a while, a soldier appeared and shouted, "Come on women, let's go." And we'd go to the bathroom in large groups. If we needed to go at any other time, that was too bad.

The German soldiers ignored us except for the scheduled feeding and toilet times. A few of the prisoners suffered some kind of emotional breakdown and screamed or cried. I tried to sleep the time away. Most people simply sat there. They were too hurt to cry and at the same time too hardened to give expression to their pain.

I did befriend a very young mother. Her husband and the husband of a neighbor had been drafted into the Soviet army and were gone. Both young women had babies the husbands had not seen. The woman and her friend had been taking turns traveling to the countryside, trying to trade clothes for food from farmers. The other one stayed with the infants to nurse them. One day, the woman was caught with some food. That was her crime—for which she had already been imprisoned a month. She didn't know what happened to her baby.

After I was there a few hours, the heavy doors opened, and Grisha was thrown in. He was relieved to find me. He had gone looking for me after curfew so he would be arrested. Once we could talk, Grisha started worrying about us. He said we were in a bad situation. He feared we might be in prison for months upon months and saw no way out of Crimea even if we got out of prison. I was too young and stupid to know fully what danger we were in.

We lost count of days, but one day soldiers appeared, a few names were called, and we were among them. Grisha and I scrambled to our feet. The Germans let us out. We were dirty, unwashed, but lucky to be out of prison. We ran home and washed. Of course, there was no food, and Grisha's condition was worsened by his being in prison. I had to find a source of food.

The Germans had taken over half the first floor of the house we lived in and set up an infirmary with about fifteen beds for their wounded. A male nurse named Feldscher was in charge. I asked him if I could work in exchange for food. He hired me, and I started to work washing floors, cleaning beds, and doing other such jobs. I got leftovers—whatever was cooked that no one ate and other scraps from the kitchen—which fed Grisha and me.

Not long after I started to work there, Feldscher told me one day to clean his room. I went there and started work. A few minutes later, he appeared and forced me onto his bed. He was so fast and so definite about what he was doing I couldn't stop him. He acted as if it was not a matter of any importance to have sex with a worker. He told me I could be tossed out onto the street and someone else would scrub floors. He said I could scream but anyone who could hear was under his command and would laugh at me. Apparently, it was his routine. There was no choice for me—just fear and humiliation. I got pregnant and was told to have an abortion. I was sixteen years old.

Again, there was no one I could tell. Grisha was the only person who cared, and telling him would cause him to feel anger and misery because he could do nothing or to go after Feldscher and be killed. I blamed myself. I felt so sad I could hardly talk or move. I could feel grateful only that Feldscher left me alone.

At least, I could feed us if I kept working there. At least, Grisha was not starving.

Every so often recovered patients left, and new sick soldiers arrived. One day, a young soldier who transported a sick one to the infirmary told me to go with him. The way he looked at me told me what he intended. He guided me to an empty room and started to undress me. I resisted him, and he tore my underwear. I struggled more, and he became wild. He cursed me in German and shook me. I don't know where I found the courage—or the foolishness—to resist him. He could have killed me right there, and no one would ever have questioned him. He indicated if I wanted to stay alive, he'd better have his way. Once again, I learned a man like that considers only his pleasure, his need. Once again, I became pregnant, and again I had an abortion.

Both those men left me feeling dirty and sick. My body, which was already drained by years of insufficient nutrition, was traumatized by two rapes, two pregnancies, and two abortions so close together. My mind was no better.[11]

Grisha continued to get worse. One day, in the late spring of 1942, I was upstairs practicing German with a Russian teacher. When I went back to our room, I found Grisha dead. He died alone at age thirty-one. I ran out of our room crying. Neighbors came and helped me get a coffin, and an old man with a wagon and a horse that was barely alive took Grisha to a cemetery in Simferopol. Neighbors went with me, for which I was grateful. I don't know who paid for the burial. We had no priest, no stone, no marker. He was covered with dirt, and that was the end. That day I cried.

Many people died like that. There were no doctors. No more than a week earlier, an older woman in that house went screaming to me, asking for help. Her husband was complaining of feeling hot and cold. In a short time he died. Malnutrition killed him just as it killed Grisha.

I was sorry Grisha had to die alone.

I was very, very sorry Grisha never got to the West, never became a fulfilled artist.

After Grisha's death, I kept scrubbing floors to eat. I don't think I had any thoughts or feelings about myself and my situation. I couldn't have done anything with them. I was just sorry Grisha had died. For almost six years he had been my only contact with my family, my guide, my strength, my decision maker, my teacher. He was the only friend I had. I suffered a great loss. But Grisha had lost more. He lost his plans, his talent, his ideas, his health, his contacts with many friends, his chance for a productive life, his hopes for a better world.

I couldn't find any addresses or letters from Mykola and Jasha. Grisha had written to them and had told me they had it worse than we did. But I couldn't let them know what happened. Maybe there was no mail service by then anyway. I did find the two documents Grisha received when he was trying to locate our parents. I wrapped them in another piece of paper to keep with me.

In self-defense, I needed to improve my German. I didn't want to learn German any more than I'd wanted to learn Russian, but I worked daily with the lady upstairs. She tutored me, and I gave her scraps from the infirmary. I shared as much as I could. Even with my physical problems and limits, I was young and had a better prospect for surviving than older people.

One day in October or November of 1942, soldiers knocked on our doors and ordered all young people into the courtyard. We didn't have to know the word *Schnell* to understand we were being told to hurry. As soon as we were assembled, the soldiers told us we had ten minutes to get our clothes and get back to the courtyard. My clothing, as it had been for years, was limited—two dresses, one coat, one pair of shoes, a change of underwear. My only other possessions were my little cross that never left my neck and the documents about our parents. Some of Grisha's paintings and books were still there. I couldn't take even one of them. I would have nothing of Grisha's as a keepsake.

The soldiers loaded teenagers and children into trucks and took us to a big hall where we slept on the floor. The next day, we were put in railroad cars with no seats—just straw on the floor. The doors were locked, and the train left the

Eugenia Sakevych Dallas

Simferopol station. We had no idea where we were being taken.

My Mother

My mother with her tender care
Looked at me with so much joy
She watched over me always
with so much pride in her eyes

      I was her life
      She always hugged and kissed me
      She always talked to me asking for my advice
      making me feel I was Special

My mother was taken away from me
at the tender age of five.
I lost her steady love and care
My World crumbled around me

      My joyful, happy childhood was over forever.

My little friend in the second grade
Her mom was tender just like mine
with pride, love and kisses,
Just to watch, would make my heart tremble.

      I would burst into tears
      So much pain for a child to bare
      without loving care of a Mother
      I wish I had my Mother

Country Two: Austria and Life as a Forced Laborer

Chapter Five
Graz, Austria 1942–1945

We were on the train over a week, many young people crowded into a large railroad car with straw on the floor and a wood-burning stove for heat. Doors were locked at all times; if the straw had caught fire, we'd have died. From time to time the train stopped—sometimes for minutes, sometimes for hours—and we were fed or allowed to go to the bathroom alongside the tracks. There was no place to wash, and, no matter how long the train was stopped, we had to get back into the railway car immediately. The guards allowed no activity and told us nothing about our fate.

With all the changes from the time I left my room in Simferopol, I became ill and ran a high temperature. I lay in the straw, soaked in sweat, some days not knowing where I was or what was happening. Finally, the fever went down. I regained my consciousness, my mind, my thoughts, and, slowly, some strength.

During those days of partial consciousness, there was one incident that made its way into my awareness. A Russian-speaking woman with her teenage daughters was accused of being Jewish. By whom, I didn't know. She denied the accusation, saying she was Rumanian, but the guards took that woman and her daughters off the train. Before they were outside, they were crying. Then, the anguish of the woman's cries came back through the closed door.

Eugenia Sakevych Dallas

When we arrived at our destination, sometime in November 1942, soldiers there told us we were in Graz, Austria. We were taken to a sort of military camp and put into big wooden barracks. Along the side walls were long rows of bunk beds. There was no other furniture, and there were no separate quarters for men and women. The only separation was that younger people slept in the upper bunks. There was only one bathroom in each building. Around the barracks were soldiers with dogs, barbed wire fences, and big gates. At night, the barracks area was brightly lighted; no one could step outside without being seen as easily as in daytime. There was absolutely no way to escape.

Our first day, the soldiers rounded us up with rifles in their hands and made us march a long way, perhaps two or three kilometers, to a large building. Soon, I was working in a wagon factory that had been changed to a munitions plant where all kinds of ammunition and weapons were being made: shells, bullets, rifles, everything. I was put at a machine that cut threads into bolts. I don't know to what use the bolts were put. I only remember that cold, milky water ran all the time to keep the metal cool. My hands were constantly numb and painful from the cold. I made the same five or six motions again and again without stopping.

Often, I have been asked what I felt to be dropped into a distant country, to be in the West for the first time, to be in a forced-labor camp, and to be exposed to bombing. I have to say I didn't feel anything one way or another. I'd already seen starvation, had already been under control of authorities, had known some bombing, and had just lost a wonderful brother whose great desire was to be in the West. At the time, I was too numb to feel fear or excitement or anything else that might be expected. I simply didn't care where I was.[12]

The work in the munitions plant was not only tedious but also continued for long hours seven days a week. The mind and body were so drained we wanted nothing more than

72

sleep. We weren't allowed to sleep long enough, but we weren't allowed to do anything else. I had little sense of the passage of time. One day someone said it was the first day of the new year, 1943. I couldn't tell whether I had been there two weeks or six.

The laborers in my camp were mostly teenagers. Some of them were badly affected by the experience. It was sad to see those who, away from their parents, forgot their own languages. One of the most damaged was a girl who spoke every language at once. Words from German, Ukrainian, Russian, and French were run together without any pattern I could detect. A person who didn't know all those languages couldn't understand her, and often, even when I knew every word she spoke, I couldn't tell what she meant.

Forced laborers from many different countries were working at the factory. In addition to people from Slavic and east European countries, there were people from Western Europe, especially French and Italians. Curiosity about people from other cultures replaced some of my apathy, and in a limited way I became enchanted by the variety of people, their tongues, and attitudes. I not only learned to speak French by talking with laborers working side-by-side with me, but I also learned something about French people. The Westerners seemed somehow more refined than our Soviet people. Their behavior was kinder, softer, more civilized. But I had to remember that Soviet soldiers and Party officials—who deserved to be called boorish—had so dominated my life I didn't have a fair basis for comparison. I'd had limited contact with well-mannered Soviet citizens.

I sometimes talked with one of the Austrian women who worked in the factory. She showed as much sympathy for us as she could and seemed to take pity on me. Every so often she'd have a sandwich for me, which I appreciated. We were fed but not well and not enough. Of course, that was true for everyone.

In a sense, we were lucky there was any food in the country. More of us could have died. As it was, many young men died, collapsing right there on the factory floor from malnutrition. Or sometimes as we were walking from the factory back to our barracks, someone collapsed from exhaustion. A guard dragged the body to the side, and we never saw that person again.

The only interruptions in our work and sleep schedule were Allied air raids. If we were working, we ran to the basement of the factory when we heard sirens. If we were in the barracks, we ran to a bomb shelter. When there wasn't time to get to the basement, I'd lie on the floor of the factory, holding the floor with my hands as if the earth would save me. We might be in the basement for a long time, or the all-clear signal might sound after a few minutes, and we'd go back to work only to hear the sirens again a few minutes later. Some entire days were spent running from the work floor to the basement and back.

The raids were horrifying. The sounds of an air raid—the penetrating, pulsing cry of sirens, the screaming whistle of bombs falling, and the explosion of bombs—are frightening even in movies. The raw sounds are worse, different and worse. Yet there were times when I felt no horror, no fear. After a while, I stopped running from the barracks to the shelters. Other laborers also took the attitude that whatever would be would be. We were simply too exhausted, our bodies too run-down to spend the energy running and then pushing our way into shelters. We just didn't care anymore. I'd lie in my bunk thinking if a bomb hit me at that minute it would do me a favor. But sometimes—for what reason, I'm not sure—I ran to the bomb shelters with everybody else.

What those raids meant in the progress of the war we didn't know. All through 1943 and 1944, we heard Soviet troops had just recaptured some area in the Soviet Union. Places in Ukraine were mentioned, mostly large cities. In 1944, it seemed the areas the Nazis lost were closer and closer to us, places in Poland, Hungary, Czechoslovakia, Bulgaria. In 1945, the raids became more frequent, and we guessed that might mean the end was near.

One time I was fired at by a low flying plane. I guess we were walking between the camp and the factory when the sirens sounded. Allied planes flew in and started bombing. One plane flew very low, firing bullets at everybody on the ground. I crawled under a little wooden fence, which, of course, was no protection, but I needed to be on the ground, gripping the earth. As I lay there, I thought I heard voices from above screaming, "Shoot her! Shoot her!" I know it was impossible for me to have heard voices from a plane, but that's how terrified I was. I was told Allied planes would not be firing on prisoners. Maybe pilots didn't know who we were. Maybe there is another explanation, but the attack was real. People near me went down, dead. Afterward, the living stood, and the German soldiers marched us on as if nothing had happened. I felt strange to be walking. I was surprised I wasn't dead.

About a year and a half after I arrived, bombs did hit the munitions factory. I was in the basement, and though the explosion and the shaking of the building made me think I'd surely be dead that time, I wasn't hurt. The factory was damaged far beyond repair. When the all clear sounded, German soldiers were outside to see that no one escaped. We were marched to our barracks, and soldiers made certain fences and gates were still in place.

The next day, we were marched to another munitions plant, that one perhaps three or four kilometers from the barracks, and sent immediately to production lines. I was given a few minutes of training and put to work wiring electrical motors. Besides the additional time it took us to get to that plant, we worked longer hours and got less food. The Germans had children working there, standing on their feet all day long.

Children fainted. Children died. Nobody paid attention. Other laborers kept working, or they would be dead. Just as happened with the famine in Ukraine, people stepped over the dead and kept going.

In 1944, I met a young Hungarian man named Franz who had recently started working in my factory. I fell in love with that tall, handsome Madiar. For the first time, I loved someone and was loved in return. I was in a new world. The love of a man was distinctly different from anything I'd known. I had painful reasons to recoil from the physical presence of a man, but, as strong as that instinct was, it didn't make me turn away from gentle Franz. The way in which we were thrown together during an air raid gave us a feeling in common: we hated the Nazis and wanted the Allies to beat them, but the Allied bombs might kill us.

In fact, it was during bombardments of Graz that Franz and I had time together. We told each other what we knew and what we thought, and everything we said pulled us together. We spoke in German because neither of us knew the other's language, but we understood each other. When bombs exploded close to us, we felt shivers of fear the next explosion would destroy the building and us, so we held each other closely, feeling some security and temporary comfort in each other's arms. And, exhausted from the war and bombs and from work and malnourishment, we found some strength in each other, in feeling we were not alone.

It was strange and pleasing to feel physical attraction for a man. We let the war make us say, "Live for the moment—what will be will be." There were precious few times we could be together, and we expressed our physical love without concern for the future. (Neither of us knew anything about birth control anyway.) Too soon my big love, my man, was sent to some other place where his mechanical skills were needed. We said we'd find each other again.

After Franz left, my old anxieties came back. I could

be pregnant. I became depressed and confused. I promised myself I would never look at another man, and then I thought of the joy and pleasure of feeling affection and passion. How could there be any affection if I stayed away from men? But if I didn't stay away from men, how could I stay away from trouble? Collectivization and the war had taken away my life at Kamjana Balka; I could not grow up in a loving home and get married and make a loving home in a happy village. That was forever lost to me. But other people endured the same and greater loss. I couldn't let that loss excuse me. Still, I was disgusted with myself and kept telling myself everything was my fault. My mind kept spinning, bumping against contrary thoughts; it would not rest. My body wanted rest; it would not be strong enough to be pregnant and continue under the strain of work and air raids and my own emotional turmoil.

The Germans were getting desperate, and laborers started to smile because we knew they were going down. Soldiers were getting upset. In some ways, they were getting softer, less brutal, in handling us, but they still looked at us with contempt. One time, I saw a fat German soldier and his partner taking two laborers to another part of the camp. The soldiers had their rifles drawn, one in front, the other behind. The two prisoners were little more than skeletons. One of them fell and couldn't walk anymore. The soldiers made the other prisoner push him in a wheelbarrow. I could only hope those poor souls made it until the Allies arrived.

All kinds of rumors were going around about the end of the war. Somebody said it was over but the Germans in Graz wouldn't give up. The big questions for us were about what would happen to us. Would anybody be in authority? If so, who? Would we be sent back to our native countries? Would we have any choices? Would we be on our own? The French with whom I'd made friends invited me to go with them to France. I could converse pretty well in that easy, charming language and liked the idea of going to France. I definitely did not want to go back to USSR. To my old Ukraine, yes. To Soviet Ukraine, no.

We were working in the second factory about six months before it also was bombed. We heard the sirens, ran to the basement, and almost immediately heard and felt the building being hit. My ears hurt, and I was shaking with the building. After a while, no more bombs were hitting the building, but the procedure that always followed an air raid was not occurring. Something was different. Whether there weren't as many guards or they weren't as hostile wasn't clear, but after a long wait, we were told to leave the basement. We had to pick our way around debris, and when we got outside, we saw the factory was badly damaged. There'd be no more work there. On the way back to the camp, we were talking, and the guards were not ordering us to be quiet.

The next morning, no guards appeared to march us to work at another factory. There were no guards at the gates, and the gates were open. Some of us set aside our fear and ventured outside. The need to see what was out there was too strong to ignore. Many stayed in the barracks, some too afraid to leave, others too weak. I was weak but went anyway. I was curious, and I might find some food. We might have done that two days or maybe only one day, but we did see some fighting.

We could tell we were getting closer to some action and got behind a bombed out wall where we could watch without being seen. People were running in all directions. I heard bullets whistling and saw them hitting walls near us. Maybe we weren't safe after all. Then I saw tanks and soldiers, driving and running from one street to the other. Someone screamed, "Russians are there!" People started running in other directions. Tanks were driving fast, turning the curves of narrow streets without slowing. I couldn't always tell who was who, but wounded soldiers were falling. Everything was one ragged confusion, but Soviet troops were definitely in Graz.

I remembered watching that scene, but the next thing I remembered was waking up in a German hospital. I didn't seem to be hurt or wounded in any way. Nobody talked to me; the doctors and nurses were too busy. The hospital was overflowing with wounded soldiers, German and Soviet and maybe others. The German doctors treated everybody equally. It was as if they weren't a part of the war. Whether someone from camp took me to the hospital or helped me in some other way, I never knew. I was kept a couple of days and let go. Maybe I was pregnant and had a miscarriage. Maybe I collapsed from hunger. I never knew.

Back on the street, I learned the war was finished. I stood there, detached from everyone and with no place to go. I didn't know whether I was free or whether some other authority would grab me. I thought about looking for Franz, but I had no confidence he would be looking for me. Of all the possibilities I could think of, I most wanted to join the friends who asked me to go to France, so I started walking toward the camp.

Down one street, I saw some Soviet Mongolian soldiers and became uneasy. They frightened me, and I moved quickly to get out of their sight. In the next block, I encountered a Ukrainian girl from camp named Katia. I told her I didn't want to go back to Ukraine, that all of my family was dead, and that the Mongolian soldiers terrified me. She felt the same way. As we were talking, two young Soviet soldiers approached us. One grabbed me by the arm and ordered me, "Take off your watch." He had watches all up and down his arm, probably taken from Germans. I got so scared I screamed at him in Russian he should be ashamed of himself and I didn't have a watch. When they heard the Russian language, they ran as fast as they could away from us. I don't know who was more terrified, they or we. (And neither he nor I knew all his stolen goods would be confiscated when he got back to USSR.) I was still shaking after they ran off.

Our adventure did not end with the Soviet soldiers. After a few hundred yards, we encountered a drunken Soviet officer with heavy medals, an ordinary looking person with dirty curls. He was standing in front of a house, looking like a village farmer. He ordered us to go into the house where Soviet women soldiers were sitting and talking. We were getting nervous around those people. They did not pay any attention to us, so Katia and I stepped outside into the back yard. There we saw a tall young man with an intelligent face. He was a Soviet officer but was wearing civilian clothes and started interrogating us in Russian. I told him about my parents, Natalia, Gabriel, and Grisha, which left me with no family except a forty-year-old brother who had difficulty supporting his wife and children. I had nothing to go back to and didn't want to be a burden to anyone. The details of Katia's life were different, but she also had no promise or hope in Ukraine. The man stopped asking questions and said to us softly in Ukrainian, "Jump over that fence and run." He walked away from us, and we disappeared quickly. We were profoundly grateful to that man.

We ran as fast as we could toward camp. Somehow Katia and I got separated. As soon as I reached our area, I began asking about the French prisoners and, to my surprised disappointment, learned they were gone. I started asking other people what they were doing and where they were going. I saw a fourteen-year-old Serbian girl I'd talked with before. Milena was a tough girl who spoke every language and had been in Tito's army as a partisan and in German camps since she was ten or eleven years old. She told me there were enough French laborers in Graz to make up a train, which was the reason they were gone, but there weren't yet enough Italians. Apparently, some authority was making some decisions about moving people.

Milena said the Italians in our camp were going to the train station to wait for more Italians from farther north to make the required number and she intended to go with them. She said the men didn't care whether she went and wouldn't care if I went but both of us better get out of camp as soon as possible.

One thought of encountering more Soviet soldiers was all I needed to tell Milena I wanted to look for Katia and get my things from the barracks and I'd be ready. Milena went with me. On our way, I saw a Russian soldier inside our camp. He looked jubilant. Behind him were more Soviet soldiers, all Mongolians. I pulled Milena back, and we went another way. Then as we moved past one of the barracks, we saw a group of Soviet soldiers a short distance away. A commander was passing out loaves of bread to his men. They saw us, but made no attempt to stop us. I considered leaving my coat and my other dress in the barracks, but we were so close I ran in and out. We didn't see Katia anywhere.

Milena led us to the Italian men she had already talked with. All of them seemed to be telling all the others what to do all at once. Using her Italian, with some pointing at them and herself and me, Milena asked if we could both go with them. I smiled my best smile, and the men, true to the reputation of Italian men, said *si, si*. Milena looked at me and said the two of us would make a good team and should stick together.

Eventually, the men reached some kind of agreement. They seemed ready to leave, and minutes later we started walking to the train station. Milena and I walked with men all around us, hoping to stay out of the sight of Soviet troops. Other Italians were already at the station, and we settled in to wait. I supposed someone in the group was checking to find out when we might leave.[13]

Milena spent much of the waiting time talking to different men. One of them she introduced to me. His name was Mariano Fanti. He was a dentist who had been a prisoner of war in the north of Germany. He was in his mid or late twenties and quite pleasant. He and I had a good conversation, in

German, and continued the conversation at other times.

Waiting was unnerving and tiring. Sometimes, we got word our train would arrive soon, which made us excited until we concluded it was a false report. It was risky to leave the safety of being in the middle of the Italian soldiers, so I went quickly with my head down to the bathroom. Still, I was drawn into conversations with other people at the station. I talked with a German who spent three years as a prisoner in Graz because he was a German Communist. He was happy to be returning home. I said, "How curious. Here I am fleeing communism and you're happy to be Communist." We laughed. The whole thing seemed crazy to me.

Another time, I passed near an old German man who was trying desperately to talk to a Russian soldier. They did not understand each other and were getting nowhere. Wanting always to help, I stopped and offered to translate. I spoke broken Russian because I did not want the soldier to think I was Slavic and send me back. As soon as I translated enough to make them partially understand each other, I left. The old German kissed my hand in gratitude, but I was wondering whether I had been foolish to let myself be noticed by that Soviet soldier.

At last, a real train was arriving that seemed to be for us. We were told to line up four abreast. Fanti put me on the inside of a row close to the front, and I bent my knees so my height would be less noticeable. The movement must have attracted the attention of the Russian soldier I'd helped. He yelled at me from across the platform. My heart fell to my heels. Wanting to help might have me on my way to Siberia instead of Italy. My protector dentist told me to keep still and pay no attention. Anxiety was building in me, but I was calm on the outside; Grisha had taught me well to show no emotion. The Russian soldier started pushing his way through the crowd. Somebody stopped him, and the two of them were both talking at once. While he was detracted, we boarded the train.

I shrank even more and lowered my head to be out of sight Under my breath, I was saying, "Train, please go. Train, please go." Time stopped, but I continued saying, "Train, please go. Train, please go." When the train whistled and the wheels began to turn, relief washed over me. As we moved away from the station, joy swelled inside me. I lifted my head. Milena poked me and grinned. She had become my way out, and I said to her we should stick together, and she said we would.

We were on a transport train without any roof. We had no tickets, no documentation, no money, and no possessions. I had never held a passport, yet there I was, a Ukrainian, leaving Austria and headed for Italy. All I had on me were papers documenting my parents' arrests. I had the clothes I was wearing, the shoes on my feet, another dress, a coat, and my cross, which was hidden under my dress. I was rich! Slowly, we moved away from the station. Then, gradually, the wheels went around faster and faster. We were on our way out of Graz. It was May 1945, and I had been in Graz two and one-half years, working seven days a week. I was nineteen, almost twenty, years old. I had not felt so happy or so free since I ran through my father's fields.

Mariano Fanti kept close to me, continuing our earlier conversation. He asked what I would do when I reached Italy. I had not thought beyond getting away from the Soviets, had not one thought about living a normal life. I couldn't give a good answer. I supposed I'd go to work. After I said what I was thinking, Fanti said, "Come with me to my home. I have a mother, father, sister, brother. They will not mind." I was happy to say I would be pleased to go to his home, but I had to tell him about my agreement with Milena. He readily said she was welcome, too. I would later wish he hadn't been so willing because I paid a price for my friendship with Milena. Fanti's offer was worth breaking my agreement and wouldn't likely have bothered her.

During our happy train ride, no one slept even though we were exhausted. No one complained about being hungry even though we were starving. The Italians were so glad to be going home they sang almost without stopping. We asked over and over, "Is it real? Is the unbelievable real?"

About eight hours after we left Graz, we reached Linz, Austria. We were nervous about going north when Italy was to the south, but somebody told us Linz was a center for relocation. We were transported by British soldiers to a camp outside Linz and put in tents near the river. And we were fed. Our first meal outside camp was powdered scrambled eggs and sausages with bread and tea. What a delicious meal that was. I couldn't remember the last time I'd eaten—at least two or three days—and couldn't remember the last time I'd seen or eaten eggs and sausages—fifteen years perhaps—but I would always remember that special and delicious meal. And I savored it that day.[14]

Milena and I were in a tent by ourselves and appreciated the chance to wash in the river. We had seen no other women on our train from Graz or in that camp. Officially, our train was repatriating Italian soldiers, and more arrived from other places. The identification as Italian was fortunate because, as we learned, Soviet people were being held in another camp, and the Soviet government was pressing British and American forces to repatriate all Soviets. Luck was with us two women.[15]

After a few days, still in May 1945, we left Linz. Feelings of relief, joy, and excitement began building well before we got onto the train, and continued building until well after we were outside Linz. When, at last, some of the soldiers thought we were near the Italian border, first one and then another said he was sure we were in Italy. Each time one said we were in Italy, we all cheered. Then someone else said we weren't there yet. In minutes, there was another announcement we were there and another cheer. The excitement built, and when it seemed it couldn't go any higher, it did.

Later, I would recall good memories of Franz and the satisfaction of meeting people from other countries and learning other languages, but on that train I felt only joy to be escaping the pain and hunger and depression of the camp and factories of Austria. Even more, I felt a great sense of release, of freedom, to be out of the area of Soviet control.

My Childhood

I was robbed of my childhood
Happiness to me was denied
I went through turbulent life, but somehow survived
Why my life was spared?

I think I was chosen
to bring the message to the world

Ukraine by evil force was occupied.
Million souls were crucified
The rest conveniently russified

My parents were arrested
Their identity stripped
Why their destiny was so cruel?
Today I ask for what reason were they punished?

Me, when I first started modeling in 1946.

Country Three: Italy and Life as an Illegal Refugee

Chapter Six
Clusone and Milano 1945–1946

The whole village of Clusone was at the station that day in May 1945 to welcome Mariano and other soldiers. Never had I seen so much hugging or heard so much talking. Friends and relatives surrounded Mariano and were pushing and squeezing to touch him, embrace him, greet him. People were laughing and crying at the same time. The ones who could not get close to Mariano shared the joy with each other until they could get closer. Other soldiers had crowds around them, and the circles spread into each other. Some of the men were friends of Mariano's and were going to stay with him a few days before going to the south of Italy. Milena, who could speak Italian, was mixing with the people. I stood off to the side, watching. The whole scene was beautiful, and I was enjoying it immensely. Even without comparing what I was seeing with the labor camp, it was a wonderful scene.

No one can remain against the wall on such a joyous occasion, and I was pulled into the crowd. When the first burst of celebration passed its highest point, most of the crowd moved to the Fanti house without any break. People stood in the street for hours, laughing and talking, grouping and regrouping. Some sang songs, maybe at Mariano's' request, with everybody joining at times. Wine appeared, and toasts were made.

While the celebration continued, Mariano's sister, Tina, took Milena and me into the house and showed us a nice, sunny, bright room where we would stay. Tina gave us beautiful pajamas and personal items and showed us the bathroom. My first real and private bathroom. A bath there was a heavenly experience.[16]

Like the wine, delicious food appeared. People were in the house and in the street. The celebration continued long after I went to bed and into wonderfully satisfying sleep. I had just learned that being tired from joy is much better than being tired from misery.

Fanti's apartment was big and spacious: balconies, nice sized rooms, and a kitchen with a fireplace—a comfortable home for the family, now including us. In the following days, Tina gave Milena and me nice clothes. I had more garments and better food than at any time I could remember. One of Mariano's cousins, a cordial, charming, and educated lady who knew German, offered to teach me Italian. She was surprised at how well I knew the German language, and we made good progress from the beginning.

The village of Clusone, in the mountains near Bergamo, was a beautiful place. The slopes were green; flowers were blooming everywhere. Church bells rang often, providing tranquil music. It was spring, which revived my body and mind. I was charged with energy and happiness. Life became precious. I was a young woman, no longer starving, and began to think I had a life ahead of me.

The Fantis ran a delicatessen which sold butter, sugar, coffee, meats. They had stayed open during most of the war, and the end of the war would make it possible for them to get more goods to sell. I wanted to help Mariano's parents around the house and with their family business, but they insisted I relax, rest, and get healthy. I could do some housework when they weren't home, but I wasn't useful in the shop. Still, I did spend many hours with Tina and her parents, becoming another member of the family. They helped me with my Italian and encouraged me to look around Clusone and to meet other people. I liked them from the first day and felt good around them.

Mariano was a busy young man, going places with his friends day and night. He was young, handsome, blond. Naturally, every girlfriend he ever had in his life wanted to see him, and he was with one or another of them every night. When we were on the train, he seemed to be interested in me, but with so many women around him constantly, Mariano didn't pay any romantic attention to me. I was like family to him, and our conversations, although brief, were enjoyable and satisfying. I felt quite close to him and was confident of his concern for me. After two or three weeks of enjoyment, Mariano started to work setting up a dental office and building a new practice, which kept him busy all the time.

Even if I didn't see much of the person who invited me to stay in his home, I felt blessed to be there. I was fed, got to stay in a pretty room, no longer had to worry about suffering and starvation. Death was no longer a companion. Depression was leaving me. I forgot about getting to France. Destiny is destiny. I accepted what came and began to think that what happens, happens for the best. Besides, Italian is a lovely language, too, and I couldn't ask for better people than the Italians I'd met.

The one negative part of my life was Milena. I was struggling to speak Italian, and she mocked me during family dinners or found ways to get me to say words in German which doubled for impolite words in Italian. One time she pointed to a picture of a cat and asked me in German, "What is that?" I answered her in German, "*Katze*," then realized the Fantis were looking at me strangely. What they heard was "*cazzo*," an Italian word for the male sex organ. Mariano explained to the others when he heard about it, but I was still embarrassed and grew more and more uncomfortable around Milena.

She was also stirring up trouble within the Fanti family, turning brother against brother. I never knew exactly what she did or what was happening within the Fanti family, but the fights grew so bad Mariano's brother left for Argentina. Not long after that, Milena left, too. I never knew whether there was a connection, but I'm sure everyone was thankful no one would see her again.

To practice my Italian, I listened to everyone and talked with anyone who had the patience. I mastered at least ten new words every day. Many words I knew because French words were nearly the same—and the roots of French and Italian were the same. Of course, I had to watch for words that might once have been the same but had developed different meanings. Within three months, I spoke Italian well enough for ordinary occasions.

As I started exploring Clusone, I discovered there were many displaced Yugoslavians in the village. I started making friends, and we'd have coffee together at the local cafe. Some of them had lived there for a while, apparently preferring a fascist Italy to a communist Yugoslavia. They were always arguing what regime, what government, would be better for Yugoslavia, anarchy or democracy. They all had one thing in common: they had lost or given up their homeland; they were refugees. Their destiny was to live their lives in foreign lands. I had that in common with them, and some of them were quite interesting in other ways, so I enjoyed our coffee sessions together.

When I was with them, I wanted to practice my Italian although I could not always understand their Italian. Most of them understood Ukrainian and some Russian. One day some of us were sitting in a cafe, and a Yugoslavian who came in to join us told me a Russian man wanted to talk to me.

A tall, blond man wearing a Soviet army uniform with lieutenant's insignia did approach me. I froze. Speaking Russian, he introduced himself as "Leonid" and told me to call him "Lenia." He said he was in Italy trying to find Soviet people who wanted to get back to USSR. "I'd like to help you," he said. Then he asked me for leads on other Soviet refugees staying in Clusone. I disliked him immediately and told him I didn't know anyone from USSR. The last thing I wanted was for him to gather I was from Ukraine. He laughed, saying, "I'll be back."

As promised, Lenia came back. He appeared outside the Fanti house a few times. He never went inside the house or even knocked at the door. He waited down the street. Or he caught me somewhere in town where I was more vulnerable. He was usually friendly. He'd say he just wanted to "say hello." He made small talk, but he began asking questions: "When are you going back home?" "Why are you wasting your time here?" Or he'd say, "Your place is in the Motherland."

I couldn't tell whether he had information about me, so I tried to be vague and say as little as possible. I might say, "I don't have anything in USSR," and add nothing else. To many of his questions, I said. "I don't know," or "I'm not sure." I talked with Mariano about Lenia. Mariano was worried about my safety and wondered what he could do to help.

One day, I left the Fanti household and found Lenia was waiting for me in a fancy car. He was like a little boy wanting to show off a new toy, and in a few minutes asked if I wanted to join him for a ride. He said he had some business to take care of at the local police station and would then take me where I wanted to go. I didn't want to go with him, but he was insistent, and it seemed not going would be worse than going. He seemed to be trying to impress me with his importance. Being a Soviet officer in Italy did give him a certain amount of power. Soviet officers were swarming the place to take advantage of the governmental chaos in the breakdown of fascism.

We drove to an Italian Republic Police Station. When we entered, a police lieutenant saluted Lenia, and the whole office treated him like a VIP. While we were sitting in the lieutenant's office, there was a knock at the door. A man, in his forties, was pushed in and called *Fascisti*. The lieutenant asked the man a few questions and then asked me what I thought. I pulled together some courage and opened my mouth, "Well, each to his own. You have your ideas on politics; he has his." I wasn't going to take sides, but I didn't want to endorse any bad treatment. I simply looked into that prisoner's eyes, and the fear I saw there reminded me of when the Bolsheviks dragged villagers away.

The prisoner was taken to the basement, and I heard two shots. I was already nervous and started getting scared. Lenia enjoyed the whole spectacle. He walked around the station like a big shot, as if he owned the place. I felt sick at what happened to that poor family man. Just because he was thinking differently about life, he had to be killed.

After we left the police station, Lenia again brought up the question of when I was planning to go back. I answered simply, "I want to stay here in Italy." He told me he had to go away for a few days but would be back and I should be ready to go. He said he would take me to a place where many people from USSR would meet and be taken back. I was feeling uneasy by the time he let me out of the car.

I did not see Lenia for a few weeks and was beginning to hope he'd forgotten me. Then, one afternoon, I was sitting at the cafe with some Yugoslavians, practicing my Italian. A car stopped, and Lenia stepped out. He was obviously angry, and, barely saying *ciao* to the others, said he had to speak to me. I stood up and walked a few steps away from my friends. Lenia began giving me orders. "We have to go. We have to leave now." Again, I told him I didn't want to leave. "Don't argue," he said. "Let's go. Pick up what you have to, or go as you are." I was getting panicky. Lenia produced his gun, holding it close to him but pointing it at me.

I started to tremble like the smallest leaf on the tree. I raised my voice, yelling at Lenia, "I have nothing in the Soviet

Union. You killed everything dear to me. You destroyed my family, and now you're forcing me to go there." By that time, my Yugoslavian friends understood what was going on and moved over to save my head. One of them had been a Yugoslavian officer and wasted no time getting right next to Lenia, trying to calm him and blocking him at the same time. Another friend led me away from there.

They took me to the apartment of one of the group to spend the night. It wasn't safe for me to go back to the Fantis, and I didn't want to cause them any problems. Someone contacted Mariano, who advised I should go right away to a city where people don't know each other. He recommended Milano. Mariano and his sister gathered my things and sent them to me along with train fare to Milano and the name of someone to contact there. My Yugoslavian friends agreed Milano was a good choice. Everybody told me to get my name changed to something that sounded Italian and not Slavic so another Lenia would not find me. Early the next morning, a fall morning in 1945 not long after I had turned twenty (or nineteen) years of age, I was accompanied to the station. We didn't see Lenia or anybody like him. When the train arrived, we looked around again, and at the last minute, I climbed into the car.

It was sad leaving the Fantis. Even though I had been with them only five or six months, it was as though I truly had a family. I appreciated studying Italian with Mariano's cousin and sharing things with Mariano's sister. I enjoyed his parents and talking with Mariano whenever he had time. I was comfortable and delighted in their home. They were wonderful to me. I wrote to them, and years later, I visited the Fanti family, taking with me the best gifts I could get, hoping I could express to them in some limited way my unlimited appreciation for everything they did for me.

But, as always, I took things as they came. I was much better off than I might have been, and perhaps it was time for me to move on anyway. Maybe I could have lived my whole life in Clusone and maybe not. Maybe I would have met a Yugoslavian man about my age. Maybe Mariano would have run out of Italian girlfriends. Maybe I would have become restless. I don't know. "What if" might be a pleasant and tempting game, but it shouldn't be played seriously. In spite of any "what if" statement I made, I would be ending my stay in Clusone with the end of 1945 and getting a new start in Milano with the beginning of 1946.

The train was packed, standing room only for about five hours, and, in spite of my best thoughts about the way to think about leaving Clusone and the Fantis, I was feeling blue.

In Milano, I found my way to the woman whose name Mariano had given me. Mrs. Santucci was as kind and generous as the Fantis. She fed me and gave me a bed of my own in her bedroom. She and I had a good talk. She helped me with my Italian, and when I explained that agents from USSR were looking for people with Slavic names, she helped me find someone who knew what to do.

First, I let the Fantis know I arrived safely and their friend was kindly helping me. Next, I got in touch with a Russian man who was an Italian citizen working in city hall. For a fee of 3,000 lire, he helped people like me to change their names. He had two witnesses—people I'd never seen before— sign a document that they knew me. Then he said, "Now your name is Irma Simsolo, and you're Iranian, born in Tehran. These days, it's good to be Iranian." He chose the name and the nationality. He didn't ask me what I wanted, and before I could say anything, he handed me a small identification card, said "Good Luck," and walked away.

I think I said, "Thank you." I was a little dazed. I had become Iranian. And I was Irma. As I left the building, I was wondering, "God, why couldn't he have left my first name as Eugenia? Why Irma?" I did gradually go back to Eugenia, and for years I was Eugenia Simsolo from Iran. (I still have an

94

ID card and my United States Green Card with Eugenia Simsolo on them.) But I was a new person. I could blend in. My name would not mark me. I felt much more secure.

At that moment, I most needed a job. I was hungry to start working, and in the next few weeks I tried so many jobs I lost count. At first, I wanted definitely to work in a bank and made some attempt to do that. I must have thought a bank job would give my life stability. Of course, it was impossible for me to get a job in a bank. My Italian wasn't good enough, and I had no training or experience. How naive could I be?

I chanced to meet some Russian Jewish people who seemed to like me because I was friendly. One of them, a tailor, found me a position working for a wealthy Italian woman married to a Hungarian Jew. I moved in with the family and started to work, cleaning pots, scrubbing floors, taking care of the baby. I never stopped. At the end of three days, the woman said to me, "You don't know how to do anything right. I am a lady, and I know more about cleaning than you do." I probably had as much experience being a domestic as she had being a lady, but it was her house, and I was fired. For three days' work, her husband paid me fifty lire, not even a half day's pay. I didn't complain. I took my fifty lire and left.

I heard about a hairdresser who needed help. I went to her and got the job. I was given a couch in the salon and moved in. I worked hard, did everything from cleaning the place to washing hair. My hands were strong, and her customers complimented me when I washed their hair. With time, I was supposed to become a hairdresser. I was happy there until the owner started taking in her laundry from home and telling me to wash it by hand. When I washed her linens, they didn't seem clean, so I washed them again and tore them. I told her I wasn't good at domestic work, and she said she didn't need me. Back to step one.

Somebody told me a man was looking for domestic help for his wife and children in a country house. I went to an interview, but it soon became clear he was looking for a mistress who could also tend his children.

And on it went with other attempts. In my talking with people about jobs, I met other immigrants who told me about a Center for International Refugees called Schola Cadorna. Having no money and no place to go, I went there. The former school was a huge building which was packed with people from around the world. There were Greeks waiting for their families to help them return to their country. There were Swiss men who sympathized with Italy, had served in the Italian army, lost their Swiss citizenship, and were being denied reentry to their country. There were Yugoslavians, Russians, Ukrainians, Austrians, French, and Spaniards. We were given bunk beds and fed stew with macaroni, which we were told was American food. I couldn't have been happier and thought the cuisine was marvelous. Compared with camp food, it was superb. Delicious. After two weeks, I had to admit I was becoming less enthusiastic about the unchanging macaroni menu.

At Schola Cadorna there were people whose experiences were much like mine. When strangers met, the question was: "What horrible experience did you have?" They didn't ask the question in that way, but that was the question. I met two pretty sisters from Dnepropetrovsk, both of whom had been forced laborers in Germany. Valia was very pretty and very pregnant. She was engaged to one of the Swiss men who had served in the Italian army, and they were stuck as refugees. Genia was a stunning beauty who decided to go back to Ukraine where she hoped to find her parents. I told them of my encounter with Lenia and what I'd heard about former POWs and laborers who went back, adding that I wouldn't even consider going back voluntarily.

Genia was determined to go. The two made a plan for Genia to send a coded letter to Valia, indicating whether it was safe to return. I left the Center after a month or so but remained in contact with someone who told me Genia's letter from Ukraine did arrive and indicated she was being sent to Siberia.

Valia lost her sister. Then she lost her fiancé. His mother arrived from Switzerland with her whole family and a young girl she planned to marry to her son. If he married a Swiss citizen, he would be able to reenter Switzerland. In the face of his mother's rescue plan, the young man proved to be quite weak; his love for Valia faded, and he left her at the Center alone and pregnant. It was a pathetic and desperate situation, but Valia could do nothing to give the father of her child the spine to stay with her and the baby.

What happened to Valia I never learned. No resources for single mothers existed at that time. One heard stories about babies being sold on the black market by corrupt officials and doctors. I often thought about Valia. Her fate could have been mine.

Talking with Valia and Genia brought back memories of my family and of life on the farm. That was my Ukraine. What it became was not my Ukraine. The sadness and anger I felt made me alert for any mention of Ukraine. I was always hoping for some sign Ukraine once again would be what it was but always fearing it would never be the same.

At the Center, I had many conversations with people from Ukraine and neighboring countries. From them and from the Yugoslavians in Clusone, I remember some repeated comments about what had happened in our part of the world. Many people at the end of the war expected the United States would somehow go against USSR and remove the yoke of communism, and they were disappointed when they learned that agreements at Yalta gave the Soviets much power and influence. People who were inside USSR during most of the war didn't know the United States had supplied all kinds of war materials and supplies that saved the Soviet Union; they were told it was the might and resources of communism that prevailed against the Nazis and Fascists.

Some of the older ones remembered the start of communism. To some, Lenin was the great leader who could have made it work if he'd lived. Trotsky was the great strategist and organizer who made things happen and a spellbinding speaker who made listeners believe in communism. Stalin was the infighter who got rid of Trotsky and took over everything.

There were contradictory statements about the differences between Eastern and Western Ukraine. There were stories of the Nazi's taking rich Ukrainian soil to Germany. And many other comments about what was lost.

For a while at the Center, I was deep in nostalgia. With the closing of the Iron Curtain, however, I wouldn't be getting news of Ukraine and would push all memories to the back of my mind for the next few years.

One day, I met a Yugoslavian woman named Slavitza who, like Valia, was engaged to a Swiss man who had served in the Italian army. They had lived at the Center for a long time. She had a job at a theatre, and I asked her about getting work. She said, "You want to work? I'll introduce you at *variete* theatre."

The next day, she introduced me to the director of a new show. He looked me over and said, "Stand straight. Turn around. Walk." He put me through a few minutes like that and asked me some questions. Having been in the opera production, I could honestly say I'd had some stage experience. No more than half an hour later, he hired me to be a showgirl for a revue called "Bataclan." He wanted someone who was tall, slender, pretty, and graceful, and apparently I met his definition. But I was young. All young people—to me—are physically beautiful. They are fresh; they have energy. Even after all I'd been through, and even though there would be health problems traceable to those early years, I still had the attributes of youth.

"Bataclan" was a variety show featuring singers, dancers, and comedians. The leading lady of the new show was

Marisa Maresca, a beautiful, dark-haired woman, who was a wonderful singer and dancer. To me, she was a prima donna. Her brother, Mario Maresca, a polio victim, managed our show and was the one who actually put me into the cast and onto the payroll. Several members of the cast, such as Walter Chiari, were well-known and popular. I discovered it's important to performers that people know what work they have done, so I learned all about them and didn't make any mistakes when I talked to them. All the performers seemed worthy of recognition to me. Maybe I was inexperienced and uncritical, but I thought they were good.

I rehearsed all day long. I was coached to be more graceful in movement and to have pleasing posture and appearance while standing still. I was shown where I should look for different effects and how to look at the audience without looking at anyone. I was taught about stage costumes, ways to make something look right from the audience no matter what it looked like up close and without stage lights. I had instruction for application of stage make-up, also different because of distance and lights, and I had to shave my legs (something new). Everything was fascinating and exciting, and I had a job that was going to last more than three days.

Rehearsals often ran late. If we missed the last tram, we had a long walk back home. Slavitza and her fiancé occasionally had other plans, so I started looking for a place near the theatre. I moved to an old lady's house and shared her bedroom. She had one room, which was like a living room, dining room, and kitchen all together. The next room was the bedroom, which had two beds.

During rehearsals, I had bouts of anemia, one of those problems that likely began during the years of poor nutrition. One morning, I felt ill and was late for rehearsal. The producer was angry and yelled at me. Our top singer, a Hungarian actor with whom I had often talked, saved me from being fired. That was one time my talking to people helped. My friends told me to eat horse meat for anemia. I did, and the illness passed.

In the show, Slavitza and I were to stand near a water fountain on stage and look gorgeous. With an Italian girl, we were the Three Graces and were supposed to hold large bowls above our heads as the fountain turned. In reality, the bowls were attached to the fountain, and we held our hands against the bowls while water was cascading from bowl to bowl and splashing us. We wore tiny bathing suits (the kind that became known as bikinis). The manager wanted us to appear without the top part, but we started crying, so he compromised on a top about the size of a shoe lace. Flowers covered the base of the fountain. I was often told that the scene, as viewed by the audience, was spectacular. I don't know how such a scene would be judged today, but it was fun at the time.

At the end of each performance, we did a procession, walking past the whole audience. The theater had about eight hundred seats, and every night it was filled. The many men in the audience expressed appreciation for us girls.

By the time the show opened, I had been in Milano two or three months and would be in that show for more than five months. The theatre was good to me. It was a beautiful spring and summer in 1946. I had work and money for food. I had friends. I felt good. I was busy. My Italian continued to improve. Oh, I had only one suit, one dress, and no purse (I used a knit bag with handles, inside which I carried a shoe box to hold makeup, keys, money), but those matters were of no concern to me. My only concern was my identification, so I learned to avoid anybody who asked many questions. That was the best period of my life—better even than being with the Fantis because I was supporting myself.

After the show opened, I started getting invitations to go to dinners, parties, nightclubs for entertainment and dancing. Milano lived by night; all kinds of places were open until the early hours of the morning. Once I went with a group to a place to dance. After we'd been there for a while, a man asked, "What kind of ballerina are you if you don't know how to dance?" He was right. I danced some on stage—routines taught by a choreographer—but I had done no ballroom dancing. I soon learned and enjoyed dancing so much it became a favorite activity.

As I went out more, I began to realize Italian men can be very persistent. I either had to be strong or inventive to get away from some of them. On one occasion, two men insisted on walking me home. Each one was holding one of my hands. I pulled their hands behind my back, each one probably thinking I wanted his arm around my waist. Instead, I joined their hands. Soon enough, they realized what had happened and pulled their hands away as if they had been contaminated. They laughed when I did, but neither one tried to grab my hand after that. To many of the men I met, saying "no" meant nothing, so I invented something else. Once, I told an insistent man who wanted to go inside with me to wait until I could clear the way, but I left him standing where he couldn't see which door I entered.

The director of "Bataclan," had an assistant who made everything work. For us showgirls, she made sure our costumes and grooming were always right, had us in the right place at the right time, and took care of any problems. Near the end of the run, she introduced Slavitza and me to a man named Jasha Holborn, an impresario. He said he would like to hire all three of us to go to Switzerland to work in a nightclub. I was pleased to be asked, but I didn't think I had sufficient documents to travel. My ID card with Irma Simsolo on it did not make me feel secure. I had visions of getting to the Swiss border and being told I would have to go to USSR. After our show closed, the other two girls went, but I chose disappointment over risk.

I never learned what happened to Slavitza when she reached Switzerland or whether her relation with a Swiss man had a happy ending or a sad one like Valia's. My personal experience with a Swiss man was not good. The man was quite presentable and attractive, and he was quite pleasant to be around. When I started to earn money at the theatre and moved to the apartment with the old lady, he wanted me to cook for him, which I did several times. I was always thrifty with my money, and there I was buying and fixing food for him. Next he started to press me for sex. He wanted me to cook his meal, then pay for a hotel. The man became repulsive to me, and I told him to leave me alone, but he wouldn't. He was more persistent than most Italian men. He would go to the theater and wait for me. To avoid him, I used the back door, which was always locked. It was only when he saw me with another man that he left me alone.

One evening after the show, I was walking fast near Piazza Duomo on my way home. It was midnight, but everywhere, cafes were open, and many people were sitting at tables. My thoughts were elsewhere, and I was caught by surprise when someone reached out and hooked my arm with an umbrella handle. I screamed and turned to see who my assailant was. There was Jasha, the impresario. He asked me to join him for some ice cream and said he might be able to help with my documentation. I sat down, and we began talking in Italian but somehow changed to Russian. He had dealt with the matter of documentation for years and had his own problems but did know more than I knew.

The conversation changed, and Jasha told me about himself. He was a Ukrainian Jew who left Kyiv before the Revolution. He settled in Milano where he became an opera director and impresario. He had been involved in many, many productions and had worked with many well-known performers. I was quite impressed by all he'd accomplished. He lived alone but had lived with a German girlfriend for several years until she found an Italian businessman with a more regular income. He seemed to know everybody and everything in and about Milano. Jasha was twice my age, and I saw him as most handsome and completely charming.

We talked for hours. I was caught up in the night spirit of Milano. Street lamps lit the night sky, giving the city a special beauty, and, even though a great war had just ended, Italy was blooming, bursting with energy. And I was floating on air.

Jasha knew my theatre job was almost over, that I had no immediate prospects for being in another show and wouldn't go to Switzerland because of my lack of papers. We talked about documents—mine and his. He suggested I might want to add modeling as another career and said he could help me find work as a model. I had to ask, "What's a model?" I had no knowledge there was such a job. As Jasha explained modeling, I thought it sounded interesting and told him I'd like to try.

Night was becoming morning, and Jasha saw me home. He was a gentleman, kind and refined. Perhaps I was a naive and gullible young woman to be as taken with Jasha as I was, but I felt safe and secure with him. (And without his ever knowing it, he did cause that Swiss man to leave me alone.)

Jasha and I made plans to meet the next day. I enjoyed being with him so much I was certain I was safe and secure with him. And it didn't occur to me to wonder what he saw in me.

My interpretation of the extermination of millions of Ukrainians by slow starvation under Stalin's tyranny.

Seated, left to right: Jasha, Father, me, Mother, Gabriel
Standing: Mykola, Natasha, Grisha

Me at 2 or 3 years old

Crimea, 1941
At 15 ½, I sang and studied opera.

On board the
USS General John Muir.
I was given a job helping children with
their trays of food.

Gene feeding the pigeons
in Milano, Italy 1956.

Geneva, Switzerland
1972

Today, my son is a
successful business-
man and songwriter.

Stewart and me

Eugenia Sakevych Dallas

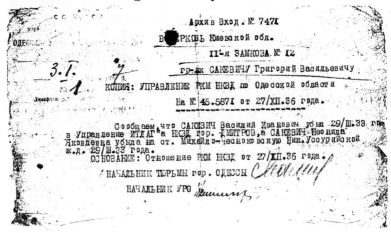

Архив Вход. № 7471

Б[...]РКОВЬ Киевской обл.

11-я ЗАМКОВА № 12

гр-ж САКЕВИЧУ Григорий Васильевичу

КОПИЯ: УПРАВЛЕНИЕ РКМ НКВД по Одесской области

На № 45.5871 от 27/XII.36 года.

Сообщаем, что САКЕВИЧ Василий Иванович убыл 29/III.33 год в Управление ИТЛАГ'а НКВД гор. ДМИТРОВ, а САКЕВИЧ Неонида Яковлевна убыла на ст. Михайло-чесноковскую Ник.Уссурийской ж.д. 29/III.33 года.

ОСНОВАНИЕ: Отношение РКМ НКВД от 27/XII.36 года.

НАЧАЛЬНИК ТЮРЬМЫ гор. ОДЕССЫ

НАЧАЛЬНИК УРО

One of the documents sent to my brother, Grisha, from the NKVD following
his inquiry about our parents' imprisonment.

THE WHITE HOUSE
WASHINGTON

Ms. Eugenia Dallas
6702 Hillpark Drive
Hollywood, California 90068

Your thoughtful gift means so much to me. Thank you for
remembering me in this special way.

Hillary Rodham Clinton

THE WHITE HOUSE

August 28, 1991

Dear Ms. Dallas,

Thank you for sharing the fascinating
and moving story of your life and its
historical context. I greatly appreciate
your thoughtfulness.

George joins me in sending best wishes.

Warmly,

Barbara Bush

Ms. Eugenia Dallas
6702 Hillpark Drive
Hollywood, California 90068

Appreciation from two First Ladies.

Chapter Seven
Milano and Modeling 1946–1951

Jasha made arrangements to take me to a *sartoria*, a fashion designer's salon and showroom where dresses were created and modeled for wealthy clients. The designer, Mrs. Marconi, had me put on a beautiful black velvet gown. The fit was perfect. An assistant pinned my hair up, and I looked in the mirror. Something changed in me. I was a new person. I knew that person, and I didn't know that person. When I walked out of the dressing room and in front of Jasha, Mrs. Marconi, and her staff, my shoulders were straight and my bosom forward. I carried my head proudly. In that dress I felt powerful, completely sure of myself. The assurance I felt in the stage show was nothing by comparison.

I could hear the others saying what I was feeling: "The gown was made for her." "She must have been modeling for years." "Grace, elegance, sophistication—she has everything a fashion model must have." I didn't know a thing about the business, but I was sure I had just found my profession.

It was late summer, 1946, and fall fashions were almost ready. Mrs. Marconi engaged me, and we arranged some times for me to go to her salon while "Bataclan" was in its last few days, after which I would be available full time. In the first days, many dresses were tried on me. I was admired and complimented by the seamstresses. They were happy to have the right body for the beautiful clothes on which they had worked long and hard. Mrs. Marconi started teaching me what

105

would be expected of me.

My natural feeling for modeling was good, but it would take me only so far. I had much to learn about styles and fabrics and colors and designing, about each single clothing item (a casual dress, skirt, or blouse, a dinner dress, an evening gown, a wrap) and combinations for different occasions, about what appeals to which buyers, about techniques and practices that show clothes to their best advantage, and about a business that involved long periods of preparation, last-minute rushes of getting clothes ready, and short, intense, compressed periods of showing clothes to potential buyers. I had to understand that the glamour would be in the shows, but the test of shows was whether or not sales were made.

All at once, I was seeing Jasha often and getting busy with my new job. The rush of preparation for fall shows was just as demanding as I'd been told. I started with Mrs. Marconi but soon met other dress designers and many models.

Designers taught me well about the business, and two or three of them taught me something about myself. In different ways, two or three of them told me I had sad eyes. They said I had a beautiful smile and good features but sad eyes. One said everything else about me looked twenty, but my eyes had the expression of an old woman. I looked at myself and knew they were right. I began telling myself I must look happy, that I must look as if I'd never had a problem. With effort and time, I created a new image. I thought about happy occasions, those rare times when I had spontaneously said something that caused others to laugh or smile. I forced myself to joke, to offer some light comment I wouldn't have made in most conversations. I became much more nearly an extrovert among the models and designers. Slowly, the new me seemed natural.

The models with whom I worked helped me more than I can say. Some of them did not intend to help me, I'm sure. Modeling was, after all, a highly competitive occupation. Even the most successful models could never relax, and the less successful models had to scrap and fight to survive. Pettiness and jealousy were common, more so at the smaller shows than at the larger ones. Among the many models whom I met—with their wide range of personalities—were some who were at best never friendly and at worst cold, inconsiderate, selfish, nasty. Even from them I learned. I observed and learned. Having said all that, I would add that most models accepted me and were considerate of me, and a special corps of models taught me all the things daughters usually learn from mothers and from social training in good schools: manners, grooming, health and hygiene, and they taught me the methods and practices models needed to know for taking care of the face and body and clothes. (Ways of handling things such as hairdos, manicures, and pedicures or folding and hanging clothes could easily make the difference between achieving and not achieving the necessary chic and sophisticated look.) The designers were experts with fabrics and colors and ways to use them, and the designers could help models with the wearing of each, but the models were the ones who taught me techniques and tricks for wearing clothes. I am grateful to many models and especially so to a few who became real friends. They made possible my transition from poor girl with two simple dresses and no knowledge to sophisticated woman with a stylish and extensive wardrobe.

Although the transition didn't happen overnight after an appearance by a fairy godmother, there was a Cinderella aspect to my change of fortune. A poor child with no advantages in Kyiv became a transient child with no permanence, then a teenager with no promise, and after a brief period of mixed calm and tension, dropped into a world of high fashion and income. My conditioning had made me accepting of whatever came. I was not given to thinking and analyzing. Even so, from time to time in that period, I closed my eyes and visualized myself wearing a threadbare dress and walking a dreary street, then visualized myself wearing a costly designer dress made exclusively for me and walking a spotlighted runway. I didn't know what to think. Whatever emotional or psychological progress I'd made, I hadn't reached the point that I could draw conclusions or make statements of insight and perspective. When good things started happening, I simply accepted them and appreciated them.[17]

I was most appreciative of Jasha's getting me the job. Jasha said getting the right people to the right places was his business. He and I spent time together talking, going to restaurants. He sent me flowers. At some point, it could be said we were dating. I continued to feel secure and comfortable with him, realizing gradually I loved him, and then that I was in love with him. He was an attentive, romantic man and felt the same way about me.

Part of my work was under contract, and part of it was freelance. Much of the work was in Milano, which was second only to Paris in fashion, but I went to different cities, also. Because I was hired late in the preparations, my appearances were somewhat irregular, and in fall 1946, my schedule was changed several times.

Starting in spring 1947, there was a definite pattern. The spring shows ran about two months, and the fall shows ran about two months. Each fall and spring, I worked shows in Milano and in other cities such as Rome, Naples, Venice, Genoa, and Palermo. There were also summer festivals in various places, and I worked them, also. At other times, there were photography sessions or other activities. The actual schedule and the cities visited changed from year to year, but the pattern stayed the same for four and one-half years—all of 1947 through 1950 and the spring 1951 shows.

During most of that time, there were great political clashes and crises in Italy. Demonstrations, confrontations, strikes were frequent, but I was not directly affected. I tried to understand what was happening, and Jasha helped make some of the issues clearer. What concerned me most was the strength of the Communists. Jasha and others told me Italian Communists were not the same as Soviet Communists, which was some comfort, but the presence of Soviet agents in Italy continued to bother me.

After the fall shows of 1946 were over, I moved to Jasha's place. He had a lovely sixth floor apartment in a good section of town. He had a room for his office with desk and telephone, a living room with a balcony (only slightly damaged in the war), and a bedroom-sitting room. There were a nice kitchen (also with the balcony) and bathroom. Living there was truly a luxury for me.

Just before the spring 1947 shows, Jasha and I stood for a marriage ceremony in an Orthodox Church. We weren't citizens of the country or members of the church, we had false identity papers, and I did not change my false name to his, so our marriage was not legal or official in any eyes but our own. That was enough for us.

One day, Jasha came home with a puppy, a mixed bulldog and boxer. It was the ugliest thing I'd ever seen. So ugly, it scared me. The puppy jumped into my lap and started licking my face. I named him Bill after an American actor I'd seen in movies. I was certain the name Bill was fresh and original but later found out every other dog in Milano was called Bill. It was all the rage. Bill and I became inseparable. By the time he was grown and trained, he went everywhere I did. He posed with me for photographers and sometimes worked with me in fashion shows. We were called Beauty and the Beast. He did look the part with his long and pronounced lower jaw from which two teeth stuck out, and he worked quite well.

During the parts of the year I was not modeling, I could spend more time with Jasha—if his work did not take him out of town. Jasha introduced me to a completely new way of life. He gave me an education in opera, theatre, music, art. He had wonderful, cultured friends, people whose enriching experiences had given them a greater capacity for enjoying life. We went to beautiful places together. His knowledge of what we were seeing made me see more and appreciate more than I could have on my own. Life became fuller and more interesting. References to artists, composers, and singers no longer went by my head like words in a language I'd never heard. For many years to come, I would appreciate the great opening of my life that Jasha produced.

I also had time to experience more of Italy. I could restore myself in mountain hideaways; I could absorb the history and culture of Rome. Whatever people told me I should see, I tried to see and often explored unfamiliar regions, always discovering delightful people and places. I had time to write letters to the Fantis, and in my third and fourth years in Milano, Tina sometimes visited me for a few days. I could take her around the city and show her a good time. The Fantis asked me to visit them in Clusone, and I thought I would but somehow never went the short distance from Milano to Clusone. (It would be several years later I would go to Clusone from the United States.)

In my first year as a model, photographers from New York arrived in Milano, set up a photo session at a castle, and took many pictures of several models but did not engage anyone that day. When I didn't hear from them, I took another job, then was told they wanted me to pose for *Vogue* USA. I lost them, and they lost me. Opportunities, I learned, could appear and disappear with no warning in the modeling business.

One of my first shows was the Venice Festival of Fashion at the Excelsior Hotel. That wonderful production confirmed my original feelings about modeling. First, the clothes were ideally designed and made for a country that had so recently ended a dreadful war. The designers were full of inspiration and imagination. They drew upon the marvelous Italian sense of color. They combined beauty and practicality to create dresses of great appeal. They fashioned fur pieces that were striking in their luxurious beauty. (Nobody thought of objecting to furs in those days.) They were dream furs, long sable, mink, and fox. Second, hair dressers and makeup artists were superb. With speedy strokes, hair dressers could create in seconds special hairdos that highlighted each garment to its best advantage. Makeup artists highlighted each model's features for each outfit. Third, with those garments and with the expert attention to our appearance, we models walked out, knowing we were indescribably beautiful.[18]

It was that confidence which let models walk as they did—gliding, almost floating, taking off slowly the treasured coats and dragging them alongside on the runway.

As I stepped onto that runway, I felt beautiful. The clothes and the grooming gave me the power and the confidence that made me feel beautiful.

Off the runway, I did not have such confidence. Because I spoke Italian with an accent, people often tried to guess whether I was Yugoslavian or German. I would say, "I'm from Iran," and show my ID, but with my accent and light skin, I was not believed. Having no legal papers kept me nervous all the time.

Attention from Italian men—at least a certain portion of them—contributed to my nervousness. The new me, with runway attractiveness, was noticeable, and there was something in my face, in my expression, which was Eastern European, closed. Some simply stared at me as if I were a painting. Others, smiling mischievously, often followed me for blocks, dressing and undressing me with their eyes and making comments. I never became accustomed to that and never handled it well. I felt cheapened more often than flattered, but saying nothing usually gave me my best chance of getting away.

When I was in a social situation that obligated me to

111

talk, personal questions made me most nervous. Men who were intrigued by a blonde model with an accent wanted to know more: where I was born, where I'd lived, what my nationality was. Some could smell my fear, and a few, aware that Italy was flooded with illegal immigrants, tried threats. When I was escorted by a man, that didn't happen, but when I was not, I was approached. If I'd had Italian citizenship, my nerves would probably have remained calm.

Despite concern about my name, I told others at the Center and in the theatre to call me Jenny. Designers began calling me Jenny Russa (the Russian Jenny). They wanted to distinguish me from another model, Genny Rossa, so called because of her red hair. I didn't care for other nicknames given to me, Mystery Woman and *Sucero* (sugar), among them.

Genny was a sophisticated model. Designers liked to use her and me together because of the red and blonde contrast. We worked well together and maintained a professional relationship that was close and friendly. Genny was engaged to an Italian for fifteen years. An Italian engagement: a waste of time for all I observed. The man married a woman he'd known for two weeks, and the sophisticated, beautiful Genny Rossa remained alone.

My closest friend among the models was Yolanda, a dark brunette with deep olive skin and dark eyes. She and I also made a striking contrast. We were the same age and height and had the same measurements. Our bodies were considered appealing, and we moved with elegance and grace. People would turn to look at us with fascination and follow us with their eyes. Yolanda and I became the best of companions. Whether we were working, traveling, or vacationing, everything was smooth and easy. There were no conflicts or misunderstandings. Perhaps our relationship was not deep; perhaps it was because we operated on a surface level that disagreements did not arise, but we did remain friends across the years.

In spring of 1948, after the Milano shows, I was engaged by three designers to travel to Rome for four days, Naples three days, and Palermo three days. Before I left Milano, my friends were joking, "Watch yourself in Palermo. They are all barons, all nobles." I smiled and took the comment as a joke. With my dog, Bill, I went from Naples to Palermo on an overnight boat. On arrival, I went right away to the designers' showroom, got acquainted with the clothes, and then went to the hotel. The Excelsior in Palermo, like the Excelsior in Venice, was an elegant place (although the big sounding name seemed more appropriate for the one in Venice). After freshening myself, I went down from my room and asked the clerk to get me a taxi to take me to a restaurant for lunch. A man who was standing at the desk talking with the clerk said he would drive me. He ushered me to his car and opened the back door. I guided Bill into the back seat where I also sat. It didn't occur to me he expected the dog to go in back and me in front. My driver, who wore a thin mustache, kept looking me over in the mirror but was shy about conversing. I tried to keep up some conversation, mostly questions about his city. I stupidly asked him if it were true all Sicilians were barons. I did not understand his response.

On arrival at the restaurant, he asked if he could join me. I said, "No, thank you," and asked what I owed him. He said it would be charged to my room and asked whether I wanted him to drive me back to the hotel later. Having seen some horses and carriages on the street, I told him I did not need him anymore. After lunch, I returned to the hotel in a *carrozza*. The same two men were at the desk. We spoke, and I went to my room for siesta time. From one to four o'clock, everyone in Italy slept.

The show was quite a success with the Sicilian ladies. They seemed to like my Bill when we did our Beauty and the Beast presentation. After the show, I enjoyed a pleasant and relaxing walk to the hotel. As I neared the hotel, I saw my driver from the morning. He asked whether I would like him to drive me anyplace. I told him I wanted to go to a good place for dinner after I changed clothes. When I went back downstairs, the driver opened the back door once more, and again I entered with my dog. The driver said he hadn't had dinner yet and asked if he could join me. That time, I didn't mind; in fact, I rather welcomed some company after the show. He drove to one of his favorite restaurants where we took an outside table and had a good meal and good conversation. He told me his name was Michele Di Stefani and later told me he was twenty-eight. I could see he was tall and dark, but beyond that I learned nothing else about him. He was, however, well-informed on many subjects, so the conversation was most informative for me. He continued to be polite and well-mannered as he had been earlier.

Dogs were allowed inside restaurants in Italy, so Bill had a good meal, too. Beggars were free to approach diners, and several did appear at our table. They seemed respectful and at a slight gesture from Michele moved on, saying thanks as they went.

On our return to the hotel, I excused myself and retired. The next morning, late, I had breakfast in my room. Going downstairs, I saw my acquaintances as usual. My "driver" offered his services to take me anywhere I wished to go or to show me a special place in Palermo. He seemed so sure I would like it that I went. It was an enchanting villa on the Mediterranean, a hotel with a beautiful view and wonderful food.

Members of the staff were most respectful, and it was clear they were addressing him as *Barone*. I had to ask him why. He smiled and said, "They are just joking. Giving customers a title," but as he spoke, he waved his hand in an imperial gesture, and three serving people who were standing near our table moved away. It was not the same gesture he'd made to the beggars the night before, but it was similar. I began to wonder: Had I been treating a baron as I would a chauffeur?

114

Observing more closely, I saw Michele and other Sicilians had different ways from northern Italians. I was especially intrigued by the ability to say things without words; hands and bodies spoke sentences. When Michele moved his head forward and closed his eyes, he meant "Go away; don't bother me."

The next day, Michele took me to another lovely place where serving people again called him *Barone*. The light became brighter. When I went to the show, I asked my dress designer about him. "Oh, yes, Michele Di Stefani is *Barone*. His sister is our customer. Very pretty lady." I was embarrassed at how directly and rudely I'd asked him whether everyone in Palermo was a baron. The designer said he had income from his properties. It was curious to me that a young man with so many possibilities resided in a hotel. That would be a boring life for me. I somehow pictured him standing at the desk every day talking with the clerk.

Back in Milano, I could not wait to tell my friends I met a real baron. They asked all kinds of questions I couldn't answer because I learned almost nothing about him, but the idea of my being with a baron was our prime conversation for a while. We laughed at my not catching on sooner, at my treating him as a chauffeur, at his being so polite as to seem timid.

After that first trip, I saw Michele twice a year when I worked in Palermo. On what turned out to be my last trip to Palermo, it was arranged for me to stay in another hotel. I was photographed on my arrival with my dog, and the pictures were in the newspaper. My driver-baron was sorry I was not staying at his hotel, but he appeared dutifully to take me touring to historical points. That time, he took me to meet his sister and her family. As the designer had said, the sister was beautiful and so were her family and her home—extremely beautiful. I especially remember all the floors in the house were marble, every room. After the new collection of fashions for that season were shown, I left Palermo, and my romance with the baron ended.

I did hear from him. After each visit, he sent me all kinds of flowers and beautiful Sicilian cakes. He wrote letters and called and called. My friends and I found the whole thing so amusing and laughed so much simply at the reference to my "Baron of Palermo" that I began to feel I was allowing us to be unfair to a decent man.

Models could be rather jaded about the men who pursued them as prizes. Many men sent flowers and notes of invitation, and they were often laughed at. (And the models could behave badly toward other models when they received the most or the fewest flowers.) I was receiving so many flowers in Milano often I didn't recognize the name on the card. Men would ask, "Were the roses I sent you beautiful?" I'd say, "Yes, they were beautiful." Then I was asked what color they were. If I guessed right, they'd think they were scoring points and send more. If I guessed wrong, they were insulted. If I found a way to avoid guessing, they'd send two different colors trying to trip me.

Models received invitations to some elegant functions. Once, near the end of my modeling in Italy, I was in Venice, as were owners of Hilton Hotels and Sheraton Hotels—there, I suppose, to buy more hotels. They took a few models out for dinner and parties on their yachts. If I could have spoken English, perhaps I could have made an American connection.

One of my other regular places was Genoa. Through my first fashion designer, Mrs. Marconi, I met her friend, Mrs. Musso. She and her husband were a talented couple who held their fashion shows in their spacious luxury apartment. They had an entire floor, with one portion for their fashion business and the other portion, tastefully decorated, for their residence. All meals were served there; everything was there. Mr. Musso was a particular admirer of mine, and when I visited, Mrs. Musso watched me carefully, even slept in the same room with me. Being in their company and in their most inviting apartment was a pleasant contrast to the hotels.

Working as a freelance runway model all over Italy continued to be a wonderful job. Handling the hectic hours of pressure to prepare for a show and then performing under hot lights for a critical audience gave me a distinct sense of accomplishment. I liked the travel except for that lingering bit of nervousness about having a phony ID. Train travel was nice, but most of the time I took airplanes because they were faster. I liked the free time modeling gave me, but the crowning glory of my job was keeping custom-fitted, beautifully designed clothes for very little money.

While I was out of town modeling, I called Jasha regularly, but he was often out of town himself with his opera jobs. Sometimes I reached him in another city, or he reached me, but sometimes we missed each other entirely. We did manage to be together in Milano at several times during the year. He would have been gone even more because there were many opportunities in other countries, but he had no passport. He had once bought a Belgian passport from a Dutchman and used it until it expired during the war, and he was afraid to try to renew it. Between modeling tours in 1948, blessed by ignorance and without Jasha's knowledge, I went to the Belgian consul and begged him to renew Jasha's passport, which he did. When I told Jasha what I had done, he became scared, thinking of all kinds of bad consequences for me and for him. Then he smiled. Then he was relieved—and happy.

There was a big demand for Italian opera in Germany, Austria, and Holland, and Jasha had always been fond of Germany and the German people even though he was terrified of the Nazis and the "demon" Hitler. With his added mobility, Jasha expanded his professional range, and in that period worked with many great singers such as Maria Callas and Renata Tebaldi, who were just getting started. Although I couldn't go with him, I was glad Jasha had added opportunities. "Impresario" is an impressive title, but impresarios at

Jasha's level didn't make much money. In fact, in the second year of my modeling, I became able to meet expenses he could not. Naturally, I wanted always to contribute my share. And I had that traditional Ukrainian characteristic: the dedication to help, to do what is needed. It was good for me to do something more. After all, I owed my modeling job—and much learning—to Jasha.

With a new passport, Jasha was immediately in action by telephone, mail, and airplanes. I was in Milano much more than he was. It was good I liked the city. Milano might not have been my first pick of Italian cities, but it was alive and active. It was the Paris of Italy in fashion, which was good for me, but it was also the nation's first city in many businesses and industries that were much more important than fashion. Perhaps the level of business activity made people more business like. The people did seem harsher to me than people of other cities. Of course, I did not personally know enough people to draw big conclusions, but I think I was accurate on that point. I did meet some people who surprised and shocked me, but I might have met them somewhere else, also.

I met a family of the nobility; at least I met the father and the mother and their son who was about my age. They all seemed quite nice. The parents were pressing the son to get married. The son spoke honestly with me. He knew I had a problem with my documents and marriage to an Italian citizen would solve the problem. He spoke of his problem with his parents that marriage would solve, but he had another problem about marriage: he was homosexual. Then he said to me he would like to get married to a nice girl, have children, and make a home together, but he wanted to be free to maintain his other lifestyle. He liked me, his parents liked me, and he suggested he and I could both solve personal problems that otherwise could damage our lives. That was certainly the most unusual offer I had. It was also unnerving.

When I began to understand what he was saying, I

think I became immobile and unseeing. I knew almost nothing about homosexuality. I did know a dress designer, an attractive woman and good seamstress, who made such an agreement. She had two fine children, and after that her married life was just a show. All her time and energy, her life, went into her fashion designing. I didn't want that kind of life, and the idea of homosexuality was repulsive to me. He was waiting for me to answer. I said only, "I could not do that." I don't remember how that meeting ended.

I remember a young woman named Mariella with a different marriage problem. She was deeply in love with her fiancé. He wanted her to wait while he tried to convince his mother to let them get married. Her fiancé said a baby would make his mother like Mariella, so Mariella had a baby. It didn't help. Mariella had a second baby, but the mother showed no sign of changing. Mariella couldn't take the disappointment, being unwed with two children. With the children in her arms, she threw herself from a cliff.

It was said mama played a vital role in the son's life in Italy. That was certainly true in Mariella's case. But I also thought of Valia at the Refugee Center who lost her fiancé to his mother's will.

Milano and modeling were being good to me. I could not have picked a better place or better job for me than the ones I had by luck or accident or fate. I was too busy—and maybe not capable—to analyze what it was. At unpredictable moments, I thought of my mother or father or Gabriel or Grisha, of the life I had known and of the life I might have known if there had been no upheaval. But I could make no sense of all of it.

Yolanda and myself (Los Angeles 1968)

Country Three: Italy and Life as an Illegal Refugee

Chapter Eight
Milano, Men, and Documentation 1948–1951

In the summer 1949, I was in Milano between shows, by myself, and in need of a holiday. While planning a trip, I was called to attend a photography session for the international edition of *Vogue* magazine. I took my dog and was driven to the park, where I joined models from Egypt, France, Germany, and other countries. Photographers were taking many different shots of models in well-known designer clothes. One photographer, a tall and elegant man, began to concentrate on me. I bent down on my elbow, and the dog got busy digging earth, burying part of my dress. I tried to stop him, but the photographer said leave the dog alone, for my face was radiant. He talked as he was taking pictures. I guessed he had plans for me. He was saying I was photogenic and easy to work with.

Everything was fine until he asked me, "What is your name in Russian?" I got panicky. I was terrified and kept repeating it in Italian. I was so scared I made myself look suspicious. My cheerfulness and happiness disappeared in seconds. I didn't know what he thought. Perhaps "All beauty, no brain." But I couldn't help think he might be a Soviet agent. Either way, I may have lost another good opportunity.

Several of us models were invited to enter a beauty contest at the Odeon Nightclub. The national title was highly desirable, but I couldn't take the chance I might win and be asked questions about where I was from, so I declined. Perhaps another lost opportunity.

If I could have taken those chances, would my life have been changed? I had to wonder, but it wasn't loss of opportunities that hurt as much as it was that I didn't belong to any country.

I could go for months being quite confident, then a question, perhaps completely innocent, brought back the child-hood fears and my conditioning by Grisha: "Be alert, stay to yourself, and say nothing." It could be the smiling face of a curious friend who could tell I wasn't a native speaker of Italian and who asked, "Where do you come from?" Or a new admirer, only trying to make conversation, who asked, "Do you plan to return to your home country?" Or a haughty store clerk who simply asked my name. First, I thought getting a new name and an ID card would give me security. It didn't. Then, I thought my marriage to Jasha would protect me from prying photographers and aggressive men. It didn't. I was always petrified about my being until I reached the United States.

In the fall 1948 season, the year before the experience with the photographer, I had a bad experience with an aggressive man. I was working an industrial show, presenting new artificial fabrics from which dresses had been made with great skill for me. It was the beginning of new era, and my job was to make the new fabrics look good. The show was in Milano; a man named Tulio was in charge. He wanted to meet with me every day for lunch and then for dinner to talk about the clothes, but he talked mostly about me in the clothes. Italian men did have a talent for charming a woman. He paid me well for modeling and then added bonuses. He presented me with nice gifts. Before I realized how completely charmed I was, I became involved with him. Quickly, I realized I was wrong and began refusing him and what came with him.

He would not accept "no" at any time. He followed me to other cities: Torino, Rome, Venice. He said he was in love with me and kept saying, "If you don't marry me, you will never be happy." I felt no love. I felt shame and embarrassment. Emotions I blocked for years seized me again. I desperately wanted to be rid of him.

When the modeling season ended, he started standing on a street so he could see the entrance to my building. When I left the apartment, he appeared and walked wherever I was going, trying to talk to me. He told me he would have me, or I would have nothing. Fears I would be harmed or killed kept me from doing anything until one day a display of anger from him provoked me to anger. I told him I would go to his superiors and tell them he was spending company time and money chasing me. That caused him to stop. He stared at me for a long time. I couldn't tell what he would do but was feeling afraid he would threaten me about my being in the country illegally. Minutes passed. Then he turned and went away, saying something I couldn't understand.

I told Jasha of my affair. He tried to understand, but he was hurt. He knew sooner or later he would lose me. Our careers kept tearing at us; we spent less and less time together and had conflicts about who could change something to accommodate the other. Our age difference was becoming more important. I was in my early twenties, and he was over fifty. All his time and energy were taken by his work. My youth and my youthful energy were dominating my life. I had a constant drive to be going somewhere, doing something. That difference probably made me begin seeing Jasha more as a father than as a husband. We were still strongly attached to each other, but—as I understood later—I was not fully and romantically in love with Jasha. If I had been, I wouldn't have been unfaithful. At the time, I didn't understand what was happening and felt I was being ungrateful to the man who started me on a highly desirable career and helped me develop in many ways.

As I thought more about it, I realized I'd already been feeling restless and hemmed in at Jasha's place—trapped and guilty at the same time. It wouldn't be fair of me to stay there if what I felt for Jasha was filial affection and he thought of me as a wife. I considered moving—tried without success to talk about it. Maybe deep down I was wanting that affair to cause Jasha to want me to leave and didn't know it. Maybe I wanted him to make the decision.

Another thing I didn't understand about myself at that time was that I wanted to learn from a man. I was interested in a man who was ahead of me, and long before I could articulate what I was doing, I responded to men in terms of what I could learn. I was drawn to Jasha in great part because he knew so much about music and theatre, people and places—and he educated me thoroughly. (In the decades that followed, I drew on what he taught me. I understood things I read and was able to participate in discussions because of what he taught me. Not just about operas and singers but on a wide range of subjects, I remembered or used something he taught me.) I didn't learn all he knew or could teach me but had probably learned all I could. I also learned from Mariano and from Michele. There was never any intimacy with either, and I don't know whether there could have or would have been, but I liked being with them—among other reasons—because they gave me something new: they had information and could answer questions.

Among the men I met because I was a model, my first impressions were in terms of whether they had knowledge and experience that would be good for me. Scores of men pursued models. Wherever we went, men were waiting for us. We were like magnets going near pieces of metal. It was definitely flattering to be the object of attention and admiration, and I liked giving pleasure to viewers, men and women, at shows. But I didn't want to be like a painting at which people would look and look and keep looking.

Admiration could be amusing. Male employees in industrial buildings guided me over heating grates to watch my skirt blow up, but I was across the grate before they could see more than a few inches of a leg. And I could laugh with them.

At some point, however, admiration was too much and became annoying. That was so if attention came from vain and fawning men who pressed for dates only because they wanted to wear a model on their arms the way they would wear a medal on their chests. They didn't show any individual character I could respect and admire. On the other hand, attention was not annoying if I immediately saw something of particular interest in a man.

Few interesting men appeared. I was finding again and again that to be attractive and have sex appeal could be a curse for a young woman. Men like Tulio appeared, attacked, and pursued. They wore down resistance unless a woman found a way to get rid of them. For some time, when I got rid of one, another appeared.

Then, at one of the fashion shows in the fall of 1949, I met a gentleman, an industrialist, who made me feel there was more in life than I was seeing, made me excited about what he might show me. I knew I would be learning from him. His name was Leonardo; to me, he was Nando, and he became my prince. Nando was a special man, cultured and distinctive, refined and strong, handsome and funny, well-mannered and perfectly groomed.

It was fascinating to listen to Nando explain the business and political forces at work in Italy. His enthusiasm and firsthand knowledge turned subjects that could be dull into exciting descriptions. He had political aspirations, which was interesting for me because the only political people I'd observed were Party functionaries in Ukraine who got their jobs by doing the dirty work for somebody above them—not by being elected to office.

Nando represented safety and protection insofar as my papers were concerned. No one would bother me about them when we were together. He also made me able to suppress most of the bad feelings Tulio had aroused. I could tell myself I was a better person. That may have been, in part, because Nando was much older than I. If I didn't have a father complex, I at least found older men more interesting. Nando was divorced with children, with whom I had little contact. His ancestors had been in navigation and shipping; his family traditions were strong, which appealed to me.

Not long after I met Nando, I decided I would move. I didn't think I should be dating Nando from Jasha's apartment. I rented a place, moved my clothes, and left a letter with my keys.

Nando introduced me to an Italy and a way of life different from that which I had known. We traveled to Sorrento, Amalfi, and the Island of Capri, seeing them in rich detail as fully as Michele showed me his beloved Palermo. We heard the top operas and concerts from the best seats in the house. I had dined in fine restaurants, but we dined in finer restaurants than I knew existed. I was accustomed to modeling the latest styles in clothes, but Nando put me into more dresses and furs in a wider range of designs so whenever we were seen in public I was wearing exactly what was best for me for the occasion. Nando had a chauffeur always waiting for him and homes in different parts of Italy. He introduced me to a life of luxury, beautiful places, and good times—a lifestyle I might have seen in the movies but did not know actually existed. I was in love with my Italian prince.

He was attentive and complimentary, frequently saying something about me or my appearance—and saying it with his special expressions. Once, for example, he said, "You look like an elegant Arabian horse." For me, it was an unusual comparison, but I liked it.

When Jasha returned to Milano, he found me and asked me to come back to him. He confronted Nando and charged him with destroying our marriage. It was not pleasant. I would have run away from both of them if Nando hadn't been so calm. He knew Jasha and I didn't have a legal marriage and had class enough not to feel threatened. (I doubted, however, that he would endure much challenging.)

I told Jasha all my good feelings for him, but added that I needed freedom. He begged me to go back home, telling me I could see my prince. I didn't think that would work. He said, "You are my family; you are my child." That change in him took away my resistance. He continued to tell me he appreciated me for my qualities, saying, as he said before, "You are a real *mensch*." I was terribly confused. My feelings were so mixed I couldn't think clearly or act sensibly. In that state, I went back to Jasha's after no more than a month away.

I began dividing myself, trying to meet the expectations of Jasha and Nando, of my employers and my friends. If I didn't think about everything, I was all right, but at low moments, I was feeling walls closing in.

Jasha helped by being more like a father. Nando was so confident of himself the arrangement didn't seem to disturb him.

Nando was sensitive enough not to invade Jasha's area. When we had our dates, Nando called for me but waited in the car. He was such a busy man with his various companies and businesses and was so much in charge he didn't need me for support of any kind. Such strength was both comforting and exciting. It was pleasing to know he was making time to see me. I did need some assurance and did ask him one day whether as busy as he was, he would always find time for me. He said, "Remember this, dear: If a man wants to see his woman, there is nothing that will stop him."

Yolanda was so impressed with Nando she urged me to marry him at the first opportunity. After we took her on a trip to Lake Como, she was even more excited and happy for me. The drive was delightful. Yolanda and Bill were in front with the driver, and Leonardo and I were in back. All the way there, we were joking, talking, and having a happy time. I

I listened to Nando with much admiration; at that moment, my heart was melting with joy.

My prince had a reservation at a luxury lakeside hotel with windows facing a marvelous view of Lake Como. Yolanda and Bill had a big, sunny room. Nando and I took a corner suite from which we could see the beauty of the lake from all directions, an enchanting view. Whenever Yolanda and I were alone, she said, "Please get married to him. I will be your companion."

Nando told me he wanted to get married, but he didn't put pressure on me. He was always patient and gentle, and that was good because I was feeling definite pressure just from the situation. As considerate as Nando was, however, he was still overpowering. He was incomparably strong in every way: physically, mentally, emotionally, sexually, financially, politically. As much comfort and security as that strength gave me, it also began to make me a little uncomfortable. Nando had told me about his first two wives, both of whom had had some kind of breakdown, and I couldn't help but wonder whether there was a connection.

I had a wonderful year and a few months with Nando. Then, early in 1951, there came a governmental order that people who entered the country illegally had to get out. For some time, there had been talk that all refugees in European countries would have to leave. Countries such as Australia, Canada, the United States, and some in South America would welcome the poor souls that did not belong anywhere. As I've said, not having a country does produce its own kind of fear and panic. Being illegal in Italy, which had long been pressing on me, had just become critical.

The obvious solution and apparently my only possibility for Italian citizenship was to marry an Italian citizen right away. Nando was ready to marry me. The obvious solution would be the perfect solution. But I began to experience what is called "getting cold feet." It struck me that living under

Nando's roof would be quite different from dating him.

While I was trying to think that through, I recalled the Swiss man who left Valia so he could have his citizenship, and I thought about the homosexual man who wanted an arrangement to serve as a marriage. Marrying Nando to stay in Italy would be an arrangement—a better arrangement but still an arrangement. I was sure I loved him, but even if the marriage remained exciting, there would be the underlying reality that I married a man primarily to stay in his country. If that was not the case, I reasoned, we would have already made plans for spending the rest of our lives together as expression of our love for each other.

What had probably been deep inside for a long time came to the surface, and I began to think it would be good to emigrate to get away from present problems. I was telling myself I would never be able to have a normal relation with a man and would never be free from authorities who would take away what I called a normal life. But I did continue reminding myself there were good reasons for wanting to stay in Italy, so I tried to find alternatives, some other way that would let me stay even temporarily.

I had to miss part of the spring season to look into all possibilities I could find, but I had no choice. In the process, I turned to the IRO—the International Refugee Organization—which had offices in Rome. There, I talked with a man whose name was well-known as one of the last breaths of Russian aristocracy. He was formerly Prince Nicolai Nicolayevich Engalichev, but when I met him, he was simply N. N. Engalichev who was helping Soviet refugees to repatriate to different countries. I would not have thought that as the grand-daughter of a serf I would have anything favorable to say about a member of the royalty that owned serfs, but he was a prince in the best sense of the word. Without saying much about USSR, we understood we were united in aversion to Stalinist communism, which combined the worst of all systems.

We talked about my situation, and Mr. Engalichev told me in essence what I already knew: "You have two choices. One, marry an Italian. Two, go to another country." Somehow, when he said it, the two possibilities cut away all others; the alternatives I'd been thinking of were self-deception. Once more, I said to myself, "Get married to stay in the country?" The response followed with certainty, "No, I can't do that." My decision was made.

Presenting my Irma Simsolo ID card, I told Mr. Engalichev I understood Canada was much like Ukraine with fields of wheat and cold winters and strong people, and I wanted to apply for a visa to Canada. He asked what I wanted to do in Canada. I told him I wanted to continue to be a model. He explained that modeling jobs would be in New York, so, at age twenty-five (or twenty-four), I applied for a visa to the United States.

I received my visa two or three weeks later. During that time, I said my good-byes to friends and to the city. Nando was understanding and said he would wait for me if I changed my mind. I promised to write him often. Yolanda still thought I should marry Nando, but she was excited about my going to America. She and I promised to keep in touch, and she agreed to look after Jasha. She had a boyfriend, but they were not close to marriage, and, at my insistence, she moved to Jasha's apartment. The designers said they were sorry to see me go, and most of them seemed quite sincere. They hoped I would send them any hot new fashion ideas. Other models said they would miss me, and some of them probably did. Several friends and co-workers gave me names and addresses of people in the United States and insisted I contact them. Grateful for possible assistance, I took good care of all those names.

Jasha was despondent I was leaving, but he understood there was no peace for me in Italy. It was a painful situation for both of us. He offered to follow me to the United States, but that wouldn't have worked. We belonged to different generations. I told him I would always be in touch and would return to visit him. Jasha gave me the names and numbers of friends he had in Los Angeles. I gave him Bill—my dog, our dog. I told him I would always be grateful to him for his help and love, and that was a true and sincere statement. I had been in Milano more than six years and had been close to Jasha in one way or another for all except the first few months. I would stay in touch with him for the rest of his life.

Departure time arrived with sadness and tears. Packing was easy. I had my clothes and jewelry, and I still had the documents about my parents and my little cross. Leaving Italy was not easy. Italy was special. I was quite sensitive to the reality that in the rest of my life, I might never have such experiences again. But, having decided to make a move, I could not, did not, look back. I had been making important decisions on my own since I was a child, and, right or wrong, big or small, the choices were mine.

From Italy, I went to a huge relocation camp for displaced persons in Bremerhaven, Germany. There, I encountered hundreds of people of many nationalities. Some families had been there months. Because all my clothes were high fashion, I drew attention, which I didn't want.

At headquarters, I pleaded with the American immigration officers to allow me to go back to my original family name. I confessed to them Irma Simsolo wasn't my real name. They laughed, and one of them said, "Oh, you green-eyed Persian cat, don't worry about it. You won't have this name for long. Someone in America will marry you soon." I was already upset and became more so with that remark. I wanted my father's name back, but they refused. They gave me no reason, so I didn't know whether there was some regulation or it was too much paperwork.

After two or three days, I became restless and found relief by going to museums, visiting castles, touring the city. But I still checked departure time for the ship several times daily.

In the camp, I saw many Russians going to church for confession. One day, as I walked past the church, I encountered the priest. The man was tall, and his dark, hypnotizing eyes said he could be French, Italian, Spanish, Russian, German. His petrifying gaze terrified me. He spoke to me in Russian. He knew my name, who I was, and everything about me. He knew my parents were arrested and I had changed my name. I started getting scared again. He asked me if I would like to ride with him to the headquarters of another camp. I said to him, "I have no business there." He insisted I go along just for the ride. My brain flashed back to Lenia. I was afraid to go; I was afraid not to go. The priest was extremely nice, sensing perhaps I was afraid of him or uncomfortable in an unusual priest's company. We went. He made small talk on the way, did what he had to do in the office, and we drove back. On the way back, he told me he had lived for many years in Estonia, Finland, France, and now Germany. He spoke every language like a native. He said it was simply easy for him to learn anything and learn it fast, even the priesthood. That statement made me wonder why he learned the priesthood fast, but I did not ask him anything. He was much too clever for me.

He insisted I return the next day to help him make holy bread for communion. That morning, he must have been doing some kind of physical labor, or else he was careless about cleanliness, for it was with dirty hands and filthy fingernails he mixed the flour and water. He was not very priest-like. By then, I began to assume he'd become a priest to cover his real business of recruiting people to work for communism.[19] When some Russian people arrived to talk to him, I took that opportunity to disappear.

The next evening, I was told by someone in my dormitory he'd been there a couple of times that day looking for me. My heart started beating like a hundred drums. After that,

I avoided the church, taking a longer way around to go any-where. Another day, while I was at breakfast, he appeared, approached with a smile, and sat down at my table. He asked me to go with him a few miles to deliver some papers. I was trapped. There was no way out for me. I started to think, "Why didn't I stay in Italy?" I hated myself.

We drove away from the camp with my destiny in his hands. For a few minutes, he was silent. Then he spoke to me with a kind of sorrowful pity for the way he had to make a decision for my life. "I like you," he said. "You are a nice, intelligent girl. You speak a few languages, can pass for any nationality. A pity you're too old. If you were sixteen or sev-enteen, you would go to America, but before that for a few months you would be trained our way. You would learn to gather information for the Soviet Union." I was almost get-ting sick to my stomach. Despair overwhelmed me, and fear kept me silent. It would have been a great mistake to tell him what my family had suffered and what I thought of the system he served. I could only be happy that, at twenty-four, I was old.

He showed me a family from Yugoslavia but of Rus-sian or Ukrainian descent. He said, "You see that family? They will never go anywhere. They will rot here because the man was working against communism one time."

A day or two later, early in August 1951, I was told I would board the U.S.S. General John Muir for New York the next day. I couldn't sleep that night and was truly a nervous wreck the next morning. When I did get in line to board, anxi-ety to get onto that ship began building. A German cleric, working for the IRO, started to talk to me. This German man could not know what was going on in my heart and my head. My tranquil look, calm and indifferent, fooled people. But in my panicky situation, the inside of me was turmoil and terror. My mind went to America and returned. The cleric gave me his card and address, asking me to write to him to let him know how things worked for me. Just before I stepped onto the ship, I saw my "priest" looking at me, blessing me or cursing me. I will never know which. Maybe I was blessed because he let me go to a new life, a new country, a new hope.

The Red, White and Blue

The Red, White and Blue - my precious flag
I wish I were born in the country of freedom and liberty
I wish I were in my youth, in the country of justice and serenity
I treasure and I am proud of my flag

Soviets took by force my land

Suddenly black clouds of terror
From the neighbor to the North.
Darkness blew over the green hills
The peaceful golden steps of Ukraine.

Bullets riddle my country
They took my freedom and my land
And brutally turned us into a colony.
Run by hostile outsiders.

By Force they made us give them
All our food to the last morsel
In return they give us prisons in Siberia
And genocide in Ukraine.

I respect my country and my flag of the Stars and Stripes.
I am grateful to the red, white and blue
It means to me a blessing of the freedom
That gave me a right to live in prosperity

Fulfill my life in tranquility
The United States of America.

Written by Eugenia Dallas July 4th. 1999

Country Four: The United States of America and Life as a
Free Woman

Chapter Nine
New York City, Los Angeles, and Dallas 1951–1953

On the ship, I was assigned to a cabin with many
women and children and was told to report to the cafeteria
where I was given a job helping children with their trays of
food. Mothers with small children simply couldn't handle their
own trays and the trays of children, too. They also needed
help at other times.

The trip was to take ten days, which sounded long but
in actuality seemed short. When I wasn't helping the children,
I walked around the decks, thinking about my new country
and chatting sometimes with some of the hundreds of other
passengers. I wrote letters to Jasha, Nando, and Yolanda, and
notes to others, but I would not let myself begin missing them
and Italy. That would have been painful.

While I was a forced laborer and working with French
people, I wanted to go to France; I planned and learned the
language but didn't get to go there. That made me supersti-
tious: I was afraid that if I studied English for two months
while I was waiting to emigrate, my chance would never come.
I avoided English while I was in Bremerhaven and was still
reluctant on the ship to try English. Consequently, I was only
a few days away and knew almost no English. Of course, I
was familiar with a few words that had been adopted by Italians and a few from the movies, but I couldn't put together a
sentence or ask a question or understand an answer even if I

had been able to ask a question.

One of the ship's officers started to talk to me one day. He said "Hello." I said "Hello." What he said next, I didn't understand, but he kept talking. When I tried to tell him I didn't understand, he talked some more. That went on for several minutes before he realized I had no idea what he was saying. He found an interpreter, and the three of us talked about the trip and such things. He gave me his name and address and asked me to contact him in three months after his ship returned to the United States. I did so, and we agreed to meet for dinner. That time, I took along an interpreter, which did not seem to please him.

As we got closer to New York, I studied the list of names given to me in Milano and decided I would first call a number given to me by my good friend, Lala, who was born in Russia and whom I met through Jasha. Lala, a petite and lovely woman, owned a nightclub and told me interesting stories about her life. She came from a family of Armenian nobility, and her husband was an officer in the czar's army. When they were young, she wouldn't pay attention to his admiration and love for her. He was so depressed at being rejected and unwanted, he joined the Foreign Legion. Years passed, and with hope he called upon her again. She was older, wiser, and poorer, and she was pleased to see him. He was handsome, blue-eyed, fair, tall, and well-mannered. They were married and had lived in Italy a long time.

Lala had a cousin named Mary who had lived many years in New York and was working in a boutique. The way Lala described Mary, I thought she would know something about modeling and would be as nice and friendly as Lala was.

We reached New York late in the afternoon Friday, 17 August 1951 and anchored overnight. I stayed a long time outside that night, standing by myself and wondering what would be waiting for me and what my life would be. I couldn't help being apprehensive. I'd gone into new countries before but under much different circumstances and at younger ages. For a grownup person to get used to different customs, a different life altogether, would be very difficult and maybe require passing through some misery before getting used to the new land, the new world, and the people.

At the same time, I was highly curious and excited. Wasn't the United States a big country with wonderful opportunities? Hadn't thousands upon thousands of other refugees stood where I was standing, watching the lights of the city and wondering the same things I was wondering? My thoughts and feelings remained mixed, but more than anything else, I was positive. And ready. I had papers. I was legal. I was official. I had a green card that would allow me for the first time in my life to live and work without fear.

The next morning we disembarked. I saw no false priest looking at me and no one in Soviet uniform. A good feeling welled up inside and washed over me from outside. I was hearing in my head, "Free. I am free. Nobody will deport me. I am human. I can live." I laughed at the crowd and the lines and the push to get on busses. I was in the USA. I was on American soil.

(Later, I chose to celebrate my birthday on 18 August instead of 24 August, which was arbitrarily selected. The day I set foot in the USA was a true "birth of freedom" for me.)

Dozens of us were taken to a hotel somewhere around 20th Street. I deposited my things in the room and immediately telephoned Mary. We made arrangements to see each other the next day. I was so thrilled, so excited, so eager to be a part of my new country I couldn't stay in the hotel. On the sidewalk, I looked around, picked a direction, and started walking. It was late afternoon, warm and quite pleasant. I carefully copied the name of the street, "One Way," but I did not get lost. I just walked and looked, walked and looked. I walked long enough to prepare me for a good night's sleep and went back to the hotel tired and happy.

Mary was as nice as I expected and assured me I could work as a model, in fact, suggested several kinds of jobs I could get. She even called her friend who worked at Seventh Avenue and 43rd Street. When Mary asked where I was staying, I showed her what I copied. She laughed, and I did, too. It was good the room key had the name of the hotel. Mary then invited me to stay with her in Queens until I got settled. I went back to the hotel very pleased and happy.

Monday, I reported to IRO as I was supposed to do and told the person there I had a job and would stay with an Italian family. He looked at me in surprise and said IRO had a job for me, that I'd signed papers to go to a home to work as a nanny or domestic near New York before I even got on the ship. Yes, I said, I was signing many papers, the clerk was in a hurry, and I didn't know what I was signing. The man said I could go, but IRO wouldn't help me if I needed it. I thought about that possibility only two seconds. I was confident I'd get a job, thanked the man, and left for new opportunities.

The next day, with some advice from Mary's friend, I went to Seventh Avenue and 43rd Street and introduced myself to an Italian designer. I was hired and began working in the showroom, modeling dresses for buyers from retail stores. The lady who hired me wasn't always available to translate, so from the beginning, I had difficulty because of my lack of skill with English. My employer was Jewish as were most of the workers, and with them I was practicing and learning Yiddish, thinking it was English. I was happy my knowledge of German was going to make it easy to learn English, but when I started taking night classes in English, it was with some embarrassment I discovered my error.

What a lot of things I had to write to Jasha, Yolanda, and Nando! And to the Fantis if my fingers didn't wear out.

After one week, the designer fired me, telling me my not knowing English was not good for business. I thought she liked my work. I did feel the strain of not understanding conversations, but I was sure I made the dresses look good. It would be only a matter of time before I'd be everything the company wanted. When she told me, I was crushed. I'd never been fired. I'd started my first job in a new country full of confidence—confidence enough to tell the IRO I wouldn't need help. I'd struggled to keep my confidence up during those days, and all at once it was gone.

I left the building and outside picked up my confidence again. There were other similar companies nearby. I'd watched people going in and out the buildings, so I went to a company that seemed very active and presented myself. Once again, I was hired by a Jewish company to work in the showroom, modeling coats. It was a pleasant place to work, and I got by with mostly Yiddish from German. Specialized terms created problems. Although I knew the fashion rag business, as they called it, very well at that time, I knew the terms in Italian. Often, I didn't know the appropriate German word, or the Yiddish word was entirely different.

In the showroom during the hour lunch break, someone was always telling stories. I listened intently, carefully, trying to follow and understand the joke. I usually picked up the last word, the one I shouldn't have, the dirty word for which I had to ask the meaning.

Not being able to speak English also made it difficult to go from the east side to the west side. I mastered one subway route, but if I missed a transfer or my stop, I was lost. One day, I was late and took a taxi. I showed the driver a piece of paper with the address, but when I said something, the driver turned to me and said, "You are Italian." He became very excited to speak Italian. While staring at me in the mirror, he asked where I lived, then wanted my address and telephone number. He was a young and handsome man, skinny and tall, with a dark complexion and green eyes, but I had no time or interest for him. I was only glad my Italian got me to work on time.

After a week or so, I began feeling I would not be suddenly fired. I was also feeling a need to be an American fast. That would be the magic key. The sooner I got used to the country, the faster I would be happy. But I was not meeting Americans. Almost from my first day in New York, I was meeting Russian Jews. I met Russian families who were in the United States for fifteen or twenty years but who were not happy because they had not settled well. They were still living in the past and had no social contact with anyone who didn't speak Russian. It would have been easy to slip into those groups and be stuck. As much as I might like knowing Slavic people in New York, I wanted more to know Americans.

I tried to be around Americans only, but that was difficult. My night class in English was most helpful for the language, but, obviously, I wasn't meeting Americans in that class—only other foreigners. I was living with an Italian American family, which was very nicely half American and half Italian, but it was not making me American fast enough. Besides that, I had taken advantage of the hospitality there long enough and needed to be much closer to work, so, after two weeks in New York, I moved to Manhattan's Barbizon Plaza for Girls.

There, I thought, I would meet young American women and learn language and customs faster. But they were all so busy with work and dates and getting ready for work and dates they had no time to socialize with me. I didn't usually get much past "hello" with most of them. The first resident who seemed to have time was Italian. She had been living in Argentina and had gone to New York to see whether her family could transfer their silk business to the United States. She was young and very much the business woman.

Slowly, I began to establish acquaintances and maybe make friends, but at the same time I felt quite isolated. I could, of course, find Italians or Russians and talk with them, but I couldn't walk out of my apartment and talk with any New

Yorker: couldn't make comments about the weather with another pedestrian, couldn't ask a shopkeeper about price, availability, or features of any item, couldn't discuss objects or ideas, couldn't solidify friendships, couldn't have full exchanges with mainstream Americans.

A fortunate meeting opened the way to meeting many interesting people over the next eight to ten months. In the coffee shop at the Barbizon, I met Ham Fisher, the cartoonist. He knew scores of young and creative people—artists, actors, musicians, writers—who were in New York to establish themselves, and he was at the center of many activities that pulled groups of those people together. His home studio seemed always to be so filled with artists and performers I wondered how he ever did his cartooning. If he said, "Let's go to Coney Island," to three people, there were thirty by the time we got there. Ham Fisher accepted me as a friend and included me in gatherings over the coming months. Through them I would meet those interesting people, become friends with some, and see the names of some in newspapers as they achieved successes. I also met and became friends with Ham Fisher's mother, a highly educated woman with whom I spoke German.

At one gathering at Ham's studio, I met Eddie Fisher, skinny and arrogant, very much in love with himself. When we were introduced, he said to Ham, "Where did you find her?" He seemed to be pleased with his remark, but the way he said it had the sound of an insult to me. I said nothing. I was afraid he was a relative of Ham's and was relieved to be told he was not.

During that period I began to know some other models, and sometimes they took me on blind dates. Those occasions were certainly good for learning American ways. I met many kinds of American men, some of them as assertive and persistent as the most assertive of Italian men, some of them quite passive. Some were polite and well-mannered, and some were not. Some of them were pleasant to be with, but I met none on a blind date who could be teachers the way Jasha and Nando were. I learned much about social life in the United States, however.

One thing repeatedly struck me, astonished me. Women would order beautiful, huge steaks, eat two or three bites, and push the plate away. I was flabbergasted. Again and again, I asked what would be done with the rest of the steak, and I was told it would be thrown away. No matter how many times someone gave me reasons for that practice and no matter how clear it was to me there was no way to get uneaten steak across an ocean to feed the hungry, I never adjusted to the waste of such superb food.

Living with the Fantis for several months made it easy to become accustomed to Italian foods. By the time I began eating frequently in Italian restaurants, I could read and speak the names of most dishes and knew what they were. Two weeks at Mary's house did not prepare me for American restaurants. For lunch, my model friends helped me order. Most of the time they ordered eggs hard-boiled because they thought that would keep them slim. I learned to say "meat," and one day when I was alone, I asked for meat. I suppose the waiter was asking me what kind of meat I wanted. My brain struggled, but it could only produce "eggs, hard-boiled." I developed an aversion to eggs before I learned, by listening, asking, and pointing, to order other food.

After a month at the Barbizon, I found a studio apartment two streets away that was central, cheap, and convenient. I'd spent many years living in rented rooms and with little money. My concern was not comfort; it was financial security. Clothes I obtained through my work. Food I often didn't buy. If I spent little on rent, I could save more.

After two or three months at my second job, the company stopped making coats and concentrated on suits. My body size was not compatible with the designer's suits, so I looked for another job. I spoke with an Italian dress designer with whom I was immediately quite comfortable—and I guess he was with me, for he agreed to try me. We worked well together, and it was not long before he was designing dresses especially for me. My body gave him the spark to invent new designs for very practical but chic dresses. Very simple. It was also pleasant to be speaking Italian.

Even before I went to work there, I started to feel homesick for Italy. I had refused to let myself miss Italy when I first left, but I began missing Italy in a way I never missed the country of my birth. I wanted to go back for a visit as soon as possible. In my daydreams, I had many conversations with Jasha but not with Nando. I wrote long letters to Jasha and shorter and shorter notes to Nando, which is the way his writing went until at some time we stopped writing.

Besides missing Jasha, I also missed my dog, and in my third month in New York I asked Jasha if he could send me my Bill. When Bill arrived, I was happy. I was surprised he didn't understand English. I thought intonation of commands was enough, but it wasn't. Dogs learn language as we do; it's just that they cannot speak. I had company and a reminder of Italy.

Another reason for wanting to go to Italy began growing. Often, I thought of Prince Nicolai Nicolayevich Engalichev who was helping people get away from a totalitarian regime, and I wanted to tell him about the fake priest in Bremerhaven who was working for that regime. I couldn't put that in a letter. But I thought of it in quiet moments, and I thought of it when I heard sad stories of people who struggled and failed to escape the totalitarian regime in USSR and of those who did get out of USSR but still had great difficulty getting visas. The world seemed to distrust people from the Soviet Union. Maybe my Persian name did help me.

For years to come, wherever I went in the United States, I met people whose lives were so miserable in USSR they risked anything and everything to get out. Most of the people I met were Jewish—and they and their friends and relatives often assumed I was Jewish. Many were Orthodox Christians—in background if not in belief. We all had that one thing in common, and the strength of that feeling created a bond among us.

Gradually, my English improved, and my modeling job seemed more secure. I understood that in my new country I would, as the Americans said, have two strikes against me: the language and the competition. In Italy, I was unusual; not many models were tall, blonde, and fair with gray-green eyes. In America, there were many tall blondes with blue or green eyes and fair skin, many beautiful women who wanted to be models. I worked hard, and I was fortunate, so I stayed employed.

It was necessary to adapt to a different kind of modeling. In New York, I worked 9:00 to 5:00, five days a week. I did not travel to perform in seasonal shows at fashion centers as I did in Italy. Ways of walking, standing, and turning were not quite the same. In both places, however, models were to be chic, sophisticated, and mysterious. And in that era, models walked with the hips in and forward ("tucked in"). Swinging the hips was considered vulgar. Women simply did not move the hips or shake the body in any way.

The little tricks and methods I learned in Italy, with some variations, were still useful, and there were others to learn for showroom work. The most important lesson I learned from observing my employers was what kind of clothes to show to which buyers. That was the key to success.

An Italian advertising agency that was just getting started used me to make a few television commercials for Italian products: Cinzano, spaghetti, cigarettes. In 1952, having no idea that making commercials would become such a highly paid business, I thought of making commercials as nothing more than an interesting way to earn a few extra dollars now and then. Another missed opportunity.

In that first year, however, I became certain America is the land of opportunity. I met buyers from, and owners of, department stores from different cities, including Mr. Larry Marcus who asked me to go to Dallas to work for Neiman Marcus stores. And if for any reason I stopped modeling, I saw other jobs—hairstyling, manicuring—that I could do any time and almost anywhere.

For a few weeks, I also considered starting my own business. An older gentleman, originally from Ukraine, took a liking to me and wanted to help me open a fashion boutique. He was a former opera singer who was living at the Waldorf Astoria hotel and who knew many people in high society. His idea was that he could introduce me to some very wealthy ladies and it would take only fifteen to twenty of them to keep me busy. He would invest money, and I would invest time and knowledge; he would take 25 percent, and I would take the rest.

The details would have required careful thought, but the idea seemed workable. First, I knew fashion extremely well. I could look at a person and visualize what style clothes and coloring would be most suitable. Second, I knew where and how to buy the most fashionable items in Italy. Third, and maybe most critical, I could work well with the women who would be my customers. But I also knew the fashion business is difficult and competitive and that businesses do fail unless everything is taken care of at all times. That led me to think about the day-to-day and month-to-month operations. I would have to put my shop above all else; it would dominate my time and energy.

I thought about the people I knew who gave their entire lives, all their waking hours, to their businesses. They had little time for family life. The question for me was whether the business would be interesting enough, satisfying enough for me if I had nothing else. Always, I'd had a strong feeling for family. I remembered my own family, the family of Grisha's Jewish girl friend, the Fanti family: that was what I longed for. When I was with Jasha, I had someone, but he and I spent more time apart than together, and there were no children to complete a family. I longed for a husband and children with whom I could build a life. That was fulfillment. I sifted all those things, then quit thinking about starting a business.

Time passed very quickly in New York. Working in wholesale showrooms took regular blocks of time the seasonal shows in Italy did not. Night classes in English took time. My social life became fuller month by month. Slavic and Germanic people, many Jewish, and Italians were always inviting me to some function. The creative people were going to art shows and theatres and often had parties. Models, designers, and other people in the business were telling me I added some life to their dinner parties. Correspondence with friends in Italy filled many hours of reading and writing. The letters to and from Nando had stopped, but those to and from Jasha were long and regular. The exchange with Yolanda was not as regular, but there was no doubt it would continue. Occasionally, I wrote to the Fantis, and I heard from them when something special happened. I was waiting to hear Mariano was married. (Eventually, he did marry.)

I thought about trying to write to my brothers, Jasha and Mykola, but I was afraid a letter from the United States— if it reached them—would cause trouble or at least unwanted attention. I'd heard too many stories of such problems. Whenever I thought about writing a letter to Ukraine, I was reminded of the freedom in my new country. I was free to go anywhere any time without fear I would be stopped and questioned, perhaps arrested. I was free from the threat of being found by a Soviet agent and sent back. I was free to work anywhere I could get a job. I could buy whatever I could afford. What a wonderful country. I was learning about paying taxes, and I would learn about voting. If I paid my taxes, what

I owned would not be taken from me. If I voted, I would be part of the governing process.

New York, I learned anew every week, was an exciting place. Art shows and museums, movies, stage plays, operas, and ballet, grand stores and small shops, fancy restaurants and sidewalk stands: there was more of everything than I could have imagined and more than I could see and do. I took in as much of everything as I could. Naturally, I visited landmarks such as the Statue of Liberty, which I appreciated very much. Going to dinner or a show or both was almost a nightly activity. The Metropolitan Museum of Art became a favorite and frequent stop. Events such as the St. Patrick's Day parade were a new excitement. I marveled at the simple pleasure of going ice skating whenever I wanted.

I was enjoying meeting many people and gaining new friends. I dated different men, some of them quite nice, but no long, romantic relations developed. As much as I wanted a family, I have to say it was good a serious relation didn't develop. Guilt and fear and suspicion still cast a shadow over me. Being free from any involvement helped me adjust to my country faster, and I was definitely becoming much more American.

After August and September slipped by, I appreciated the cooler weather of fall. I was not at all accustomed to the heat and humidity of a New York summer, and it seemed no matter what I put on, it was soon dirty. Fall was quite pleasant, but winter weather was different from any I'd known. I'd experienced cold winters in Ukraine but found it difficult to stay warm in New York.

It was easy to catch the spirit of celebrating December holidays in the American way. In the New York tradition, I rang out 1951 and rang in 1952 with a large group of interesting people. Spring was quite pleasant. As the weather grew warmer, it struck me I'd already been in New York nearly ten months. It wouldn't be long before I would complete my first year in the United States.

My thoughts turned to a vacation. I wanted to see more of my new country, and I needed a break from the concentration and the work. Jasha had told me about a friend of his, a poet named Sasha, who lived in Los Angeles, and he'd told Sasha about me, so I decided to go to Los Angeles. My employer said she would have a job for me when I got back and gave me the name of one of her friends in Los Angeles, Gemma DeVillard, who was in charge of Perino's restaurant. My English continued to improve, which made me more sure of myself, and that made me happier. I planned to move from my apartment to save the rent. Having accumulated very little, I could store a trunk in a friend's basement and take everything else with me. I'd rent a little apartment in Hollywood for two months and stay a longer or shorter time, depending on what happened. I then splurged and booked a sleeper for my dog and me from New York to Los Angeles in July 1952.

When I reached Los Angeles, I called Sasha and Gemma. Gemma and I became good friends even though our age difference was significant. Sasha and his wife and I also became good friends. He was proud of a fellow Ukrainian who was succeeding in a glamorous business and admired me for my worldly attitude and self-confidence (neither of which I possessed to the extent he thought I did). Another friend of Jasha's, an actor-producer named Volodia, introduced me to many people, most of them European. Loda Halawa, a Polish actress-dancer, visited my little place with a handsome friend. I met Akim Tamiroff, the actor, and the son of Feodor Chaliapin, the great Russian basso. From there, the circle spread.

The people I met were somebody in Europe before WWI and tried to live in the same style in the United States, but they had no money. I was fortunate enough to meet Russian nobility that emigrated all over the world in 1917 during the revolution. Slavic men got excited to meet me, and there was always talk about my getting married. One attractive man began seriously to court me, but when he learned I had no money, just elegant clothes, he dropped me faster than that hot potato. I enjoyed the people I met, but I also felt sad about those who had lost what they once had.

I got to know many interesting places in Southern California. Every day someone was there to drive me to some different city to visit and look around. Friends I knew from New York invited me for a day at their Malibu ranch. The woman who knew me was there with her husband. Her father and mother were also there. That old grandfather tried to make a date with me. Then, when I rejected his interest in me, he told his wife I was propositioning him. I was very hurt, but I didn't know what to say. Happily, that was the only unpleasant event in California.

Two months passed very fast. It was time for a good vacation to end, but I thought that on my way back to New York I should stop in Dallas to see the Neiman Marcus store, which I learned had been in business since 1907. (The store was founded by A. L. Neiman, his wife Carrie, and his brother-in-law Herbert Marcus. Mrs. Neiman set the standard in fashions.) I arrived early in September, two days before the biggest show of the year and was immediately hired to work the show. The store and the fashions were impressive, so impressive that instead of staying no more than two or three days as planned, I agreed to stay a few more weeks. My contacts were with Larry and Stanley Marcus, and they made it easy for me to stay: I was treated well, paid well, and not asked to make a time commitment.

I moved from the hotel to the home of an older Jewish-German lady, and naturally we spoke in German. I became very attached to my new friend, Mrs. Wolf. Even when I moved away from Dallas, our correspondence went on for many years.

As had happened in New York, I quickly became associated with Orthodox Russians, Russian Jews, Italians, and Germans. Somehow, the word spread that the new model at Neiman Marcus was Slavic and also spoke Italian and German. Then when a newspaper article about me appeared in October 1952 (with a certain number of errors and a picture of me and my dog), more people became interested in me, and I was invited to different homes. I enjoyed meeting those groups, and it was comfortable to slip back into other languages.

As I became acquainted with the larger population, I realized Dallas was a very different city. People were different. They spoke differently, which gave me an added language problem, and they interacted differently, which sometimes confused me. My popularity increased, however, and I met new people every day and went out every night to shows, dances, parties. Those "few more weeks" went by quickly— as did the rest of 1952.

In my letters to Jasha, I always gave a report on Bill. At some point, we talked about my sending Bill back to Jasha, and I did that early in 1953. I missed my dog, but he was probably happier in Italy.

Every Wednesday all models were driven to the second Neiman Marcus store, which was new and featured a beauty salon. There we had our hair and nails done. The driver took the same route each time, going along Airline Avenue and crossing Bryn Mawr Avenue. I admired the beautiful homes and was enchanted by the manicured gardens and yards. I noticed one peculiar colonial two-story house with slightly messy bushes and remarked to the other models, "I would like to have that house."

I met an appealing Jewish man, visited his home often, and became friends with his charming mother and sister. The man and I dated on quite a few occasions, all of them enjoyable and interesting. One night, early in 1953, he took me to the home of some of his friends where I met an American who had been in the American army in Italy and who spoke Italian quite well. I chatted with him for a few minutes, but compared with my date, who was very dynamic, the man seemed rather dull. The next day the man called me and reminded me, in Italian, his name was Charlie. (He didn't tell me how he got the telephone number.) We talked about Italy. I told him I was just passing my time and counting the days until I could get a visa and go back to visit.

My new acquaintance started calling me every day, talking at great length and asking me out to dinner. His fondness for Italy gave us one definite thing in common. He'd learned to speak Italian and French during the war, which I could admire. I couldn't say I found him especially interesting, but it was easy to be with him. Actually, he was a comfortable contrast with the man who introduced us and who was in some ways too strong.

Charlie was polite and could be funny, especially in the way he made fun of himself. I did laugh at many of the things he said—although I didn't understand some of the remarks that made other people laugh. Once, we went out for dinner and dancing with other couples. One of the women said, "Let's go to the john." I felt embarrassment because there was a gentleman in our company named John. Confidentially, I shared my embarrassment with Charlie, who said loudly enough for others to hear, "Well, tell them, 'Let's go to the Charlie.'" The others laughed, but I wasn't sure how to respond.

Charlie's father, a very severe man, was born in Greece, found his way to Dallas as a young man, and after other jobs and businesses started a laundry service for restaurants and turned it into a highly successful operation. Charlie, who was thirty-one, was running the business. Charlie's Scottish-Irish mother died when Charlie was eight. Her death had a strong and lasting effect on him.

Charlie had been twice married and had a young daughter. He told me often American women didn't make good wives and he was only interested in European women, who do. Soon after he met me, Charlie announced he had stopped drinking. He was bragging to everyone, "I don't drink anymore. Because Eugenia doesn't drink, I stopped." I didn't understand why he was so proud of himself. What did it matter whether someone drank or not? It never had among the people I'd known.

Soon, I was dating Charlie exclusively. It wasn't my idea, but he was the only one asking me. I didn't realize that others, having seen us together on a few occasions, assumed our arrangement was exclusive. I wasn't thinking of anything permanent, but Frau Wolf looked at me one day and said, "You're going to marry that man." I laughed and replied that my only plans were to return to New York, which I would be doing almost any day.

In the next few weeks, I increased my contacts with my New York employer, and with my Dallas employer, I discussed the time I would leave. I'd changed my original plan to stay in Dallas two days to a plan to stay a few weeks, which became three months, then let that stretch to five, six, seven, eight, nearly nine months. And I began to be nagged by a feeling that staying away from New York was a mistake. Charlie tried to talk me into staying in Dallas, but he realized the more he pushed about staying, the more that made me want to leave. I hadn't become a citizen yet, but with my green card I could get a visa, so I applied for one early in 1953. Needing to go back to New York before I went to Italy, I made the break, and in May 1953, I left Dallas.

Country Four: The United States of America and Life as a Free Woman

Chapter Ten
Dallas and Los Angeles 1953–1969

On my way back to New York, I began to realize how much I missed the artistic and intellectual life of the city. One of the first persons I called was Ham Fisher. He was the fastest way to renew contact with interesting and exciting people. Hearing their discussions once again made me realize just how provincial Dallas was by comparison.

I moved into an apartment with a friend named Nina, a Russian refugee from China, but between work and social activities, I was seldom at home. During my first week back, Charlie called many times when I wasn't at home, and at all hours when I was. He always asked when I was going to Italy. I said as soon as possible. He was afraid if I went to Italy, I wouldn't return. Before a second week passed, Charlie—wanting to get to me before I left—drove in one stop to New York. His arrival made me feel uneasy. He asked me to marry him right away, which made me more uneasy. I couldn't answer.

I hesitated because Charlie had been married twice already and was not a man from whom I would learn. I couldn't say that I was in love with him. On the other hand, he was likable, he said he wanted children, and having a family was my strongest wish. He was persistent, maybe I felt a little sorry for him, and he was ready to go to Italy for a month without going back to Dallas. (In Italy, I had wondered about the possibility of a good relation with a man in the future. I didn't think about that.)

Some of my friends met Charlie. At least one of them, my roommate Nina, had a good impression of him. Ham Fisher was having a big party, and in his home Charlie announced he wanted to marry me and wanted Ham's blessing. Ham was hesitant and not enthusiastic, but Charlie interpreted his remarks as a blessing.

Not quite able to say no, I agreed to marry Charlie. We were married 7 July 1953 in City Hall, New York. The clerk asked us to join hands. I was nervous and raised my hand, thinking he meant, "Raise your hand and swear allegiance to the United States." The gentle laughter made me relax.

Two days later, we left for Italy. I was happy to see my friends in Milano, but some of my old fears did return. As soon as we got off the plane, I felt less safe. At the same time, I definitely felt American. I was a different person; I had a right to exist.

Jasha and Yolanda were happy to see me, and the four of us spent much time together visiting old friends and favorite places. In private, Jasha and I talked about the directions of our lives. He was still working in opera and going to more places. He had new lady friends but not one special one. When we talked about me, Jasha said, "I wanted you to get married but not to that."

In Rome, I went to IRO to see Mr. Engalichev. He was sad because his French wife was very ill. What I had to say could not be made cheerful. I did first express my appreciation and admiration for the good he was doing, for seeing that people like me who had lost their homelands could have a chance for new homes. Then, I told him all the details of Bremerhaven, of how, covered by the robes of a priest, a Communist agent was working on young people to convert them and was hurting many families. I told him I still had goose bumps just thinking about that priest. Mr. Engalichev became pale, his face showing great anger. I added, "You work so hard organizing and helping refugees, and just before they are to leave to go to new countries, the priest in the camp decides their destinies. It's not right."

Mr. Engalichev thanked me for choosing to tell him what was happening and for taking the time especially to see him. Before I left his office, I returned the conversation to the good things the United States was giving me and thanked him once more. To be the bearer of bad news to a man who was already sad made me feel bad, but the visit was the completion of something unfinished. It was the high point of the trip.

On 8 August 1953, Charlie and I left Italy and returned to Dallas, Texas—to my new home. Charlie had a nice, big house, which needed attention. He had been divorced six months before we met and had been living there. He had a part-time maid for cooking and some cleaning, but the place needed much cleaning and painting inside and out. It was past time to replace drapes and carpets, and the furniture was not in the style of that in the nicer houses I'd visited in Dallas. The grass was mowed, but plants and shrubs were neglected. Immediately I began a full-time job cleaning, rearranging, and repairing. Charlie kept all the money; purchases and hiring of workers went through him.

As soon as I had inside and outside looking presentable—but long before I made things satisfactory—we gave a party to introduce each other's friends. House and yard were overflowing. Our guests seemed to be having a good time, and I was complimented profusely that night and in the notes that followed. I thought it was a nice evening but couldn't avoid thinking of social gatherings in New York and Italy that were characterized by a certain sophistication or elegance missing that night. I hoped I was not being snobbish; it seemed a simple observation.

One of my Russian friends asked me, "What are you going to do now you are married? Will you join the club or a charity?"

I didn't understand a life that turned on activities like that. I said to him, "I have a husband, a home, and responsibilities."

When I was single and working, I was always going somewhere and doing something, and my residence was only for sleeping and getting ready to go out. Getting adjusted to married life meant making my residence a real home; going out was something additional. I made no attempt to become a part of the social set whose activities were featured in the newspapers. Even so, I still attended many events, for Dallas did have an active social life, and Charlie and I were invited to many functions by different sets of people.

My strong ideas about family made me entirely dedicated to my husband. He was to be the focal point of my life, and whatever I did was in terms of what he wanted. We both wanted a baby. Often, Charlie said, "Give me a son," and in due time I became pregnant.

During the holiday season, we drove to New Orleans and on to Charleston. I enjoyed the lovely and interesting cities and the pretty countryside. In America, I had found a wonderful country.

Maybe I worked too hard at making Charlie my focal point. Maybe he didn't know how to accept that even though he had complained about American women as wives, but he started drinking. He had announced he wouldn't drink because I didn't, and, as far as I could tell, he hadn't been drinking, but six months or seven months after we were back in Dallas, he was definitely drinking. And sometimes he was moody or inconsiderate. On one occasion the two of us went out for dinner. As we sat in the bar waiting for a table, he started to flirt with a girl and put her on his knees. I was sitting right there, heavily pregnant and embarrassed to share my humiliation with everyone.

On 19 August 1954—only one day from my adopted

birthday—our son, Peter Eugene, was born. I was ecstatic. Charlie was happy. I spent almost every minute of the day with Gene. Although he was only four months old at Christmas, he received all kinds of presents. He already had almost everything any child could have, and I bought toys, toys, and more toys for him. I couldn't remember having had a toy when I was a child, so I compensated with my son. He seemed to enjoy the toys. Like most mothers, I thought my baby was special—that he was the handsomest, smartest, best-behaved baby there ever was. I certainly enjoyed him and think I made him feel wanted and loved.

When Gene was about five months old, Charlie was playing with him one day. The play became somewhat rough, and the baby cried. Charlie never touched Gene after that.

One day in summer 1955, I went walking with Gene, taking a different path from my usual one. On my return, I saw the house from an uncustomary direction. Something about the house made a strong and different impression, but I could not say what it was. Moments later, it struck me I was living in the very house I had admired so much on my trips to the hairdresser two years earlier. I was living in a colonial two-story house I said I wanted. The realization brought a strange feeling—and questions.

August was at hand, and I had a birthday party for Gene. I wasn't sure I could depend on Charlie, so I invited only a few people. The party was nice, but it did not stop Charlie and me from moving farther and farther apart. Six months later, he suggested I should go to Europe. He made the arrangements without telling me and told me to come back in six months. I was ashamed and confused. I had no words and could not have spoken them anyway. I couldn't get beyond asking "Why?"

At last, I accepted that Charlie was an alcoholic. First, I had to learn what it meant to be alcoholic (which taught me something about Marussia). Then I could understand Charlie's boasts about quitting. Of all the men I'd met and all the choices I'd had, I chose to marry an alcoholic. At first, I was angry with Charlie because he deceived me. Then I began to think I was still feeling guilty and ashamed because I was raped. Maybe I could let myself marry only a flawed man: I didn't deserve anyone else—and could never have the kind of relation I dreamed about.

I felt terribly alone and upset. With no appetite since Gene was born, I was losing weight. I couldn't decide what to do and didn't want to talk with anyone, so in June 1956 Gene and I flew to Frankfurt (the city Charlie picked) and stayed in a small hotel. The son of the owner and his Hungarian-Jewish wife were most helpful. They wanted to move to America with their four-year-old son to start a new life. The wife had relatives in the United States, but they wouldn't sponsor her because she married a German.

Before I left, I wrote Jasha I was going to Frankfurt. He had a new German girlfriend in Dusseldorf he would be visiting, and the two of them visited me. Jasha was upset about my marriage and upset because he saw I was upset and showed physical signs of not eating and sleeping properly. At least I could tell Jasha I worried constantly that my family was not what a family should be, that it was not the family I longed for. It did help to talk with him.

I took Jasha's suggestion to go to Viareggio, Italy. He thought the sea air and the baths would be good for me, and they were. I was still sad, but my baby was quite happy, swimming and playing and making new little friends. He wasn't quite two years old, but in the three weeks we were in Viareggio, he was speaking Italian. Slowly, I began to think about the five months I would be in Europe and decided to go to Milano and try to work. Charlie was sending $100 a month as he promised, but I needed more than that.

I was embarrassed to go back with a child and no husband to the people who had known me as a leading model.

But I was accepted before and was sure I would be again.

In Milano, I found a place for us to stay. The woman, who had two boys going to school, would be a nanny for my son. I went back to my old designers, who were happy to see me. It was almost time for the fall shows, and I was hired to work from August to November when I was scheduled to return to the United States. As pleased as I was to see the beauty of Italy, to be earning good money, and to refurbish my wardrobe, I did not consider staying. The old fears came back just as they did before. I had no problem with immigration authorities, but the old, deep fear was always there.

In November 1956, I went back to Dallas. Charlie had a girl living in the house. He would have been happy for me to stay in Italy forever. (He'd told everyone in Dallas I was the one who wanted to go.) He moved out, and I was left in a big house with my son. Charlie told me to file for divorce. In spite of all that was bad, I still was not thinking about divorce. I guess I was letting my longing for a family of my own deceive me because the words "file for divorce" tore me apart. Charlie had told me American wives weren't good. Now, I wasn't good either. I said to Charlie, "But what about the innocent child? His destiny is gloomy to grow up without a father."

Charlie's response was that his daughter from his previous marriage was without a father. I didn't understand how not taking care of one child explained not taking care of another child. Every contact became unpleasant, and when Charlie was drunk, he was abusive. I had to accept that Charlie would not be a husband and Gene would not be fortunate enough to grow up in a family with two parents. I filed.

I'd returned to Dallas seriously underweight, and the realities of the situation in Dallas made me even less able to eat and sleep. In January 1957, a series of physical problems started. After having my teeth cleaned, I caught an extremely bad cold; then, all at once, the left side of my body was paralyzed, and I was in excruciating pain. My physician, Dr. Uhley, went to the house and started giving me penicillin. The paralysis ended in about a week, but I continued to have intermittent fever. My temperature could be quite high one hour and near normal the next hour.

At some point, I was in the hospital semi-conscious. Dr. Uhley later explained that an infection of the blood caused streptococcus intercarditis, which affected my heart. My heart was not right. My mind was not right. At thirty-one years of age, I was a complete mess. I lay there, partially aware, and every four hours I was given a penicillin shot.

A friend I knew through Charlie, an Italian-American woman named Betty, made arrangements with the owners of a day nursery to take care of Gene full time. Betty took Gene to visit me. The child, only two and a half years old, was ready to burst into tears at any second. My friend told my son, "You must not cry." His lips twisted—how hard it was for a little one to understand—to hold in his emotions. I didn't know to tell her to let him cry. My heart was in pain to see my baby in pain. Making the matter worse, his body was covered with insect bites—chigger bites. He was not being cared for. It was an unbearable moment for both of us. My child just looked at me, eyes full of tears. Betty took my little one by the hand, and I don't remember what happened for a long time.

Later, I learned that Charlie's friends advised him to take his child home, take his help back, and have his baby with him. Charlie took over the house but rented it instead of moving there himself, and he did not take the child. He told somebody it wouldn't work. I guess he didn't want to be bothered. It wasn't expected I would live, and the plan was as soon as I died, Charlie's sister would adopt my son. I would have survived to block that—if not for my son, then for myself.

My life was indeed hanging on a very thin thread. My memory of events is not clear, but after four months in the hospital, I started to feel stronger, better, more aware. The infection was destroyed but with serious consequences. I had holes in two heart valves, which allowed leakages. My heart was probably already damaged from streptococcus that caused rheumatic fever when I was a child, and it was possible my trip to the dentist let a kind of streptococcal organism, always present in the mouth, get into my blood. I wasn't offered any immediate hope the condition could be corrected but was told of new work being done for heart problems.

When I was able to leave the hospital, Charlie got us a small apartment. I was glad not to live in the house. I was so happy to be alive and to be with my child I didn't care about anything else. That attitude was not in my best interest. Charlie sent one of his laundry trucks to move my clothes from the house to the apartment. The house was being rented by three men, but only the maid was at home. She said I couldn't take the crystal, silver, and dishes; they were being rented along with the house. The driver hurried me. I felt as if I was a thief stealing my own clothes. Some clothes, coats, and alligator bags were gone; where I didn't know. I threw clothes into boxes as fast I could. My child was crying. He wanted to take his rocking horse and big stuffed animals, but the driver was saying, "No room, no room." I wondered later why I let myself be pushed aside and did not insist on better treatment. I was an intimidated immigrant, not strong physically or emotionally—not strong enough to stand against Charlie or his driver.

It was June 1957 and time for me to start building a new life. First, I wanted to give Gene the attention he hadn't had for months. When a hotel offered swimming privileges, I signed up for the summer, and we spent many hours every day at the pool. Gene learned to swim and then, with encouragement and help, developed the confidence to dive. He was happy to be at the pool and, with great delight, called out again and again, "Mommy, watch me."

I was delighted to watch him but saddened to see he was emotionally hurt. He was afraid of anyone who tried to talk to me. When someone approached, Gene stood in front of me, holding me as tightly as he could. When Gene and I were not at the pool, we played games in the park or at home.

When Gene and I rested from playing games, I read to him. After six or eight weeks of not being out of his sight, I accepted an invitation to a small party in the same building. I hired a baby-sitter, a high school girl, and asked her to read to Gene before he went to sleep. She started reading, and Gene started correcting her: "You don't read good English. My mommy reads different." The baby-sitter agreed I read differently—and added I read the wrong way. I didn't know how, but Gene understood the words I pronounced improperly even if I did not understand the words myself.

When it was certain the divorce would go through, three of Charlie's cousins became my good friends, and I remained in contact with them many years after I left Dallas. In Dallas, I thought I was the one they didn't like. From them, I learned more about Charlie. His family and friends told him he couldn't win the hand of an elegant and attractive woman, and he pursued me to prove he could. He didn't want to be married; he wanted his freedom—and his bottle.

The rest of 1957 passed in the same way, as did most of 1958. I did little other than take care of Gene. In September, at age four, Gene started pre-school. There was a full program, and I had a few hours to myself. I felt quite well by then and was unable to stay still. Soon, I was involved in several activities. I needed job skills and enrolled in cosmetology school, starting with manicuring. I responded to friends who had been calling me. Talking to some Russians led to my attending the Orthodox Church, becoming a close friend with the priest's sister, and singing in the choir, sometimes as a soloist. Singing was a good exercise for my chest. Talking with some Italians led me to various social events. On one of those occasions, early in 1960, I met a young Italian doctor and told him about the trouble with my heart. He paused and said, "You give me the inspiration to specialize in cardiology."

My spirits were quite high, and talking with the young doctor sent them higher, but throughout that spring I felt myself getting more and more easily fatigued. Maybe I was doing too much. People who were aware of what was happening were very kind to me. In summer 1960, a Russian couple, on the pretense they had to go to Houston anyway, drove me to see Dr. DeBakey and Dr. Cooley. They could not help me, but they, too, told me much progress was being made, so I started doing some research about my problem and work being done.

As long as I paced myself, I could care for Gene and keep up with some activities, but, as time passed, I could make less and less exertion and abandoned everything except my son. (Gene would listen to my heart and, hearing the irregular sounds, say, "Mommy, you have two hearts.") In that time Gene went to a Catholic kindergarten, then on to the first grade. He was not demanding, but he was an active boy and participated in many things. He was in school programs and went often to the homes of other children or invited them to our place. He was in a Captain Kangaroo television show, which was exciting, but which also meant taking him to the studio, assisting him, and waiting and watching for several hours. An active boy takes a great deal of energy, and lack of energy on my part was depressing.

One event in 1960 gave me a great lift. I was in the company of Jewish friends from Estonia and saw an envelope I recognized was from the Soviet Union. I asked about it and was told times had changed, that one could send letters to relatives there. I was intrigued and said I had two brothers in Kyiv with whom I'd had no contact in almost twenty years and had been afraid to try to write them, afraid that, if they were still alive, my letters would put them in prison. In Stalin's time anyone who kept correspondence with the West was automatically an enemy of the people. The friend with the letter not only encouraged me to write, but practically dictated a letter and showed me how to address it so my brothers could be located. I was quite excited and put in the mail that very day a letter to Jasha and Mykola.

A few weeks later, I was surprised and delighted to see a letter from Kyiv. Jasha wrote that they were happy to hear from me and that Mykola had searched for me through the Red Cross, but, of course, when I changed my name to Irma Simsolo in 1946, Eugenia Sakevych disappeared forever. Jasha said he and Marussia were both working. They had two sons and three daughters, all in the university. Our brother, Mykola, had been a soldier and a POW and was working as a photographer. He was married and had two children. I had a feeling of change, of something new and at the same time a feeling of going back to what I already knew. I had a feeling of family—I was not alone anymore in this world. I began a regular correspondence with my family.

In March 1961, my efforts to gather information about my heart were rewarded. I was called by the doctors of St. Paul's Presbyterian Hospital in Dallas and offered surgery. I was told the open-heart surgery was new and risky but necessary. On the appointed day, many doctors were there, including my Italian doctor who had done research with dogs to develop the procedure. After I was sedated, I kept talking. The anesthesiologist asked me what I was saying. I repeated: "I wish you good luck, doctors. You have to succeed. There is no other choice. I have a child."

That was the last I remembered. My body was chilled to 90 degrees Fahrenheit. My heart was then chilled to 82 degrees with a saline solution. After that, the doctors went to work for over eight hours. (One newspaper article reported it was two hours and ten minutes. That would have been a blessing for me and the operating team.) They opened me and repaired a hole in a leaflet of the mitral valve, repaired another leaflet in the aortic valve, and replaced two worn ones with plastic leaflets. The procedure was successful.

As I recovered from the trauma of the surgery, my body felt better, and I gained strength. After eleven days, I was sent home. There, I started to think about what I had gone through and got so scared my temperature jumped. I got hold of myself, chased away those dire thoughts, and got better. My worst pain came from the sharp knuckles and twisted fingers of a nurse who had very bad arthritis. A bath from her was a minor form of torture, endured with grimaces and tears. But I survived and prospered. Having a strong will for survival took me through the surgery and kept me upbeat after the surgery.

The surgery generated much interest and attention. It was described in medical journals and covered by newspapers all around the country. It was reported as one of the first surgeries of its kind. The doctors and I were described as pioneers of open-heart surgery. Few humans had survived such difficult surgery at that time. (Another woman who had a similar operation for a less serious problem that same day never woke up.) I received letters and telephone calls from all over the United States and Canada. Some were inquiring about my operation in hopes for themselves or their loved ones. Some were congratulating me and wishing me well.

After two months, the pain from the opening had become only slight discomfort, and that was fading. Gene's school had ended for the summer. I wanted to get out of town and registered us for a vacation on a ranch outside San Antonio. There, we had a wonderful time horseback riding, swimming, and eating excellent food. We returned to Dallas renewed in spirit.

A few days later, I received a letter from Ursula—a fashion model I knew in New York who had moved to Los Angeles—suggesting I visit her. More vacation would be good therapy, so we went. Ursula reserved a room for us at the

Capri Hotel, which was too expensive for me. I called Diane, someone I knew from Dallas and moved to her place for two weeks. In that four-apartment building were three divorced women with small children.

I liked Los Angeles. The climate was good for me. I spent time with Ursula and other people I knew. We went to Catalina, and my six-year-old son had much fun sliding down the sandy dunes. The fresh air and sun made us look very healthy.

We returned to Dallas after our vacation, and I couldn't stay still. I had a tremendous burst of energy and wanted to be busy. I went to work as a manicurist while my neighbor cared for Gene.

A week or so later, I received a letter from Diane, telling me about a job taking care of two children on Saturday and Sunday in exchange for half the house. The idea was appealing. Charlie had paid for our apartment and medical insurance, but there were signs he wasn't going to continue to pay, and I had used my savings. I would have to support Gene and me. After a period of looking at reasons to stay in Dallas, and for going to Los Angeles and after talking with Gene, I decided to go.

We moved to Los Angeles in August 1961. I went to the house Diane told me about. The man was the boyfriend of Diane's neighbor, and he had the two children only on weekends. The situation was somewhat unclear, and I didn't feel good about it. I determined I wouldn't stay there.

My first concern was to get Gene into school. He'd seen a boy on the street dressed in a military uniform and wanted very badly to be like that boy. I managed to get him enrolled in the Brentwood Military Academy, where he would soon begin second grade. I found a very inexpensive apartment in Bel Air, where we sat and slept on the floor for a few months until I could buy some used furniture from a friend.

My medical records were transferred to doctors at

UCLA, and I was put under their care. The doctors thought it was much too early for me to work and wanted me to apply for welfare. I refused. I felt privileged to be in the United States and was too proud to accept handouts. Besides, I thought my health was good.

I took a job as a model at Saks Fifth Avenue for a few months and went to school to get a California manicurist's license. Once I was licensed, I got a job at the Beverly Wilshire Hotel and worked there five days a week, including Saturdays, for a year. It was a good job, but I quit because I wanted to be with my son and take him places on the weekends. An English girl who ran a travel agency in the hotel advised me to study and become a travel agent. I worked for a few months for a Brentwood travel agency, but I wasn't good for that job. I was alone in the office with no one to answer questions and had to do correspondence in English. In spite of the Saturday hours, I went back to manicuring, which paid well.

Of course, with all of that movement, I needed a car. I had learned to drive in Dallas but did not gain much skill. In Los Angeles, I learned to drive with the aid of traffic tickets and became proficient enough to get around.

Gene did well at his academy in his classes and with trumpet lessons. (He was the youngest pupil taking instrumental lessons.) In spring 1962, he completed second grade. Several people told me the Beverly Hills schools were especially good, so I moved to Beverly Hills and enrolled Gene there for the third grade. He didn't do well, so I enrolled him in another military school where the supervision was constant. He seemed to do better there.

In the fourth grade, which began in fall 1963, he showed some talent with his trumpet. That year and for the next several years, I arranged for him to have horses to ride and to pursue any musical or athletic activity in which he showed interest.

Also in fall 1963, my friend Yolanda arrived from Italy

for a visit. Our friendship was still strong in the same ways it was in Italy. Wanting her to stay, I introduced her to male friends I thought she would like, among them a Polish Jew I met in 1952 with Loda Halawa, and in time he and Yolanda were married. After they had been married a few months, I suggested she get a job. She would learn to speak better English, and she needed to be busy. I assured Yolanda she knew enough English to work as a sales lady and took her to Saks where I had worked. She was hired and worked there 29 years, retiring only when computers were installed.

Yolanda wanted to know why I wasn't married. I told her that illness, surgery, and recovery accompanied by a divorce had pushed marriage and dating aside for the past six years, and I still wasn't ready. I didn't tell her I had met men who seemed serious about marriage but that I ran away from the prospect. I didn't know whether I ran because of the reasons I gave Yolanda or because of my old guilt, a need to be with my child, or lingering concern about my health. Some men I met through my circle of friends seemed interested and said they wanted to be married. I met many men—all sorts of men—on my job. Some of them were looking only for sex, a few seemed genuinely interested, but I didn't date any of them.

A dashing journalist regularly said to me in the presence of others, "Eugenia, let's go to Las Vegas."

I ignored him a couple of times, but when he persisted, I had to invent something to protect myself from that wolf. I told him, "You do know I am foreign, and I am sure your wife would not like me to go on a trip with you. She could deport me from the USA." He laughed then and whenever he saw me after that, but he stopped his teasing.

On 28 May 1964, I became a citizen of the United States. I had studied. I had taken the test. I raised my hand and said, "Yes, I want to be an American." I accepted the good wishes of my friends. It was a proud time, and I was radiating joy and good feeling. Actually becoming a citizen was a complement to the feeling of arriving in the United States. As I said before, the day I put my feet on American soil—18 August 1951—my life began. Immediately, I was free. I could feel like a human with a right to live.

In spring 1964, Gene was halfway through the fourth grade. During the same period I was becoming a citizen, Gene was becoming aware his mother was not like the mothers of his friends. He would say, "I wish I had an American mother." I wanted to tell him I was American, but I understood what he meant. I had absorbed too many cultures to be like those who knew only one. I understood his discomfort, but it still hurt to hear him express it. I tried to be more like other mothers. He did seem content at military school, and it was delightful to observe him teaching one of his friends to play trumpet or ride a horse English style.

In fifth grade, Gene was promoted to lieutenant but was caught smoking and demoted. I thought the demotion was enough punishment, but I talked to him about the harm of smoking and the need to follow rules. I couldn't tell whether I made either point.

Since that first letter from my brother Jasha, I'd been writing regularly and getting closer to making a trip to Kyiv. Jasha had sent me pictures of his whole family, including Kolia and Ura, the two sons, Galina, Lida, and Valia, the three daughters, and their spouses and children. I had a large family.

In 1965, I began definite preparations to visit them, and in summer 1966—after Gene finished the fifth grade—we went. An efficient travel agent arranged our flight to Moscow (of course, we had to go through Mother Russia, not directly to Ukraine), rail passage to Kyiv, and a hotel stay of twelve days at a very low rate (that would show the West what was possible under communism). As an American citizen, I was able to get through most of the bureaucratic red tape and inefficiencies, and with my clothes and look of self-confidence, I was assumed to be American.

The whole family was waiting for us at the train station in Kyiv. The welcome was overwhelming. I couldn't count how many people were there. From the pictures Jasha sent, I recognized Galina right away, so I knew it was my family, but when an old man stepped forward to embrace me, I had to say, "Who is this?" I guess I still had my 1936 image of Jasha. Not since I arrived in Clusone after the war had I stepped off a train to so many greetings. It was exciting at that moment and then gratifying to know my parents had many descendants and I had family.

In the coming days, Gene and I looked around Kyiv (insofar as we were permitted) and in the evenings we visited with my family. It took hours for them to tell me what happened during the thirty years since Grisha and I left Kyiv, and it took me hours to tell them what happened to Grisha and me from 1936 to 1942 and to me after Grisha died. The few letters Grisha and Jasha wrote covered very little.

Jasha, Mykola, and I talked about our parents and life on the farm, about when I was born, about Kamjana Balka, our village. Travel was restricted. A trip to my birthplace would not have been possible, so I didn't have to consider whether to go. Probably I didn't want to. If the village had been destroyed, I would have been devastated; if it had been just as I remembered it, I would have been overcome by thoughts of what we had and what was taken from us.

One link to the past did have me in tears: photographs. Whatever family pictures remained were with Jasha. There weren't many, and the quality wasn't good, but I was happy to see pictures of my parents and my sister and brothers. I sat and stared, completely absorbed. On a later trip to Kyiv, when I again wanted to see the pictures, Jasha gave me some of them, which I keep and treasure. I still look at a picture of me taken when I was two or three years old and ask: Is that me? Am I that little girl?

Living conditions in Kyiv had not improved. My family lived in drab and dreary crowded buildings. There were no goods for them to buy even when they had money. The food—even that at the hotel—was heavy and greasy. It was difficult for me to eat it; for Gene, it was next to impossible. Gene learned appreciation for the United States, and my great appreciation of my new country swelled even more.

The most striking thing about the visit was that my own family did not entirely trust me. Life under the Soviets made everyone suspicious of everyone else. Although they were probably thinking I had a secret job and was somehow wealthy, no one asked me directly, "Why would someone so well-dressed and obviously so wealthy be in Kyiv?" At least, no one did on that first trip.

Jasha's oldest son, Kolia, was certainly curious about me. He and I had some slight memory of each other from the three years I was in Kyiv with Jasha's family. That would have been about Kolia's second, third, and fourth years and my seventh, eighth, and ninth years.

I took some things with me for the family (shirts, sweaters, coats, shoes, lingerie, toiletries). I learned there was a legal market for used clothing, so when it was time to leave, I emptied our huge suitcases. Kolia asked what I would wear, and I thoughtlessly joked we would have an excuse to go to Italy to buy new clothes. It occurred to me the statement said things I didn't intend: that we were wealthy or ostentatious, that we had freedoms they didn't have, that I had some special privileges like those of the Communist elite. My efforts to correct that impression weren't effective.

In spite of that, I planned to take more things on future trips. On our flight back to the United States, I realized that as oppressive and detestable as the system was, I still loved the land; Ukraine continued to hold an attachment for me.

In fall 1966, Gene enrolled in seventh grade at Beverly Hills. That year it seemed as though everything was all right.

I remember one moment that was as pleasing to me as hearing Gene say he wanted an American mother was painful. Gene and a friend were talking and listening to some loud music. The friend used a four-letter word, and Gene said, "Don't use that language in front of my mother. She doesn't know those words, and I don't want her to learn them." How much my lessons about vulgarity had to do with Gene's statement and how much was simple protection, I didn't know, but I was pleased.

Gene began the eighth grade in fall 1967, again at Beverly Hills. Something happened at the beginning of the school year (possibly earlier) that made Gene want to change schools. He would not tell me exactly what happened or what bothered him. Without knowing the truth of what happened, I resisted changing from the school that had such a good reputation.[20]

In that eighth-grade year, I received notice Charlie had died. After some hesitation, I told Gene, who wondered why I was upset. He had no more to say than "I don't know him; I know only you." I had to be sad that father and son didn't know each other, and I had to be sad for Charlie. Because of alcohol, he lost one wife after another (I was not the last), a daughter, a son, his father's business, respect of many of his family and friends, and whatever good qualities he had.

Gene got through the eighth grade and in fall 1968 started ninth grade. It was not a good year. Gene began using drugs (probably before the school term started) and later sold some for someone else. Late in the school year, another boy attacked Gene. I never learned the connections between wanting to change schools, starting drugs, and being attacked.

The attack occurred during gym class. There was a rest time. Boys were to lie on the floor with their eyes closed. While Gene's eyes were closed, a boy used some metal object to hit Gene across the face and was going to hit again, but a friend of Gene's opened his eyes, saw what was happening, and grabbed the boy. The accounts I got indicated the boy was filled with enough hatred to have killed Gene.

The school nurse called me at work, and I raced to the school. My son was lying in the nurse's office, bleeding from his broken, flattened nose and face, beyond recognition and semi-conscious. No one had called emergency. My son could have died. The nurse told me she would drive Gene to the hospital. I was too panicked to object or call emergency myself, so I let the nurse drive my son to Cedars Sinai, and I followed in my car. The doctors did patch up his nose, and it seemed as if everything was all right with his face and nose.

A week or two after Gene returned to school, an older boy, who was on drugs and selling heavy drugs, hit Gene in the face and broke his nose again. Once more, he went to the hospital and had corrective surgery followed by a long time for healing. All those events put me in a state of panic, and when I got panicky, I couldn't think straight. I didn't know what to do and took the advice of customers who said their children did well in Switzerland. As soon as I could make arrangements, we left. It was July 1969, and Gene would be fifteen the next month.

Eugenia Sakevych Dallas

The New Millennium

Some people think the World will end.
Some of us are not satisfied
With the Country and criticize this land.

Wake up, look around and be fulfilled,
 Believe me there is no better place than United States.

I am excited every day
To reach every New Year for which I pray
And hope will come in peace and harmony.

Modern advanced technology
Is an exciting time for humanity?
I am very lucky to live in comfort and plenty
United States of America is my country.

Don't criticize but think in a positive way
Be grateful that you were born
And privileged to live in USA

Don't put down your country and your people
Respect, and count your blessings to live in USA
Recognize the good qualities of the land
Honor; Support your Presidents at all times
This is your country and your people.

Wrote for the Poem Readers Club Nov.1999

Chapter Eleven
Between the United States and Switzerland 1969-1972

I stayed in Lusanne long enough to get Gene enrolled in high school. Supervision, academic program, and room and board were all part of the school. Everything seemed to be set. There was no reason for my being there, but I stayed a few extra days, just in case, then in August 1969 returned to Los Angeles and to work.

For the next two years, I wrote Gene regularly, and he responded irregularly. His letters were usually brief, communicating very little of what he might have been thinking and feeling. Sometimes his letters seemed rather strange, but when I asked him about something he'd written, he either ignored the question or said he was tired or sleepy when he wrote the letter.

I also wrote to my brothers often and started reading more about USSR and Ukraine. I worked more hours and took French classes. My time was well-filled.

It was not easy to reach Gene by telephone, but I did talk with him a few times. Little by little, I came to realize, as Americans say, he had gone from the frying pan into the fire. In Switzerland, he was even freer to use drugs. In his last year of high school, at sixteen and a half, he wrote he had fallen in love with a French teacher five years older than he. He said Catherine was very pretty and a nice girl. But Gene was a minor.

I did speak with the two of them by telephone. With her, I spoke German and with Gene, English. The two of them spoke French to each other, some of which I could follow. There was more than a language barrier, however. Gene was manipulating me, confusing me. I didn't know how heavily he was using drugs. My overriding thought was that in spite of my having paid a lot of money for his school, he hadn't been studying and might not graduate. He was perhaps selling drugs and might be arrested. But he was so skilled at lying to me that even when a statement was surely a lie, I couldn't articulate my reason for knowing it was a lie. And his accumulation of lies somehow worked.

Having gained no assurance from telephone conversations, I decided to go to Gene and closed house. Many of my possessions I packed in three trunks and shipped to Kyiv. (The trunks had to go indirectly through Poland to get them to my family.) A few items I stored at a friend's house, and in July 1971, I went to Switzerland. I made a long search for an apartment in Geneva, where I hoped my son would live and go to day school, but he refused and stayed with his girlfriend, Catherine, who was also using drugs.

Not wanting to give up and go away, wanting at least to be close to Gene, I decided to go to work for a year in Geneva, went to a model agency, and was hired by several designers. At forty-six years of age, I was successful again. During the following school year, Gene avoided me as much as possible, even when I was hospitalized for a respiratory problem, but he knew I was there.

I had sometimes said I didn't feel European anymore but was not completely American, even though Europeans often took me for American, and added I was someplace in the ocean between two continents. That was never truer than during the time I was in Switzerland.

Gene somehow graduated in June 1972, and there was

no way he could stay in Switzerland with Catherine, so he agreed to go back to the United States. We had a three-week wait for a charter flight. I wanted us to have some relaxing time together, so I talked with a travel agent and made reservations for two weeks in Majorca. I asked, then begged Gene to go, but he refused. I was sad and desperate for this child of mine. I was too depressed to stay in Geneva by myself and too depressed to go to Majorca by myself. Faced with that choice, I decided it was preferable to be miserable in some other place.

Palma, Majorca was a popular city, and the hotel the travel agent chose was also popular. Tourists were looking for company; men were pressing me to go to lunch with them as soon as I appeared. Being alone suddenly seemed preferable. I went to the manager of the hotel, who regretted his hotel did not please me but called another one for me, and I went there. I liked that hotel. It was on a hill overlooking the sea, beautiful scenery in all directions, and it was tranquil. There were two swimming pools, one connected to the sea. Gene would have liked that.

I went to the pool and, lying on my stomach with my bra unbuttoned to absorb some sun, fell into conversation with a couple from Iceland. Talking with them was easy and light, and as we talked, I noticed a rather ugly man who kept looking at me while trying to teach two little children to swim. I said to myself, there is no decency left in this world: a married man with two children staring at me. Maybe this hotel was no better than the other.

That night on my way to dinner at the hotel, I passed a big family with children and overheard a child say, "There is that lady." The next morning after swimming and before going in to change for lunch, I was sitting in a swing chair when two men sat near me to have a cocktail. They were with a chubby child, not yet two, who was running in front of me. He was such an adorable baby it was impossible to resist talking to him. The child came closer to me, then looked back at the men. I followed his gaze, saw the older man looking at me, and said, "What a nice baby. Is he your grandchild?"

He said, "No, my friend's child. Please, will you join us for cocktails?"

It seemed as though he didn't want to lose any time with his invitation. Being quite content where I was, I declined. The men were pleasantly persistent, so I seated myself closer to them, but refused a Kahlua drink. It was then I realized this was the ugly man who was looking at me the day before. Well, he wasn't so ugly up close, and the child wasn't his.

They told me they were Scottish, from Glasgow. The older one, Stewart, was a solicitor and the younger one, Lawrence, his client. Nice people, I thought, but very provincial. I was struck by Stewart's last name: Dallas. I introduced myself. They asked whether I would be attending the concert that night. I said I probably would. We talked a while, and I excused myself.

When I went down dressed for the evening, it was still light. The orchestra had started to play, and I seated myself. My new friends appeared, handsomely dressed for the evening. They stood and talked with me. They were tall, and it was uncomfortable to look up at them, so I asked them to be seated. They told me more about themselves. On vacation with them were Stewart's sister, Selina, her children, and Lawrence's wife, Janet, and their children. Lawrence had inherited a construction business from his grandfather, and Stewart, as his solicitor, had made the business highly successful. (To me, a solicitor was a salesman; it was some time before I realized that in Scotland a solicitor is a lawyer and Stewart was an integral part of a large business.)

Lawrence excused himself, and Stewart and I continued to talk. He was an eloquent speaker, well-informed and well-read. The orchestra was playing, people were dancing, and Stewart asked me to dance. From the way he held me, I thought: not bad. This man is a gentleman. His care in the way he expressed himself impressed me. After the orchestra stopped playing, we went to a nightclub. The whole evening was quite enjoyable. My depression had lifted considerably, but my thoughts were about Gene and what he was doing at that moment.

The next day I met Stewart at the pool. He was less timid and seemed to have more courage than I previously thought. He asked whether we could sit together for lunch. The waiter produced a bigger table for the two of us, and the bottle of wine I had nursed for two days went with me to the other table. Stewart took my hand and said to me, "A woman like you I would marry right away, but the climate in my country is too cold and would kill you." My woman's ego was enchanted by his quick declaration.

A while later Stewart said, "Let's go tomorrow to Tunisia."

I excitedly but jokingly said, "Why not? Let's go."

He excused himself and soon returned with two tickets for Tunisia. I didn't expect such fast action and said, "I thought you were joking."

He looked at me and said, "About an invitation to a lady, I don't joke."

The next morning at 7:00 a.m. we were flying to Tunisia. No worries, no problems, as happy as could be. Nothing was serious. He carried a light and lively conversation that kept me laughing and smiling. Even I made a few jokes. We toured Tunis, saw a mosque, ate a Tunisian lunch, and flew back to Palma.

I smiled to think again that this nice man I was now so enchanted with was the same ugly man who was staring at me, and whom I mistook to be a married man with children. Friends later would ask us how we met. Stewart always answered, "Lawrence and I sent little Stewart. Lawrence said,

"See that lady? Go talk to her." Still, I thought he was joking and asked him why he was saying that. He said, "Because that's the truth."

Days passed quickly, and it was soon time for me to leave Majorca. Stewart used his great power of persuasion to get me to stay longer, and I must say, he did move me, but I had to go to Gene and to the United States. Stewart understood that, for which I was appreciative. He did get a commitment from me to write to him and give him my new address and almost a commitment to visit Scotland.

"Visit me," he said. "See my country, who I am, how I live."

I couldn't tell him how appealing that sounded.

Country Five: Scotland and Life as a Pampered Wife

Chapter Twelve
Scotland 1973–1982

On the flight back, Gene wasn't cordial and open, but he wasn't antagonistic either. He seemed to be accepting and to understand he had to go to college or go to work, but when I could get him to talk, I didn't know whether he was being truthful.

It was July 1972 when we reached Los Angeles. I quickly found an apartment, sent a letter to Stewart, and joined Gene in the search for a college that would accept him. Of the choices available, Pomona College was Gene's preference, and he seemed to be definite about wanting to be a veterinarian. That sounded good to me. We took care of all matters of housing and living, and it appeared as if the arrangements were satisfactory. I tried not to be so insistent about drug use; I'd make Gene more determined to get drugs. He assured me he'd stopped and wouldn't start again, and, of course, I wanted to believe him but knew if he was using drugs, that was precisely what he'd say.

Stewart wrote and telephoned. He appealed his case so well I couldn't decline his invitation. He was right about going to Scotland before winter and before I got started working, and Gene was settled enough that there would be no better time later to go. Besides all those considerations, I wanted to see Stewart, and I still had my sense of adventure about seeing new places.

Stewart met me in London, and after two days we left for Glasgow. What a nice change from Los Angeles. The weather was magnificent. Sunshine during the day and rain at night. Stewart made certain I enjoyed myself during my visit. He had the right balance of scheduled activities and unscheduled time. We went to parties and to the races, where we saw one of his horses run. He took me along on business appointments. He left me alone to wander around his big, old house and lovely grounds. He showed me the countryside.

Everywhere we went, he had friends. It was obvious they adored him. People spontaneously expressed their admiration for him. He made people feel good. He was rock solid, loyal and faithful to his friends. As much as he could make others laugh, he was also calm. My first impressions on Majorca were confirmed and strengthened. The more I was exposed to his wide-ranging knowledge, the more I liked and respected him—felt honored to be in his presence. He and his friends, who were warm and welcoming to me, made me feel well-liked.

To make me feel like a native, Stewart had his driver teach me to drive on the left side of the road. I found that quite an adjustment. My test came the day Stewart was to meet a client at the Glen Eagle Hotel, which was about fifty miles from Glasgow. Stewart handed me the car keys. Driving and trembling, I was worrying about staying on the left. I hoped and expected that after a few miles, he would laugh about my driving and take the wheel himself. Hearing nothing from him, I dared to glance in his direction. He was asleep. I thought, "I must be driving all right."

We had two delightful weeks together. I learned about his life and work and the law firm he ran. I learned about his deceased wife. I learned he fought in Germany in World War II. When it was time for me to leave, I told him what a wonderful time I'd had and said although I couldn't offer him the many things he shared with me, I'd be pleased to show him Los Angeles if he wanted to visit.

Back in Los Angeles, I called Gene, then arranged to

go to work. Gene visited me briefly. He could tell I was feeling good about my trip, but I couldn't tell how well he was
doing. I hoped he was all right.

Telephone calls came almost every day from Stewart.
Sometimes, I was concerned I'd have nothing to say, but there
was never an awkward pause. Conversations were always
delightful. He said he'd like to visit and did arrive at Christmas time to spend two weeks. I showed him around Los Angeles and introduced him to Gene and to my friends. He did
have the British attitude about the colonies, but we had many
laughs about the two cultures. We found we were drawn to
each other, and marriage did enter conversations.

After Stewart left, his calls continued, and marriage
plans were made. On 5 April 1973, Stewart, Lawrence, and
Janet arrived for our wedding, which was 7 April in the Beverly
Hilton Hotel. Many friends attended our wedding in the pent-
house suite. Lawrence and Janet stayed in one of the bed-
rooms, and Stewart and I in another. Lawrence and Janet liked
America and went on to San Francisco.

Gene was at the wedding, probably on drugs, but had
nothing to say. Then and later, Stewart accepted Gene as my
son but detested what Gene was doing to himself. Gene said
Stewart didn't like him. I didn't know whether Gene believed
that or found it a convenient position to take.

Some friends from Dallas who attended the wedding
convinced Stewart to visit Dallas on our way back to Scotland. I would have preferred not to go but didn't raise any
objection. I closed my apartment and sent my clothes and books
to my new home, and we were on our way to Scotland by way
of Texas.

My Dallas friends were charmed by Stewart and made
a great fuss over him. They were so intrigued his last name
was Dallas the comments about it never ended. Some simply
repeated, "Your name is Dallas," and others constructed something humorous. Stewart, with his knowledge, explained the

name was Scottish and was given to the city in honor of Vice President George M. Dallas who served under President James K. Polk. The Dallas clan was from Inverness, but when England under King George III undertook the Highland Clearances in 1779 (punishment of northern Scotland for supporting the attempts of Bonnie Prince Charles to restore the Stuart line of kings), the Dallas clan was driven from Inverness. Many Scots left their country, and George M. Dallas's branch of the family went to America. Stewart's branch of the family moved to Glasgow. My friends listened, fascinated, for at least half an hour, unaware they were getting a history lesson.

At lunch in a private club, Stewart was presented with a certificate as Honorary Deputy Sheriff of Dallas, which delighted him. He liked his city and the people he met, but we had to be on our way because we were being given a wedding party in Glasgow.

The party was grand. A large hall. Uniforms. Kilts. Pomp and circumstance. Full ceremony. As guests entered, a uniformed attendant announced their names in a powerful voice, and his seven-foot-tall silver staff hit the floor. Well over one hundred of Stewart's friends were introduced. Stewart in his tuxedo and I in a long, pink organza dress stood as bride and groom in a position of honor to receive the guests. Never had I felt such honor, such pride. When the introductions were completed, the dancing and entertainment began. There was a fine orchestra. The singers and dancers were wonderfully precise and free at the same time. I was called out to dance with the master of ceremonies, who was in his McKenzie kilt. I didn't know what I was dancing, but it didn't matter. I danced more that night than I had in years. And I ate. The food and drink rivaled any I'd ever had. The party was grand.

My new life in Glasgow was very busy. We were accepting invitations to the homes of Stewart's friends. His friends were eager to know Stewart's American wife. I was charmed by the luxury homes of Scotland and their owners' tranquil way of living. We went almost every weekend to our country house with Stewart's driver and cook.

After my years in the United States, I had the feeling I'd stepped into the past. If I had gone to Scotland from Ukraine, it would have been paradise, but after having lived in the United States, I missed the comforts and conveniences. We were very spoiled in the United States. We had too much of everything and the very best of everything. Again, I had to adapt to a new country, a new life, but I'd had much experience and knew how to adjust. When I had difficulties, I thought to myself, "You got married, you chose this way, now do your best." I joined classes in mixed crafts, sewing, and chess to keep myself busy. I wouldn't permit myself to start missing the United States and, most of all, my son.

The first year I wasn't conversing much with certain people. I tried to learn and observe customs. One lady remarked, "Eugenia doesn't talk much."

I replied, "Just give me one year to learn about your customs. Then I will surely talk."

No more than a month or two after I moved to Glasgow, I had an urge to say something and didn't. Stewart had arranged the purchase of a vacation house for Lawrence, and we all went to see it. The house was filled with old furniture, which Lawrence said he'd have to get rid of. He was inspired to start taking the furniture outside at that moment, and we helped. We piled unique pieces, beautiful handmade mahogany furniture, some with brass trimmings, in the yard for burning. I made a mild protest, which was ignored, so I said no more. Who was I to say anything?

When Stewart said he should probably throw out his old furniture and buy something modern, I suggested we walk through each room and take a closer look. I appreciated the beauty of what was there, but it did show neglect. I told him we would bring those enchanting antiques to life. We would clean, polish, and refinish—repair if needed. When his friends saw how beautifully we had fixed the country house with all the "old" furniture, they became aware of their treasures.

Some time later, I got involved in an effort to preserve some historic buildings in Glasgow. I saw workmen knocking a lovely facade from an old building and asked them why they were destroying history and beauty. To them, it was just a job, but while I was there, I learned there was an architectural society working to preserve historic buildings, and I joined that group. We wrote letters, demonstrated, and did what we could. Once, we stood in front of a lovely building in the rain carrying our signs, which caused Stewart to smile and shake his head. To his friends, he marveled at my efforts. I continued to work with the society until I began to feel I was going beyond preservation and into politics.

In the fall, Lawrence and Janet invited us to a football game in Glasgow, which to me was soccer. I sat quietly observing and learning about my new country. Lawrence and Stewart were talking football, and Janet said they were always arguing football. I asked Stewart which was his team. He said the blue one. "Then," I said, "Lawrence's must be the green team." That was a blunder. Lawrence and his grandfather were the biggest shareholders and later directors of the blue team, the Rangers.

We spent Christmas 1973 in Glasgow, which was very nice—except I missed Gene. He declined my invitation and enticements to spend the holidays in Glasgow.

After the holidays, I continued doing things to the house. I could never stop working, and it was satisfying to make the rooms brighter, more cheerful. In Scotland in the winter, the whole family gathered in one room, the doors closed, which did lower heating costs. The room got stuffy, however, especially if there were smokers—and Stewart did smoke; it was the only unpleasant thing about him. With one little heater or fireplace, a person toasted on one side and was chilled on the other. Being from California, I kept doors open and heat on centrally. Visitors kept closing the doors—afraid of the draft, they said.

We went at night to the pubs to socialize and to have meals. I observed women didn't say much in the presence of the men, but they did among themselves, and they knew everything about their neighbors—more than the neighbors knew about themselves.

Wherever we went, Stewart had friends. One evening Stewart and I were socializing with some of Stewart's close friends in the Pub of St. Catherine's of Loch Fine near Loch Lomond (where stood the house of Stewart's ancestors for over one hundred years). One man in particular, McFarlane, a military man, kept looking at me with pleasure. He was thinking of his adventures in Turkey. Did I reminded him of some Turkish lady of whom he had beautiful memories? I think so. He did ask me, jokingly, if I was Turkish.

McFarlane told us about one amusing episode in his life of which he was especially impressed. The British army had been trapped in North Africa for a year, and when they were liberated the men went wild, frequenting places denied them for so long while living in the trenches. After one particularly long night of drinking and socializing at a pub, McFarlane couldn't remember anything about the events of the night before. He woke up in a strange, dark room unable to recall how he'd gotten there. Disoriented and still drowsy, he looked around. In the dark room, all he could see was the big white teeth of the female he'd spent the night with. The sight of those grinning white teeth scared him so much, he jumped to his feet in his birth costume. His eyes soon adjusted to the darkness and all turned out well, but it was an event he would never forget. Nor would we.

Another evening we were invited to dinner at the home of one of Stewart's friends, also a solicitor. Four couples were there, and we were discussing everything in lively conversation. People were interested in my life and experiences in different countries, and I was asked many questions. I discussed all matters of life freely. The ladies were curious, listening. Cecelia, the hostess, remarked that I expressed myself easily and Scottish women thought about things but didn't say what they thought.

Cecelia and I went together to Edinburgh one sunny day. Cecelia showed me historical points of the city. Then we went window shopping. I was never a shopper; I went to stores to make specific purchases, but if I was browsing and saw something I liked, I bought it. That day I saw an appealing sweater, a sort of sport jacket sweater and bought it. Cecelia was bewildered and said, "Don't you have to ask Stewart before you make this purchase?" Later, Cecelia was angry with her husband one day and told him, "You should have Eugenia for a wife. She would fix you for good." I wasn't sure whether that was a compliment to me or if it meant I was a threat to him.

The country house was in County St. Catherine on the shore of Loch Fine, which opened into the Irish Sea. I watched a fisherman in a dinghy putting a long net into the water and later pulling beautiful fish from the net. We had a dinghy. I asked Stewart to buy me a hundred foot net. Stewart said, "I will buy you the fish. Don't go through all the trouble."

I said, "But it is not the same. I want to experience the accomplishment on my own."

Yes, it was a hard job, but as always I was ambitious to finish what I started. In the morning, in the dinghy, I'd pull myself by the net to the end, and there I'd find beautiful salmon, mackerel, and plaice.

I had many experiences in the dinghy. Sometimes the waves washed into the dinghy. Sometimes the plug was pulled out by the net, and the dinghy started filling with water. Then I got to the shore as rapidly as possible.

Christmas time 1974, we spent a month in Los Angeles, which became our custom for several years. We escaped the cold of Glasgow and enjoyed life in southern California. It was good to be there and to see Gene, even if he didn't spend much time with us and didn't give me much information about himself.

We entertained often in Glasgow and in the country house. Stewart's relatives from Canada visited, and we made trips to Canada to visit them. Charlie's cousins from Greece, Lela and Anna visited. Friends from Dallas and Los Angeles were curious enough about me as a wife in Scotland that once or twice a year someone arrived. Stewart always made everyone feel welcome.

In addition to the invitations from Stewart's friends to lunches, dinners, parties, dances, sporting events, and other gatherings, we were also invited to formal dinners and ceremonies because of Stewart's service and commendations from World War II. His tuxedo was often in use, and sometimes he wore all his medals. Of course, I enjoyed dressing accordingly, and I must say I was stirred by British ceremony. (On some occasions, the Queen and King or Princess Margaret appeared, and I wondered how one of my background could possibly be in the presence of the Queen of England, but being with Stewart made it seem right.)

In summer 1975, after much long distance planning, we had two special visitors: my son and my brother. Gene took everything in stride, but Mykola truly experienced culture shock. There were no lines in stores. Shelves and racks were filled. He picked up item after item and asked, "What is this?" He was so excited he didn't know what to buy. I was delighted to watch his delight—especially so because Mykola had grown bitter about the way his life had gone, about being put into an orphanage and what followed—but sad because I knew what he would go back to.

One day, we decided to have a picnic on a little island called Sea Gull. (Stewart had named a boat after me, the

Eugenia.) Stewart anchored the boat, and Gene, assuming the water would be like the water in California, jumped into the ocean. Obviously in trouble, he struggled back to the boat and, when he could talk, said it was so cold he couldn't catch his breath.

We had a good time together, but I was sure Gene was still using drugs. He always found them, no matter where he was or how little time he had. The visits were brief. My son departed; then my brother departed, leaving me to envision each of them back in his corner of the world.

The next year, 1976, Stewart received an invitation to a reunion of his army unit. He'd been invited before but had never gone. I said, "Let's go," and we went to England from Scotland.

There, I heard more praise for Stewart and more details of what he'd done. He was highly decorated for his leadership and bravery in taking 800 British soldiers into battle. He'd suffered a severe head wound, which resulted in the loss of his left eye. The soldiers—one after another, all day—spoke of Stewart with great admiration and respect. To go with Stewart's letter of commendation from King Edward VI, I had this praise, in heavy dialect, from one of the soldiers: "I would give my right arm for Major Dallas."

Stewart hadn't talked much about the war before that day and added very little after that, except to say he was lucky in battle. The commendation from the King and the medals, which I have lovingly kept, said he was brave in battle, and that day made me especially proud of Stewart.

In one of our conversations, I did tell him I encountered British troops in Linz, Austria, and he did tell me that at that time he was in Germany, working in prisoner exchange. We had to say, "What if we had both been in Linz? What if? What if?"

The exchanging of prisoners by Stewart's unit was strictly "a hundred of ours for a hundred of yours." When

Soviets didn't want to be repatriated, the British officers had no choice but to send them anyway. Stewart said he heard of Soviet male POWs dressing as women in an attempt to avoid being sent back. Soviet soldiers went around lifting prisoners' skirts to check whether they were really women. The British at least would have had a nurse check in private.

During our annual winter trip to Los Angeles that year, I saw Gene fairly frequently. He was spending more time with music and had several very nice instruments, which he could play with some skill.

Back in Glasgow, in January 1977, Stewart and I returned home one evening after dinner with friends. The telephone rang. It was a collect call from Gene in Los Angeles. He told me he had become famous with his music and was going to buy me a Rolls Royce and all sorts of other things, then ended the call quite pleasantly. Not more than ten minutes later, another collect call came, and Gene started to plead with me to go right away to Los Angeles and rescue him from the people who kept him in a room with no food or clothes or blankets, just a dirty mattress. He had descended from the euphoria of the first call.

As I pieced it together later, some other drug user had supplied Gene with drugs, taken Gene's van that was filled with expensive musical instruments, and left him to survive or not. Gene managed to get out through a window and run, naked, to the house of a friend, another drug user, who gave Gene a shirt and a pair of pants to wear. That is where he made the second call and perhaps the first, also.

I begged and insisted he get out of that little city of Pomona where he was supposedly attending college. My brain wasn't working well enough to tell him what to do but did produce one place he could go at any time. Kappa was a Ukrainian opera singer who never hesitated to do favors for friends. She knew Gene, and he knew where she lived. "Go to Kappa's," I said. "I'll be there as soon as I can."

How I held together, I'm not sure. Kappa and her husband met me at the airport with my son, whom I barely recognized. He was an old man, a wrinkled, dried out old man with chopped up hair, who promised he would never use drugs again. He was obviously not well in general and had developed an infection on his buttock. No matter how much I pleaded with him to let me take him to the doctor, he wouldn't go even though he was in agony from the pain and high temperature. After a day or two, he couldn't take it any longer, and we went to UCLA, where doctors cleared his big wound of puss. He immediately felt better, and at 3:00 a.m. we headed home with instructions to return the next day.

With the drug user's evasiveness and fear of authority, Gene told me not to say anything to the doctors, who, of course, knew the infection was from dirty needles. Gene was treated very nicely the next day, but I, as his mother, was made to feel at fault. I was accused of being pushy for insisting on clearing his mind of drugs. I was told not to mix myself up in my son's life. A social worker told me nothing could be done until Gene signed himself into a program, and he wouldn't do that.

I guess I was wrong to respond when he called for help. I guess I was wrong to plead with him to go back to Scotland with me. He wouldn't hear of that anyway. "Stewart doesn't like me," he said. I guess I was wrong for wanting to take Gene to a religious organization where there were other college students and young people on drugs.

Gene kept saying he wasn't going to use drugs anymore and he just needed to get a job to earn enough money to get back on his feet. Not knowing what else to do, I helped settle Gene in an apartment and got him a nice little car so he could go to work.

I hoped Gene would make a commitment and act on it. He had already lost all his musical instruments, his Bandura, a balalaika, an electric guitar, and a trumpet we bought in

France at a one-man factory. It didn't matter how much musical talent he had if the drugs controlled his life. After a while he was probably back on drugs, or maybe he never did quit.

After a month in Los Angeles, I went back to Scotland with a heavy heart, telling myself the counselors were right when they said it had to be Gene's decision.

In July 1977, Stewart and I went to Greece for a vacation with his relatives from Canada. I had no enthusiasm for the trip, but he wanted to go. Stewart and I drove to London, and from London we all flew to Athens. Charlie's cousins Lela and Anna in Athens made reservations for us at a new hotel in Pietra.

After a couple of days in the hotel, Stewart felt ill. He started shivering and vomiting. I called for a doctor immediately. The doctor from the village was there soon and said he just had sun stroke and a little cold, to give him a couple of days and he would be all right. But my instinct was telling me, "Don't wait too long." I called again, and the doctor came again. He started to give antibiotics to my husband by injection. He left the syringe and told me to continue giving him injections. I was petrified at first, but I did what had to be done. My husband was worsening, almost in a coma. I called the doctor again. The doctor bawled me out, saying, "Stop getting panicky. Give him time and he will be better."

I realized I was wasting my time with that doctor. Stewart's relatives gave me no advice and no help. I called Lela and Anna. They told me to go immediately to Athens where they would speak with their doctors. Because I was panicky, I did not think straight. I should have gone to the manager of the hotel and asked him to arrange a flight to Athens to transport my husband. We took a train to Athens, which was an eight-hour trip. Luckily, there was ice on the train, and I put compresses on Stewart's boiling head. On finally arriving in Athens, we took a taxi and tried to tell the driver in English to please hurry. I knew how to read Greek, but I could not speak it. The taxi driver could not understand me, so I showed him the thermometer, the high temperature. Suddenly we were driving on the left side, right side, and passing everybody. We arrived at Lela's and Anna's home. They immediately drove us to the hospital where the doctors examined Stewart and found he had *Klebsiella pneumoniae*, also called Friedlander's pneumonia. They started to give him antibiotics, which didn't help. The doctor told me they had to increase the antibiotics and use different ones, or Stewart would die. With the added medication, Stewart got better quickly, and in less than a week, he was able to leave the hospital.

There were three nights I did not sleep, taking care of my husband. In Athens, Lela and Anna gave me wonderful support and a place to sleep. As soon as Stewart's treatment started, I called his friend and personal physician, Dr. John McKenzie, his sister Selina, his office in Glasgow, and Lawrence and Janet, who was herself a physician in general practice. I kept contact with them and one or two others. Dr. McKenzie was surprised Stewart survived and told me there could be more problems. That frightened me terribly.

Upon Stewart's discharge from the hospital, we moved to a hotel, and I started to make arrangements to return to Glasgow. It seemed strange to be taking care of such matters for Stewart. He'd always handled everything, but he had no strength or energy.

The day before we left Athens we were sitting in a cafe, and I heard some people speaking Russian at the next table. I was excited to hear Russian in that time and place. I looked in their direction a couple of times and then joined the conversation. The man had been a terrorist after the revolution in Greece and fled to USSR, married, and with his Russian family had just returned to visit his native country. The Russian wife was teaching communism in the university. She was sure their communism would take over the whole world by the year 2000. I answered we shall see. Our excitement about conversation was finished.

On our return to Glasgow, all the people I'd been in contact with and others came out to visit. They encouraged Stewart and praised me. As Dr. McKenzie explained to me—if I understood him correctly—the high temperatures of Stewart's illness caused the cells of his old head wound to dry out, which affected the brain. Stewart's personality started to change. He began losing his delightful sense of humor. He was no longer as cheerful or gregarious. And he was aware he was changing.

At my insistence, Dr. McKenzie told Stewart to stop smoking, which he did without difficulty. I was immensely pleased. When I was young, smoking didn't seem to bother me, and when I first met Stewart, his smoking was not especially bothersome, but over the years, my sense of smell, my breathing, my sinuses became more and more sensitive to cigarette smoke. His stopping was good for both of us.

I wasn't entirely well myself when we returned to Glasgow. A month before, I'd gone to the dentist and asked for antibiotics. The dentist discouraged me, thinking the antibiotics would lose their effectiveness if I used them often. I developed another streptococcus infection. I thought I would not survive that time, but somebody was looking after me.

After getting through those illnesses, we thought it better not to go to California for the holidays but to wait until the next year, so for the rest of 1977 and into 1978, we concentrated on getting fit and strong.

In 1978, I received a letter from Milano, telling me my wonderful friend Jasha to whom I owed so much had died. I had expected that letter, but there was still a feeling a great portion of my world was gone. Because he taught me so much, I was frequently reminded of him through the years—when I heard a certain piece of music or read about some writer or performer or enjoyed some special meal to which he had introduced me. Even after I got that letter, when something reminded me of Jasha, I thought of him as still in Milano, still there if I needed him. Then, each time I was hit by the realization he was not there to answer any more of my questions.

Through 1978 and 1979, Stewart continued to work, but he was frustrated because he couldn't meet his standards, and in 1980, at 60 years of age, he retired. I suggested we keep only one residence. Because Stewart's ancestors wanted him to live in the country house, we sold the flat in Glasgow. But even without his old gregarious zest, he missed his friends and the city people. We did have fun around the house. It became Stewart's job to clean the fireplace and start the fire in the den, so I called him Cinderella. We went to the village pub for meals, but he did miss his active life.

Stewart and I had talked about possibly spending more time in California and about establishing a base there. In January 1981, we bought a condo in the Hollywood Hills. Gene seemed to be somewhat better. I wasn't certain about his drug use, but he looked better and was supporting himself. While Stewart and I were there looking at condos, Stewart began talking with Gene about the construction business, and Gene seemed interested. Stewart gave him a complete course in the business.

On our return to Glasgow, Stewart went to work two days a week as a consultant to his office. It was obvious, however, Stewart's health was declining. Dr. McKenzie talked to me about courses the illness might take, but he could not advise me about personal choices. I talked to Lawrence about Stewart's behavior, and he said he didn't see anything wrong with Stewart. Others said the same thing. Lawrence said other attorneys were not one-tenth as good as Stewart.

Then, in what seemed to be a contradictory position, Lawrence and Janet asked us to lunch and suggested we move for good to California, away from Scotland. Stewart knew too much about Lawrence's business, and Lawrence didn't want Stewart to talk to many people lest Stewart say something he shouldn't. That seemed to put Stewart in an awkward and uncomfortable position, and it was a very strange and unfair to me. I couldn't, nor would I try, to convince Stewart to move to California. I knew how hard it could be to get adjusted to a new country. Stewart had many wonderful ties to his city and his country, and he was not young and resilient. Yes, I liked to live in the United States, and I wanted to be near my son, but I could not and would not ask Stewart to leave Scotland.

Lawrence was persuasive, and Stewart decided to move as long as we kept a place in Glasgow. In 1982, we sold the country house, sent some antique furniture to Los Angeles, and gave some away. We got a little flat in Pollokschield, the Lawrence Building.

While all that was happening, I required another heart surgery. It was done in February by David Wheatley, a talented young English professor, who had just returned from Africa to his native Britain and started to work in the Royal Infirmary. The surgery was successful, and my recovery went well.

In April 1982, we moved to Los Angeles.

Scotland

Your gentle constant rain and wild winds
Penetrate my bones
Scotland with so many moods
Of different colorful Plaines

      Your winters blowing wild
      All at once: snow, rain and sunshine
      Ferocious whistling winds
      Fallen rains never mild

In the summer of nowhere
Rain comes and goes
Sunshine is very rare
Green forever Scottish Hills

      With mysterious Lochs lakes
      Bonnie Bobby Burns
      And his clans for all to be seen
      Emerald green Scottish Hills.

Back to Country Four: The United States of America and Life at Home

Chapter Thirteen
The United States 1982–

In Los Angeles, we went to the Immigration Office to establish legal residence for Stewart. Through me, as a naturalized American citizen, Stewart got his green card. The officer in the Immigration Office and Stewart were both speaking English, but I, with my European accent, had to interpret: I was translating English to English. Stewart looked at his green card and read aloud the words "alien resident." He repeated the words several times and laughed at the strangeness of the sound. The officer also gave Stewart forms to get a Social Security card. Stewart refused, saying, "I don't need welfare." We explained the card was needed for identification and wouldn't make him a charity case.

Stewart seemed to adapt to Los Angeles fairly well. I was a bit edgy, trying to make him comfortable without doing so much I would make him nervous. Gene started in the construction business in 1982, which made me very happy for Gene and for Stewart. Gene was actually working, there was a reason for them to talk, and Stewart had something to hold his attention.

In 1983, Stewart and I went to Glasgow for our holidays. He enjoyed seeing friends and being back in his place. It took great effort on my part to get that stubborn Scot to keep an appointment with a new physician, Dr. Ballantyne, who found nothing different. Like Dr. McKenzie, he said the condition would worsen, which I would have to accept, and the brain cells were self-destructing.

To balance that news, I had Gene's word in 1984 he was quitting drugs. He was beginning to stay busy with construction, and he and a friend of his wanted to end their addiction. They started a program and were going to help each other, but Gene's friend, who had a college scholarship to play football, slipped. He was found dead from cocaine. That hit Gene very hard and gave him greater determination. I began to believe he would succeed.

After Stewart's illness in Greece, I didn't write to my family in Kyiv as regularly or as fully, but I kept up the correspondence and assured everyone I would visit again and would welcome any of them to California. I wouldn't get a chance to see my brother Jasha again, however. He died in 1984.

Most of the Ukrainian immigrants I met in Los Angeles had stories of families being torn apart, of imprisonment, punishment, deprivation. While living in Scotland, I'd maintained contact with several of them and met others when I returned, mostly at the Ukrainian Culture Center. For two years, if Stewart felt up to going to gatherings at the Center, we went. After 1984, I didn't go to many functions but did have regular telephone conversations with friends and continued to read more about the land of my birth. From the contacts and from the reading, I found comfort and connections if not satisfaction with conditions in Ukraine.

I talked with a woman who, with her mother, father, and sister escaped Ukraine and made their way to the United States. She had a brother who was drafted into the Soviet Army, trained as a terrorist, and sent behind German lines. Her mother, not knowing whether the son was alive, was always thinking of him but was afraid to write. In her 80s, the mother sent a letter to the old village, and the letter was forwarded to her son. After forty years, mother and son were writing to each other, and after five more years, the son visited. During the war, he was caught by Germans, tattooed, and put into the camp at Auschwitz. Four decades later, he was still crying at the pain and humiliation he endured. Often, I heard stories like that.

Across the years when I thought of the millions who went through such pain and torture, I wondered why humans had to be so desperately cruel to each other just because ideas and understandings were different. Did a strong belief in an idea make people blind and intolerant of others?

I tried to understand why the Bolsheviks hurt their own people. In the United States I didn't have to be afraid to talk to other people or to read books and slowly realized the history taught to me was not what happened. (But I must always add many immigrants never overcame their conditioning.)

In the United States, not all Ukrainians I met had suffered; some of them were part of the cause of suffering. I had brief contact with one of those despicable Communist functionaries. He was from Kyiv. He and his wife had gotten a visa to visit their son in Los Angeles.

I took the mother to many stores and shops. The father was a well-known writer in the Soviet Union, and I arranged for all of us to have lunch with Mykola Novak, a Ukrainian movie producer. At the table, that nasty Communist became intimidating and boastful. He chose that occasion to tell me I was a traitor to my country. He was telling how wonderful communism is and how capitalism would end soon. Mr. Novak and I suffered his attack in silence.

Returning to USSR, the man thought he would give lectures about capitalism, but no one asked him, and after a couple of years, he died. The times were changing; people inside and outside USSR were saying, "Down with communism."

In those years, the mid 1980s, Ukraine received some attention. There were articles in various publications, some of which I kept. Books were published. The United States Congress in 1984 decided to study the famine. All of those things were reminders of the past to Ukrainian immigrants.

With anger, sadness, and pain, I read *Execution by Hunger* by Miron Dolot. The author recounted in detail what happened to his village during the enforced famine. His village was much larger than mine, and events were on a larger scale, but the methods and the results were the same. The author was not emotional in his writing, but his descriptions of the relentless crushing of farmers triggered strong emotions in me.

The two years, 1984 and 1985, were for Stewart and me a time of doctors, hospitals, and attempts to find health care answers. In 1984, I saw a notice concerning a research project on Alzheimer's—I think it was at UCLA—and took Stewart there, but I got no answers, nothing that could help Stewart. I consulted all the doctors I already knew and collected references to many others. Stewart got tired of my dragging him from one specialist to another, but he always went.

To break the pattern and to see Dr. Ballantyne, we went to Glasgow in 1985. Dr. Ballantyne couldn't suggest anything new. Otherwise, we had a nice but sad visit—nice because Stewart and his friends still enjoyed each other, and sad because it was obvious things were no longer the same.

Stewart and I took our last trip to Italy on our way back to the United States. Arriving in Rome, we were tired. I left Stewart in line for a taxi and went to get a newspaper. I was bending forward, asking a question of the man sitting behind stacks of newspapers and magazines, when I felt someone's hand trying to pinch my bottom. Because I was tired and irritable, my brain did not control my hand, and I turned and slapped the intruder of my body. Then I saw a little dried-up man holding an ice cream cone. I burst at him, "You old fool, at least pinch a young girl."

He said very weakly, "You look young from behind."

I didn't know whether to laugh or be afraid I might

have seriously injured him.

The next day, I was better rested and in the next three days did some idle shopping. The current fashions were pleasing, and I bought a few items. (I saw a Scottish woolen jacket I had lingered over in Glasgow the week before; in Glasgow, the price was about $100, in Rome about $600.) Stewart and I had some nice meals and some pleasant walks but decided not to go to the theatre or opera.

Back in California, I insisted Stewart should play golf again after twenty years of not playing. He insisted he couldn't do it. I made an arrangement with some neighbors who played golf to take us to the course, and once he tried, he enjoyed it. He became one of a foursome and for two years played five times a week. We went at 6:30 a.m. and while he had two hours of pleasure, I waited in the car (Stewart had already stopped driving) or walked around the golf course. As his condition worsened, it became necessary for me to walk with him as he played. I sometimes thought it was too bad I didn't play, and sometimes thought it was better I didn't play.

After golf, I attended to my errands, cooked, painted, read, cried. The sickness in Stewart was slow death, every day a funeral.

Keeping up with Ukraine continued to be an antidote for depression. In 1986, the Commission on the Ukrainian Famine began work. As reported in an article in *America*, 17 March 1986, the commission was established by the ninety-eighth Congress in 1984 to "conduct a study of the 1932–33 Ukrainian famine to expand the world's knowledge of the famine and provide the American public with a better understanding of the Soviet system by revealing the Soviet role in the Ukrainian famine which claimed more than seven million lives." The commission consisted of members of congress and of the Departments of State, Education, and Health and Human Services and public representatives from the Ukrainian-American community. The Staff Director was Dr. James E. Mace, who had been a research associate at Harvard University's Ukrainian Research Institute and had written many books and articles on Ukraine of that era.

On 14 August 1986, the *Los Angeles Times* carried an article by Dr. Mace, "Genocide in the Ukraine: Its Secret Belongs to Humanity." Dr. Mace stated that genocide in Ukraine was different from genocide experienced by Jews, Armenians, and Cambodians in that "Ukrainians bear a double secret— the interior one of what they experienced, and the world's ignorance of it." Dr. Mace explained what happened, indicated the famine occurred only in areas where Stalin wanted to wipe out nationalism, and said the West didn't know about the famine until after the war and then wasn't interested. But people should know about genocide because it "diminishes all of humanity" and survivors should keep the memory alive.

Dr. Mace moved me and other Ukrainian immigrants to do something. In that period, we did begin talking more and doing more about our nation and people.

I was saying my heart bleeds for my people; I shed no end of tears for the people of my unprotected, struggling country who suffered the harsh life imposed on them by Moscow.

We were saying to each other that Ukrainians went through terrors like those of the Holocaust; yet the world does not know that. In fact, the world thinks of Ukraine as a province of Russia and not as a nation with a thousand years of history.

We were saying it was time Ukrainians should take care of themselves and their destinies—and we who enjoyed the freedom of the United States should help.

And we were working toward some ways to do that.

Ukraine was the subject of twelve programs on cable television in Los Angeles in 1987. On 21 April, the topic was the 1932–33 genocide. On 28 April, one year and two days after the world's worst nuclear power plant accident, it was Chernobyl.

Sometime in 1987, Stewart stopped playing golf. He needed my help for more and more things. Eventually, he could not function without help. I had a child in a man's body. Mentally, he was aware and not aware. Without me, he was lost and afraid. I became his world. Making countless decisions by myself was a greater strain than the physical demands.

Many of my friends knew about Stewart's condition and offered me support, but my old instinct not to reveal personal information was still present, and besides, I thought it would be imposing on others to ask them about matters of dealing with patient care. One of the few with whom I did talk was Sarah, a Russian Jew, whom I met in 1986. She had been a physician in the Soviet Army, but her command of English was not adequate for taking the California medical examination. The medical aspects of Stewart's case Sarah understood and could explain to me.

In 1987 or 1988, one doctor we saw advised me, "It is dangerous for you to keep your husband at home with you. He is a strong man and is not responsible for his actions. If he becomes agitated, he could strike you."

I did not want to hear that. I was determined I would keep Stewart at home, no matter how bad his condition might get. At times, he did become angry, his expression became animal like, and he grabbed me, but he never struck me. The incidents became more frequent, and in 1988, I took him to the Veteran's Hospital in West Los Angeles for observation.

Three days after Stewart went to the Veteran's Hospital, my son had an attack of appendicitis. Men are sometimes beyond my comprehension: they suffer, but in their stubbornness, they don't go to the doctor. Gene endured pain well beyond the time he should have been in surgery. When the suffering went past his endurance, he called an ambulance, which took him to Sunland Hospital. He was asked the name of his doctor. The only doctor Gene knew was one who had hired Gene for construction, and Gene was given the choice of calling him. That doctor told Gene to go immediately to Downey Hospital. Gene then called me. It took me a half hour to get to Sunland and another hour to drive Gene to Downey. The doctor arrived at midnight, and surgery was performed. The doctor said the surgery should take twenty minutes, but it took two and one-half hours because the rupture had been there for days. Gene's insides had to be washed and disinfected.

I was spending time on the freeways between two hospitals for seventeen days. That is how long my son was in that hospital. He developed pneumonia. I was sure it was because of the air conditioning and asked the nurse to stop the cold air. The only way she could do it was to tape the vent, but after that Gene recovered.

Gene had no insurance. I'd pleaded with him to get insurance, even offering to help him, but young people think they will never be ill. I had to pay a deposit to have Gene admitted to the hospital, and the seventeen days there cost Gene more than ten years of insurance premiums would have cost.

The bright spot in that period was that Gene had beaten the drugs and was very successful in his construction business. He got many remodeling jobs because he was good at designing and building under difficult circumstances.

Stewart was not improving in the Veteran's Hospital even though he stayed there over two months. The doctors began insisting I should put him in a convalescent home, which I did not want to do but agreed because I wanted him out of that hospital. I had serious questions about procedures and practices that were never answered. I got a name and arranged a transfer to a convalescent home that was a forty-five minute drive from our home. I went there every day for about three weeks, determined to give the place a fair chance, but the facilities and supervision were not satisfactory. I had no questions about procedures; the care was simply inadequate.

I took Stewart out and promised myself no matter what I would keep him at home. I found help during the day, but at night I was alone again. Stewart needed to have his own room, and for long stretches, I'd lie in my room, listening for any noise. When I did fall asleep, I was waking up every half hour. Sometimes Stewart walked to my bed and shook me if I didn't wake up. More often, I fell asleep, dreamed that Stewart was calling me, jumped up, ran to his room, and saw him asleep, snoring. After enough of those times, I started to laugh and said to myself, "You cannot win."

After two or three months of having Stewart at home, leaving him only part of the day with a male nurse, I felt myself getting ill. Sarah saw that and told me that for my own survival, I could not care for Stewart at home. She said no matter how much I wanted to keep him at home, I would soon be of no use to him, and if both of us needed care, somebody else would have to choose Stewart's care.

I didn't like the sound of that and appreciated her offer to visit a few convalescent hospitals with me. Of the ones Sarah and I visited, Sarah thought a facility in Studio City— one which neighbors recommended—was the best medically and would also provide good general care for Stewart. Her observations were sharper than mine. I could trust her judgment. With sadness, I placed Stewart there in 1989, hoping against hope he had some understanding of what I was doing and why.

Each morning, I went there and walked with Stewart for him to get his exercise. I fed him lunch, after which he usually slept, and I left. The facility was close to our house, so it was convenient to go back before dinner to get him washed and ready to eat.

There was much to read about the USSR: *Perestroika* and *glasnost*, started by Mikhail Gorbachev in 1985, had made people demand more reforms. Ukrainians, Armenians, and others were agitating for autonomy. It was impossible to keep up with all that was happening behind the Iron Curtain in 1989, but I kept reading.

The report of the Commission on the Ukrainian Famine had appeared in April 1988. According to an article in *The Ukrainian Weekly* on 25 September 1988, the report was well received and went to many officials, scholars, and the public in the United States and in the Soviet Union. The Commission still had work to do, including verification of "transcripts of the more than 200 unpublished eyewitness accounts of the famine." Dr. Mace said a shortage of funds would limit the Commission's work and called on the Ukrainian community to "continue to support our efforts." We, in the Los Angeles area, did that.

In 1990, before the breakup of the Soviet Union, I read another disturbing book that showed why the other republics in the USSR wanted to be free from Russia. *The Hidden Nations* by Nadia Diuk and Adrian Karatnycky detailed how much Russia took from and how little it gave to Ukraine and the other nations.

That was the most de-humanizing aspect of life in Ukraine. When an invading army occupies a country, it is expected there will be bad treatment of the people. But Ukraine was part of the Soviet Union and was being treated by the Soviet Union as if Ukraine were the enemy. Mentally, Ukrainians were deprived of existence when their heritage and language were taken away from them. People became like frightened animals that could not figure out why they were being punished.

The Hidden Nations did help me understand the bigger historical picture as did a book I would read several years later. A friend lent me a copy in Russian, which I read, then learned it was written in English by an Englishman, Nicholas Bethell, who translated some of Alexander Solzhenitsyn's work. The book is *The Last Secret: The Delivery to Stalin of Over Two Million Russians by Britain and the United States*

(Basic Books, 1974). (The use of the word "Russians" in the subtitle is unfortunate; generically, it refers to all Soviet citizens: Russians, Ukrainians, and so on.) Mr. Bethell used official material from the British and American governments and interviews with people who were involved to explain the complex and tragic events.

The situation at the end of the war was a dilemma for the Allies. The USSR could not admit any of its citizens didn't want to return but didn't want it known citizens were forced to return. British and American principles called for giving asylum to people who feared return to their countries, but Britain and Americans still naively believed Stalin was an ally and wanted to keep him satisfied with the alliance, beside which, the Soviets had under their control British and American POWs Germans had held in the Soviet sector.

A secret agreement in Yalta called for treating all former Soviets as traitors whether they had collaborated or not, whether they were still citizens or not. The two million who went back included 20,000 Cossacks, a major problem.

I read that book, crying for the fates of individuals whose stories were told. Then I felt a chill for what could have easily been my fate. I was in the most active area for rounding up former USSR citizens—one different step would have doomed me. The situation may have been a dilemma for the Allied governments, but it was a tragedy for those who were killed and imprisoned—and a trauma for the Allied forces who carried out orders for the delivery and who witnessed the distress, the pleas for asylum, and the suicides.

Many times when I was sitting with Stewart, we did not talk. Often, at night, I couldn't sleep. At such times, my mind wandered, and frequently memories of my childhood in Ukraine flashed or crept into my mind. Many people had said I should write about my life, but I had no urge to do so. When I was a child, I wrote poetry at the orphanage school. As an adult, I liked writing letters to friends and family—informal letters, some in Ukrainian, others in Russian, Italian, or English. My command of written languages was not strong, but, because I had something I wanted to say to someone, I wasn't reluctant to write letters. The thought of writing a book, however, was more than I wanted to face.

Still, there was an urge to say something about my life in Ukraine. The urge kept coming back, and early in 1990, I started writing some pages—not a book—just pages. Sometimes, I wrote page after page without stopping. Some days I could not write a single word. Often I developed a headache. But in the next eight or nine months, I wrote quite a few pages.

For one six-week period, I wrote nothing. I was entertaining my niece Galina and her sixteen-year-old daughter, Elena. Galina, Jasha's oldest daughter, was a lawyer, as was her husband, and both had good positions. Galina and Elena were happy to spend every day shopping. I had heard of people from other countries having nervous breakdowns in supermarkets because they could not handle the choices, the full shelves, and helpful clerks. I didn't worry about breakdowns, but I did have to restrain them. They were asking me: "Is this real? For whom is this? You mean we can shop here? This is not for special people?"

And I was saying, "It's for anybody. But take only one cabbage. There'll be more when we need another."

They wanted to see more and more clothing stores, but they wanted also to go back to the ones visited to look again at certain items. They were delightful to watch.

The shopping trips were more tiring for me than they should have been, and as 1990 went along, I was having more difficulty getting things done. Some days after I visited Stewart, I was too tired to do anything else. I had to admit my health had been declining for a few years and went to the doctor.

In December 1990, I had another open-heart surgery for those valves. Before the surgery, I wanted to take my husband to Scotland in the event I did not survive my surgery.

Possibly it is for the best I didn't take him, for he was the incentive for my recovery. I was praying, "Please, I must survive. Who will take care of Stewart? I must survive."

After about six weeks, I was able to resume my visits to Stewart. He seemed glad to see me, but I wasn't sure whether he comprehended I hadn't been there for several weeks. Sometimes he could carry on a conversation; sometimes, he couldn't.

Other than a little work with friends from Ukraine, I did nothing except visit Stewart. When I went for a follow-up visit to my cardiologist, he told me I needed to socialize with people and needed more exercise. "Go dancing," he said, which would do both. It didn't matter whether I joined a social group or a hiking club. His order was to do something for my health. I got busy.

I did start going to the Ukrainian Culture Center more often and talked more with others about improving life in Ukraine. A reminder came to me when I received notice my brother Mykola had died. My brother Jasha lived until he was seventy-eight and Mykola until he was seventy-six, and had they had better nutrition and better living conditions, they would probably have lived longer. The sad thought that came to me that day in 1991 and that has come to me repeatedly since then was how much life was taken from Natalia, Gabriel, and Grisha by egotistical tyrants in the name of saving the people. Fifty or more years—half a century—of life my sister and brother never had.

Knowing that Dr. James Mace was in Washington and that he was still working with material about the famine, the genocide, of 1932–33, I made an appointment to see him at Easter time in 1991. Several friends said they would visit Stewart and look after him the few days I'd be gone. I showed Dr. Mace what I'd written. He looked at the manuscript and encouraged me to write more. He also asked me many questions. I was very impressed with his manner and his knowledge.

I don't think Stewart realized I'd been away.

During that period, I was happy to see Gene was developing good relationships with women his age. His closest relationship during that period was a delightful German girl. I felt right away she and I were friends.

The prospect of Ukrainian independence made 1991 a most exciting year. President Bush was not in favor of independence; it would be more trouble to deal with fifteen countries than with one. But I wrote to members of congress, urging them to endorse freedom for long-suffering, oppressed countries, and some of them sent me encouraging replies. I forgot my English was not perfect and continued writing to others in the national government.

After talking with Dr. Mace, I also had energy to work more on my manuscript. Something in the news made me think I'd like to send a copy to the First Lady, Mrs. Barbara Bush. (Maybe she could influence her husband.) I wrote a letter to Mrs. Bush and sent a copy of my manuscript 5 August 1991. I was told by several friends Mrs. Bush probably had five secretaries to handle her mail and one of them would send me a note saying the manuscript had been received but Mrs. Bush would never see it and no one else would ever read it. I sent it anyway. About three weeks later, I did get a brief response, which might not have been personal, but I felt better for having sent it.

I found myself wanting to address all Ukrainians and wrote some pieces, which I did share with others. On 20 September 1991, the Orthodox Church sponsored a picnic and program, and I was given ten minutes to speak. I read something I wrote in English, all in capital letters and underlining.

TO THE UKRAINIAN PEOPLE EVERYWHERE:

EVERYONE MUST GET ELECTRIFIED,

THINK LIKE <u>FREE PEOPLE</u>.
WE HAVE SUFFERED FOR SO LONG
    SOME PEOPLE ARE AFRAID EVEN TO <u>THINK FREE</u>.
HISTORY WILL NEVER SMILE ON US AGAIN
    AS IT DOES TODAY.
THIS OPPORTUNITY WE WILL NEVER HAVE AGAIN. WE MUST GET OUR <u>RECOGNITION</u> FOR <u>COMPLETE INDEPENDENCE TODAY</u> AND GOVERN OUR HOUSE BY OURSELVES. WE WERE DEPRIVED FOR A LONG, LONG TIME. WE WERE FORCED TO USE THE RUSSIAN LANGUAGE. OUR OWN LANGUAGE WAS RIDICULED AND LAUGHED AT. PEOPLE HAVE TO WORK AT AND INSIST ON OUR <u>COMPLETE FREEDOM AND RECOGNITION</u>. IF WE PERSIST, OUR FREEDOM WILL COME. WE MUST SAVE OUR COUNTRY AND DO EVERYTHING THAT IS POSSIBLE WITH ALL OUR STRENGTH FOR THE <u>STATEHOOD OF THE UKRAINE</u>. WE HAVE NO OTHER CHOICE BUT TO ACT STRONGLY, FOR WE CANNOT RELY ON ANYONE ELSE FOR OUR FUTURE. WE WILL REMAIN FAITHFUL TO OUR IDEALS FOR OUR <u>INDEPENDENCE AND RECOGNITION</u> AWAY FROM MOSCOW'S TYRANNY AND <u>RETURN TO THE LAND OF THE FREE UKRAINE</u>. <u>OUR FUTURE FREEDOM AND INDEPENDENCE FROM MOSCOW MUST BE REALIZED</u>. <u>THE WORLD MUST RECOGNIZE OUR COUNTRY OF FREE UKRAINE</u>.

Those words look simple now, but there was more passion in the writing and in the reading of those words than in the words themselves, and the passion gave added meaning.

On 21 October 1991, I went to a meeting of Ukrainian immigrants in Los Angeles. Several leading Ukrainian figures were there—businessmen, priests. I was the only woman in the group. We were members of the California Association to Aid Ukraine and were discussing how much money we should try to raise for the Association. What they were talking about as a goal for all the members of the Association was far too modest. Spontaneously, I wrote a check for a higher amount. It was more than I could afford, but it was a signal. Others applauded. Seeing people would give, they gave, too. We became excited. We wanted to help our people get rid of Soviet tyranny for good.

That meeting and the response I got when I spoke to that large group at the picnic had me boiling with ideas and activity. I kept thinking of my persecuted destroyed family and the possibility Ukraine might soon be a nation. I wrote President Bush a letter urging his support for Ukrainian independence, but I thought to give the letter more weight by getting other people to sign the letter. By the time I mailed the letter in November 1991, I had 600 signatures. And because I'd already had one exchange of letters with Mrs. Bush, I wrote her also.

When I was asking people to sign the letter, many Ukrainian people asked me, "What is your organization?" They didn't seem satisfied when I said I was doing it by myself. At first, I was surprised; then, I realized that was their conditioning. Everything was done by a committee; no one would stand out by himself or herself. I remembered hearing it said Eastern Ukrainians were too cautious—their national soul had been removed. And I thought how good is America where the individual is important, and freedom of speech is real.

Ukrainian immigrants in Los Angeles (at least, the ones I had contact with) were seeing more and more hope during 1989, 1990, and 1991, and we were happy when the citizens of the land of our birth on 1 December 1991 voted overwhelmingly for independence. For almost seventy years the country was the Ukrainian Soviet Socialist Republic. With that vote, it became Ukraine, a nation. For centuries, with few interruptions, the people had been under Russian or Soviet control. With that vote, the nation was free to determine its own destiny.

On the day of the vote, I wrote a poem in Ukrainian, then translated it into English. Once again, I felt as if all Ukrainians were my audience.

To Ukrainian People Everywhere

Finally history has smiled on us.
This opportunity we never had before.
For the first time people of Ukraine became United
as one family to strive for principles of Democracy.
Our freedom finally came; now we must teach, help, show, and direct
each other in ways to approach and build Democracy in Ukraine.
Ukraine must become a self-sufficient Democratic Country.

Sadly, however, the years of being drained by Russia left a very weak economy with the need to spend great amounts of money to make business and industry function, to restore cities and institutions, and to make life livable for over fifty million people spread across a country the size of France.

Another problem existed because Russian or Soviet control was identified more strongly with Eastern Ukraine. Western Ukraine, at times part of Europe, was usually associated with Europe. Not only did the Eastern Ukrainians suffer more prior to independence, but they also bore the stigma of suspicion they might have been part of the Communist machinery. Many Eastern Ukrainians tried to get rid of communism, but the stain was always there. No matter how much they suffered under communism, no one really trusted them. In those days, I was thinking Ukraine and the whole world should take an example from the old nation of Jewish people. No matter what happened, they still protected and valued the lives of their own people. That kind of attitude is very honorable for a nation.

Stewart was becoming less and less aware as the months went by. He seemed to know I was part of his day, that I somehow was the one in charge, but I wasn't always certain he actually knew me. Sometimes he said something to me about Eugenia. If I asked whether he wanted some different clothes, he might say, "Ask my wife about that." Sometimes he seemed confused about my identity and might ask, "Who is it that puts the flowers on my table?"

After all my involvement in the progress of Ukraine's move toward independence, I wanted to breathe the free air of Ukraine, and because I had no brothers left alive, I wanted to get to know better my nephew Kolia, who is only five years younger than I. Stewart was not being responsive to anything or anyone, but I arranged for him to have many and regular visits from people he knew and booked a short trip to Kyiv in May 1992.

Once again, I realized it was much easier to become adjusted to a comfortable life than to do the reverse. Life in the United States had spoiled me. Kolia, his wife, and their son lived in a small apartment in a matchbox building. Sounds—even ordinary conversation—from adjoining apartments went through the walls. The furniture was adequate but not comfortable or attractive. Various containers of water stood by for the times water didn't run. There were no electronics of any kind. Their food was tasty, but greasy.

Daily life seemed not to have improved very much, but I thought the people looked happier. Maybe I wanted so much for them to look happier I imagined it.

From the time of that 1966 visit to Kyiv—for twenty-six years—Kolia had wondered how I could travel so easily from one country to another and asked me all sorts of questions about travel and work. When my answers didn't reveal enough, he asked me bluntly, "For whom do you work? For whom are you spying? You are such a diplomat you must be highly valuable to some power."

I couldn't resist saying, "I'm not a spy. I'm an American capitalist." I quickly added I was joking and spent the rest of my time there trying to explain, to convince him an American citizen didn't need to be a spy or be mixed up in dirty affairs to be able to travel. I told Kolia I wasn't wealthy and couldn't have everything. I didn't have the feeling I'd convinced him but hoped I could get him to visit the United States to see for himself.

When I returned to Los Angeles, I could see Stewart didn't know how long I'd been away. Passage of time was not clear. Any time was a time I should appear.

My friends from the old country and I continued to do what we could to help with the Ukrainian cause. The election of President Clinton seemed to offer some hope for more attention to other nations. He seemed softer and gentler in his understanding of suffering. I was impressed by the energy and involvement of Mrs. Clinton, so on 7 April 1993, I mailed to her a letter and sent along a portion of my book. I told her about the nation and about Russia's attempts to destroy the nation. I said that the political struggle for power in Russia should persuade the West to support Ukraine's efforts to take greater control over the nuclear arsenal on its territory.

Also, I said Ukraine is more stable politically and does not want nuclear weapons on its land that could be fired from Russia. I asked for more recognition and for more normal security and guarantees. In about three weeks, I received a brief response.

On 3 September 1993, Stewart died. Many friends told me it was good for Stewart and for me. I understood their intent and appreciated their concern. Still, I felt the loss. I thought of the strong, vital man with special knowledge and exuberance and fervently wished he'd had more years at his fullest. And, once in a while, I let myself think for a moment what it would have meant in my life to meet that good man earlier.

Some time after Stewart died, Gene and his girlfriend decided they wanted to move from Los Angeles and chose to go to Colorado, where I had taken Gene skiing when he was six.

Not since my arrival in America had I been so alone. I still had a son in the United States and family in Ukraine; I had many friends nearby. Still, with Stewart gone and Gene no longer a few minutes away, I felt detached. I found myself wondering what I was supposed to do even though I was already busy. I was painting and working for Ukrainian causes, two activities that I found worthy and satisfying and would continue. I didn't have any time I needed to fill. I needed more time for all I wanted to do. Nevertheless, that feeling of being lost and detached did persist while I continued my life and work.

Immediately, I gave more attention to aid for Ukraine. In 1994, I went three times, alone, to Ukraine, working with other people in Los Angeles before each trip to collect things to take (all manner of clothing, vitamins, medicines, books) and buying things I could not collect. I worked through one agency for handling some materials, and directly with other schools, orphanages, and hospitals in Ukraine.

Also, I was invited sometimes to speak to a high school class or other group. I could never qualify to be a historian, but I tried to provide a simple explanation for the way a totalitarian government that didn't work could control the whole USSR. I started this way:

Russians thought of czars as gods, but life under the czars was terrible. Changes of some kind were happening. Bolsheviks wanted change to happen in another way. Lenin, Trotsky, Stalin, and other leaders were clever and forceful strategists. Trotsky especially was a powerful speaker whose magnetism convinced hordes of people Marxism was the only way to achieve a better life. People became excited to think they would have everything. They made Marxism into the new god and were energized to go to work.

Bolsheviks knew Eastern and Western Ukrainians were of different mentalities. They got the East in 1922 and waited till a pact with Hitler got them the West.

The Bolsheviks used agitation and propaganda to get people from all groups with them. They recruited laborers and intellectuals. Jewish intellectuals who saw a way to end anti-Semitism became dedicated to establish Marxism and worked extremely hard. Although there were more Mensheviks, Bolsheviks were stronger, and once they gained support of the Red Army, they could not be stopped. The more power they had, the more they wanted. They created the Communist Party to do the dirty work to build power. They said so often that communism would make everybody equal, people said it, too, even though they weren't equal.

Those who heard me talk seemed to be interested and concerned. They asked good questions about my experiences, my family, and my country of birth.

In June 1995, I returned to the place of my birth, Kamjana Balka. Someone drove me there, and all the way I was wondering what I should be feeling to see my first home after all those years. I was trying to visualize the farm and the village, but once there I felt recognition only of the house in relation to the river. The house had been partially destroyed and rebuilt, so I was less sure about it.

My driver and I stopped at the center of the village. A villager approached us, then another, then others. Soon, I was so surrounded I became nervous. But the people were talking, and I was telling them I was born there. Then they were telling me who they were. All at once I had cousins—many cousins—from my mother's side. I had even more family than I knew. My father's name had disappeared from the village, but some of the older people remembered my father and told me how rich and helpful he had been. And they told me about the years after my parents and I left Kamjana Balka. Very sad.

I was quite taken by those people. They were bright, clever, sharp. The women had clear skin, rosy cheeks and lips, no wrinkles—and they had no creams, lotions, or makeup.

An official told me what I would need to do to reclaim our property. I thought about that only a few seconds and told her that I wouldn't do it. I had no sense of ownership. My parents were the owners, and evicting the occupants of the house would not make it once again my parents' property. But I left Kamjana Balka feeling I could have belonged to the people and the village. And I would return with more aid.

Recently I was told that whenever I speak to a group, I need to give the person introducing me a list of all my actions and involvements, including the exact number of trips I have made. My trips, starting in 1966, have been frequent, if not regular, but I doubt I can establish whether there were twelve, fifteen, or eighteen. I haven't kept a record of what I've done but have kept many of the thank-you notes. I haven't kept a record of what I've spent and donated and would not state the amount even if I knew it. Some things I did have already been mentioned. From various sources, I pulled together this list of typical activities.

Served as Coordinator (with Mr. Bronislav Ometsynsky) of Ukrainian Committee of Humanitarian Assistance in Kyiv since January 1992, overseeing shipments of clothing to some orphanages and medications to some hospitals

Direct actions not through the committee:

Donated medical instruments, antibiotics, and other supplies to Dniprovsky Hospital, Department of Emergency and Accidents, remaining since 1993 in personal contact with Mr. Roshchyn, hospital chairman

Received personal expression of appreciation from Mrs. Dzuba, vice president of Children's Hospital in Dniprovsky for 25,000 antibiotic tablets

Sent shipments of clothing for children at Beriska Orphanage with help of Mary Barbey, her daughters, and her husband, a Swiss banker

Received certificate of appreciation from Kyiv Central Hospital for humanitarian aid, beginning in 1994

Remembering my childhood experience, contacted Kyiv School number 87 of O. Dobzenko and donated clothes and money for fruit juices for the year, continuing from 1994 to 1996

Responded to request from the Children's Culture Center on Illich Street for English teaching materials with textbooks, tapes, and films

In 1993, delivered a year's supply of vitamins and medications from Ukrainian American company Aquilar-Roma International on Pritisho-Mikitska Street for a pre-school serving tuberculosis infected children

Starting in 1994, supplied antibiotics to maternity clinic on Zaporozia Street, headed by Dr. Didichenco

Participated in work of United States Committee to Assist Ukrainian Orphans and Needy Children; in 1995, with that organization, sent coats for thirty children at Rodomishl School in Zitomir region

Collected money from Ukrainian Society in Los Angeles to buy a computer for the Academy of Sciences in Kyiv

Donated to school children and adults in Kamjana Balka clothing (jackets, blue jeans, T shirts, underwear), shoes and
socks, blankets, towels, toothbrushes and toothpaste,
pens, pencils, crayons

Responded to various individual requests for financial assistance

Some letters of appreciation were most touching. One
has to be humbled when thanked for providing "antibiotics to
take care of my wound that does not heal for sixteen years."
Or for "vitamins, medicine for my two boys affected by radiation." Or for "cash gift to preschool children exposed to tuberculosis" (signed by parents).

Also, after I was alone, I gave more attention to painting. From the time that I took art classes when I was a teenager in Dnepropetrovsk, I wanted to study painting. Perhaps
it was Grisha's influence from the beginning. I'd taken some
classes in the 1980s and took more in the 1990s, reaching a
fair level of proficiency painting cityscapes and rural scenes. I
won some prizes and sold some paintings. The process and
the results are so satisfying that I could be happy if I did nothing else.

Looking back, I see positive events.

I survived childhood in Ukraine where my life could
have ended and no one would have noticed, and I survived
with some good memories.

I survived teenage years in Austria, where I could have
been killed and no one would have noticed, and I survived
with one good memory.

I survived and prospered in Italy, from where I could
have been sent back to USSR and to execution or death in
prison, and I survived with many good memories.

I survived and lived in the joy of freedom in the United
States where my life might have ended in surgery—or with-

out the surgery—and survived with good memories.

I survived and delighted in life in Scotland, where heart surgery again put me at risk, and I survived with good memories.

Again, I have been a survivor in the United States, my home, going through one more heart surgery and losing a good husband, and now, at the end of this narrative of five lives in five countries, I am pleased to look forward to continuation of my free and fulfilling life.

Our Ukraine

Ten years passed, since Ukraine has become free
Ten years have passed as the Government changed the name
From Communist to Democrats.

How happy we were, Excited
That day we were united
Our hope was enormous
For Washington Day

The 24th Of August 1991 it was our destiny
And the history that did smile with us that day.
It Was a miracle
What opportunity this was.

Our independence finally realized.
We have reached Statehood for Ukraine.

The 24th of August 1991 freedom for the future
We must recognize and believe
in our homeland of free Ukraine.

Lets hold strongly our independence
We don't want to have big brother anymore
We must remain faithful to our cause.

Now we can use our Mother language
For so long we did used foreign speech, as our own.
Where there is no language,
There is no nation.

Written by Eugenia Dallas for Ukrainian Independence Day, August 24th 1991

THE WHITE HOUSE
WASHINGTON

Ms. Eugenia Dallas
6702 Hillpark Drive
Los Angeles, California 90068

Thank you so much for your thoughtful gift. We appreciate your kindness and send our best wishes.

Bill Clinton

Afterthoughts

Humans like to draw truths from experience. They like to find meaning in life—or at least what is important. At a time when I can reasonably expect no great changes, I can speak of important things from my perspective.

Having a son who has matured into a good and talented man and who is doing creative work gives me my greatest feeling of fulfillment. Not having given him the stability and security he needed when he was child has been my greatest regret.

Having had a wonderful husband who made life joyous, exciting, and satisfying, who was a real and genuine partner, gave me a sense of completion that I had concluded I would never know. We had few years together, but we packed many years of living into them. Of course, I regret for both of us that we did not have more.

Having and having had good and special friends enriched my life far beyond anything that I ever expected.

My reaching back to Ukraine was from a strong urge to do something, something in memory of my parents, of Natalia, Gabriel, Grisha, something to make more people aware of what was done to Ukraine. My feeling for the country of my birth remains strong; my affection for Ukraine and her people—for my family still in Ukraine—is deep. I feel that way in memory and when I am there.

When I am in Ukraine, however, I also feel very much that I am American. On my return from Ukraine, I think how lucky I am to live in this land. In 1951, I gained the freedom I'd yearned for, and that gave me mental and emotional tranquillity. Any other place is for visiting; the United States of America is my home.

Just yesterday, I was young. For my first years and after the Nazi labor camp, I had a zest for life. I still have. I continue to want to experience to the fullest what life offers.

I have been a person of action, not of contemplation. I can conclude that I have been positive in my thinking and willing to challenge myself, for that, to me, is the way to live and to succeed. I had courage and daring. Sometimes, I panicked, but I was never afraid to act. From those traits I drew my strength.

I have tended to abandon pursuits once I saw that I could succeed. To sell some of my paintings was, for example, a goal, but after I'd sold a few, I lost interest and preferred to keep what I painted or give a painting to a friend who was drawn to it.

I am not a philosopher. I cannot reconcile the sad parts of life with the happy parts, and it is of no use to me to hear someone say that without one, we couldn't know the other. Yes, contrast by itself has impact; going out of Austria and into Italy was a great uplifting. But I cannot think of my Natalia, Gabriel, and Grisha, whose lives were canceled before they became what they could be, or of my Stewart, whose life was canceled when he was at the best of what he could be, without feeling a sense of loss for their great loss. I would feel that whether I had ever known happiness.

And I cannot think of seeing the bigger world that Jasha opened to me, of the birth of my child, of the impulsive flight from Majorca to Tunisia, or the grand party in Glasgow, or pulling a beautiful salmon from my own net, of completing a challenging painting, without a rush of good feeling. I would feel that whether I'd ever known sadness.

When, however, I read poetry or personal reflections that speak of sadness as the means of understanding human suffering, and happiness as the means of expressing the joy of life, I can say, "Yes, that is true."

Today, living in comfort, I find it hard to comprehend—

or accept—that the hardship and loneliness I knew as a child and teenager were really my life.

Today, I can say the obvious: I have lived my life (with its sadness and joy) as I have lived it—as I have written about it in these pages. I am still positive about my life and what I do. If there are further meanings or conclusions to be drawn, I will leave that process to others. I want all my vitality for living life.

CENTURY
COMMUNICATIONS
CORPORATION

William J. Rosendahl
Senior Vice President of Operations

March 4, 1999

Eugenia Sakevich Dallas
6702 Hillpark Drive
Los Angeles, CA 90068

Dear Eugenia:

Thank you for being a guest on Century Cable Television's Public Affairs Special "Week In Review." It was informative and your comments were greatly appreciated. I hope you enjoy the enclosed tape.

Warmest regards,

Bill

William J. Rosendahl
Producer

WR:kd

2939 Nebraska Avenue   Santa Monica, CA 90404-4108   310-829-7079   Fax: 310-264-8042

Eugenia Sakevych Dallas

The Love

Love the gift of nature
Love is a sparks of life
Love was given to me so easy
The feeling of happiness

Anxiety, trepidation of my heart
Inflamed by joy for you
Beating like thousand drums
Just to think of seeing you

For many years I forget about love
I thought I never could love again
The gift of Love, that came to me
So very unaspeetfully and so easy

Complete infatuation, excitement
Instant pleasure, happiness
Like telling me:
I am yours, come to me.

Love is a gift so rare and so very precious
With emotions that arc running wild
Without any control of the mind
That is in turmoil.

My heart keeps on drumming
Just with the slightest thought of you

Ukraine: Notes on a Nation

Because Ukraine, the country of my birth, was a wonderful place, because the country and people have suffered greatly, and because the nation remains unfamiliar to many, the following sketch was drawn. The notes are not offered as definitive history. Anyone who has studied history of the Slavic world will find flaws, blurred compressions, omissions. For others, it is hoped that the sketch is clear enough to provide a better picture of Ukraine and to add some dimension to my narrative.

The Name

The word *Ukraine* was derived from the Slavic word, *okraina*, meaning "borderland," and the territory that became modern Ukraine has for centuries been a border between Russia and Europe. Russia lay to the east and north, and what became the nations of Poland, Czechoslovakia and Hungary lay to the west.

Until recently, the word was preceded by the definite article. It was "the Ukraine" as in "the borderland." Today, the name of the independent nation is Ukraine.

The Land

Much of Ukraine is part of the great Eurasian Steppe—flat grasslands covered with rich, black soil—Ukraine's great resource. That soil has produced grains such as wheat, rye, barley, oats, corn, millet, and buckwheat, which earned Ukraine the title "Breadbasket of the Soviet Union" or "Breadbasket of Europe." The soil also produced sugar beets, flax, cotton, hemp, soybeans, potatoes, and all sorts of vegetables and fruits.

The territory was rich in other natural resources such as timber, animals, and fish. Among mined products were coal, iron, manganese, bauxite, titanium, mercury, potassium, rock salt, phosphorites, and sulfur. There were two mountainous areas, six major rivers, and hundreds of lesser rivers.

The Land and The People

That land between Russia and Europe was in the path of many invaders across the centuries, among them ancient Scythians, Goths, Huns, Turks, Tatar-Mongols, and, later, Polish-Lithuanians, Russians, Germans. By the first century A.D., the Slavic ancestors of the Ukrainian people had settled in the area of modern Ukraine. In the ninth century, a state called Kievan Rus (or Kyyivan Rus) was established and remained strong for two centuries. At the end of the tenth century, a strong ruler, Prince Vladimir I, converted to Christianity, and Kyiv, called the "Mother of Russian Cities," was to become the cradle of an Eastern Orthodox Christian civilization.

In the eleventh century, the strong center gave way to weaker local princes. Invasions in the twelfth and thirteenth centuries destroyed Ukraine as a nation, with Poland-Lithuania and Russia dividing most of the territory. When Poland became dominant in part of Western Ukraine, Roman Catholicism became a counter religion to the established Eastern Orthodoxy, creating divisions and enmities that still exist. Poland eventually controlled the area around Kyiv except for Ukrainian Cossacks, who could not be subjugated. The Ukrainian Cossack state, which began in Eastern Ukraine in the 1600s, became a state within a state in the 1700s and fought wars of liberation over several decades.

Alliances shifted in the seventeenth century, leading to war between Poland and the Cossacks. The Cossack leader, Bohdan Khmelnytsky, to get help from Russia, entered a treaty with the czar in 1654 that achieved independence from Poland but led to greater and greater Russian control. By the end of the eighteenth century, the control was complete, and Ukrainian history and Russian history had become inextricably linked. In one sense, all the subsequent agonies suffered by Ukraine could be blamed on that treaty; in another sense, Khmelnytsky had no other choice.

Poland and other nations of Eastern Europe continued to influence, if not control, Western Ukraine. An already complex history became more and more so; beneath each statement in these notes are volumes of explanation and commentary.

Under imperialist rule, wealthy landholders owned not only the land but also the people who worked the farms and did so until 1861 when serfdom (slavery to the western world) was abolished. Ownership of land by former serfs became possible in Ukraine, and the new farmers became productive, self-sufficient, and strongly independent. Imperialist rule in Russia survived external wars and internal conflicts between and within classes until the Revolution of 1905 produced a division of power and establishment of a parliament. World War I and the Russian Revolutions of 1917 ended Imperialist Russia. Dissent in the early 1900s was widespread and factionalized; Russia (and Ukraine) could have taken any one of several governmental paths. The way in which the Bolsheviks, as they came to be known, dictated the path taken is intriguing, complicated, and controversial. They started with few members, were part of the Workers' Party, followed Lenin in a 1903 split from the Mensheviks, found their themes if not their methods in Karl Marx, and achieved ascendancy when they gained support of the military.

In January 1918, Ukraine declared its independence but was soon squeezed from the east and the west. In Eastern Ukraine, already dominated by Russia (and affected by civil war that lasted until 1920), Bolsheviks gained power in 1922 and established the Ukrainian Soviet Socialist Republic as a part of the Union of Soviet Socialist Republics (USSR). Western Ukraine in that period was held by Poland, Czechoslovakia, and Romania, each controlling part of the territory. In 1939, the Nazis and Soviets partitioned Poland, and Western Ukraine became part of the USSR.

From 1939 to 1991, all of Ukraine was submerged. Nadia Diuk and Adrian Karatnycky, in their moving book, *The Hidden Nations: The People Challenge the Soviet Union* (William Morrow, 1990), call Ukraine "Europe's secret nation," one that "dimly exists on the fringes of Western consciousness." They write of the millions of Ukrainians who disappeared in this century with little notice from the rest of the world.

As Ukraine gained and lost territory across the centuries, it stood sometimes as an independent nation, often as a part of Russia. Although Ukrainians and Russians are both Slavic, speak similar languages, and share the same religion and some parts of their history, Ukrainians are a distinct people. They have been told for centuries, however, that they are simply one line, one branch, of Russians and have been a truly independent nation for only brief periods in the last three hundred years. A significant portion of the Ukrainian population has long been Russian, and Ukrainians have settled in other nations in the former USSR and Eastern Europe. When all those conditions are considered, it is only to be expected that conflicting attitudes toward nationhood would develop among Ukrainians—not only conflicts between regions but also within regions and ambivalence in individuals.

In spite of those realities, people and events have somehow kept alive the sense of a nation. The life and work of poet Taras Shevchenko (1814-1861), considered the father of modern Ukrainian literature, inspired generation after generation. Mykailo Hrushevsky was established as a foremost historian early in the 1900s and eventually produced a ten-volume history of Ukraine which developed the thesis that Ukrainian history and culture were the descendants of Kievan Rus—the state established in the ninth century—and not Russian history and culture as Russians claimed. Hrushevsky's work reawakened or intensified a sense of national identity. During the period of rapid and frequent change after the Russian Revolutions of 1917 and World War I, Hrushevsky was perhaps the most popular figure in Ukraine. In a struggle for power with the Bolsheviks, the nationalists were, however, over-matched.

That sense of nationality given voice by Hrushevsky and by ownership of land by former serfs created—or recreated—a pride and spirit among farmers, the major portion of the population. They were referred to as "peasants" in Western writing, but—no matter how small the parcels—they owned the land they farmed, unlike Russian peasants, who generally shared communal land. The more prosperous, ones who owned at least twenty-four acres or hired workers, were called *kulaks* (the Russian word). Although not wealthy land-owners by Western standards, they had status.

Families lived in villages: a cluster of houses, a church, a school, and, in larger villages, stores and one or more government buildings. The fields were outside the villages. Houses were simple constructions, usually of clay with thatched roofs, often containing only one room. Wooden floors and tin roofs were rare. Around the houses were gardens, fruit trees, and livestock.

Life on the farms was hard but joyful. Cooperative work and never-failing hospitality were common characteristics of the Ukrainian people. Laughing, dancing, and singing were constant expressions of enjoyment of life. As much as the people of a village shared work and play, even more, their attachment to the soil that individual families owned was the dominant force of life.

Advocates of communism had been active from the

early 1900s, and various systems of voluntary collectivized farming were tried and discarded between 1918 and 1921. During the 1920s, there were differing pressures from the Communist Party to join collectives and to produce more wheat. Generally, however, the 1920s were stable, few restrictions or programs were imposed, and, until about 1928, the USSR held a comparatively liberal attitude toward the various nationalities in the Union. In 1929, fervent forced collectivization began, and idyllic life ended. Anyone the Bolsheviks chose to call a *kulak* became to the Bolsheviks what the decadent aristocratic owner of a thousand acres was to the revolutionaries of the previous generation: an enemy of the people. And enemies of the people suffered.

Genocide in Ukraine

From that big push for collectivization of farms in 1929 to the Great Purge of 1936–38, ten to fifteen million Ukrainians met death because Stalin wanted to eliminate peasant ownership of land and to eliminate Ukrainians. (Considering that those millions did not continue reproduction, the population loss is far greater.)

Of the fifteen republics in the USSR (which contained some one hundred ethnic groups speaking two hundred languages and dialects and all wanting to retain cultural identity), Ukraine was second to Russia in size and population, and Ukrainians, especially, were considered dangerously nationalistic. In the 1920s, Lenin, to achieve greater cooperation, tolerated nationalism, cancelled grain requisitions, and allowed an open market for farmers. Stalin, opposed to such lenience, gained full control of the Party by 1928 and for the next decade (and again after World War II) made a cruel and systematic attempt to make Ukrainians and the world forget that Ukraine was ever a nation. The target was all the Ukrainians, not only farmers.

In 1930, nationalist deviation became a crime. Individuals were accused with little if any investigation, arrested on vague charges, tried for treason, and convicted with little evidence. Ukrainian intellectuals were almost entirely wiped out. Teachers, scholars, writers, poets, artists, scientists, thinkers of all kinds disappeared. Ukrainian governmental figures were subjected to arrests and purges until, by 1938, there was in effect no Ukrainian government. The church and the clergy were similarly attacked, as were the buildings. In Kyiv, centuries-old churches were torn down; faces of wonderful buildings were made ugly with Party alterations because the original designs made Kyiv look too Ukrainian.

Because extinction of the language would mean extinction of the people, use of Ukrainian was stigmatized and restricted. Although in 1923, the Ukrainian government established priority of the Ukrainian language over Russian, Stalin in 1928 made Russian the second language, the first step toward reducing Ukrainian to the language of the peasants. In time, government, business, industry, science, and schools used Russian for everything official. (An essay concerning the Ukrainian language had to be written in Russian.)

Stalin's move to eliminate private ownership of land was set in motion by the 1929 order for total collectivization. To each village, the Central Committee of the Communist Party sent a delegation of city-dwelling Party members with unlimited authority and power. There were propagandists to sell the message of communism, agitators to move people to action, special sections of Soviet secret police to spy and make arrests, a militia to provide military force, Young Communists League and Pioneers to engage and exploit youth, and other groups—all of whom exercised some power and control over farmers as did various commissions and committees such as the Bread Procurement Commission or Committee of Poor Peasants.

Methods used by Party officials were confusing and

incomprehensible, brutal and unrelenting. Farmers were assembled for long meetings day and night. One agency went to a farmer, put pressure on him to produce more food. Another agency repeated the process. Lives and possessions were watched, controlled, or taken—if not by one agency, then surely by another.

Persons who made any resistance or disobeyed any order might be put in jail or shot on the spot. Quotas of production were assigned that could not be met, and farmers were required to pay the market value of what they had not produced. Because most had no money to pay, they lost their farms. Those who did not sign over their farms to the collectives were sent to Siberia.

Village leaders—*kulaks*, teachers, officials, priests—who could not be co-opted were removed. The arrests of Vasily and Nionila Sakevych and the loss of the Sakevich farm as described in Chapter One were but one example. Neighbors, encouraged to spy on each other by promises of favors for right information, stopped talking to each other out of fear of being reported. Villagers, who had never locked any doors, began locking them.

In 1932–33, Stalin took Ukraine's grain and other foodstuff to sell for money needed to make the USSR a modern, industrial nation. Farm families had nothing to eat. Party officials went many times to every house, searching for hidden food. They took everything edible and punished those who had hidden away so much as a small can of flour. Even the seeds needed for planting new crops were taken. That action became known as the "man-made famine," for it was neither drought nor flood that caused mass starvation. It was one part of the larger genocide.

People begged, scavenged, sold possessions for pittances. With no food and restrictions against travel, thousands of people died daily. Corpses were everywhere. Horse-drawn wagons went through towns and villages each day, workers

236

picking up corpses and asking at each house, "Any dead?"

Estimates of the number of Ukrainians who died in that brief period range from four to seven million. Another three million people were sent to Siberia, of whom few returned. With as many as ten million removed and others weak from hunger, Eastern Ukrainians were broken in body and spirit.

The rest of the world remained almost entirely unaware of the assaults on Ukrainians. A few reports appeared in the West, but they gained little attention. Some journalists did not write reports because they supported collectivization; some journalists were coerced by threatened loss of visas; others had other reasons. Newspapers and magazines may have deferred to the Soviet Union or been more interested in other matters. In *Stalin's Apologist* (New York: Oxford University Press, 1990), S. J. Taylor asserted that "Walter Duranty, *The New York Times*'s Man in Moscow," had such prestige that had he written fully about events, his reports could have informed the world.

When authoritative reports on that genocide by starvation did finally appear, world outrage did not follow. Today, much material is available in libraries and on the Internet, including special materials at Ukrainian centers in the United States and Canada, but the subject still does not draw focused attention. A short list is given here as a starting point for interested readers.

Two books by Robert Conquest may be best known:

The Great Terror: Stalin's Purge of the Thirties. Revised Edition. New York: The Macmillan Company, 1973.
The Harvest of Sorrow: Soviet Collectivization and the Terror-Famine. London: Hutchinson, 1986.

In the first book, Conquest wrote (p. 45) that the famine of 1932–33 "can be blamed quite flatly on

Stalin," was "perhaps the only case in history of a purely man-made famine," but was "ignored," "denied," "concealed" so that the rest of the world was largely unaware.

In the second book, Conquest spoke again of that lack of awareness and examined Stalinist objectives to do away with private ownership of land and to end all resistance from stubbornly nationalistic Ukrainians. Conquest then examined the actions taken to achieve those objectives.

Conquest estimated—conservatively—that in those two years five million people in Ukraine died, one million non-Ukrainians died, and one million in North Caucasus died. Of that seven million total, three million were children. From 1930 to 1937, no fewer than fourteen million peasants died.

Miron Dolot as a youth witnessed the destruction of his Ukrainian village. His writings include:

Who Killed Them and Why? Harvard University Ukrainian Studies Fund. 1984.

Execution by Hunger. New York: W. W. Norton, 1985.

In the first book, a summary of facts about the assault on Ukraine, Dolot surveyed the sequence of events, the forces at work, assessments by observers, methods for estimating the number who died, and related matters.

In the second book, Dolot described in graphic detail the systematic killing of people and crushing of his village.

The United States Congress commissioned an "Investigation

of the Ukrainian Famine, 1932–1933." The "Report to Congress" from "The Commission on the Ukraine Famine" appeared in 1988. The report (pp. vi-vii) listed nineteen findings, including:

> It was a "man-made famine" and millions died.
> "Increasingly severe measures" were used "to extract the maximum quantity of grain from the peasants."
> Stalin knew about the situation and made it worse.
> "Joseph Stalin and those around him committed genocide against Ukrainians in 1932–1933."

For visual impact of that period, a short film, *Harvest of Despair*, is available. The film was produced by the Ukrainian Canadian Research & Documentation Committee, using archival footage that shows the dead and dying, the struggle and misery of the living.

Ukraine in World War II: Borderland Battlefield

During the 1930s, Adolf Hitler rose to power in Germany. In 1939, Germany and the USSR signed a nonaggression pact. In June 1941, the German army invaded the USSR with the granaries of Ukraine a prime objective. The destruction begun by Stalinist forces would be continued by Nazi troops. Suffering Ukrainians would continue to suffer and to die.

World War II in Ukraine was brutal and complex. The loss of life and property was incalculable; the history of the forces at work was, and is, difficult to establish.

The war put the world's two largest military forces into highly destructive combat. The invaders spared nothing in their path. The defenders destroyed everything usable as they retreated. With the complexity of attitudes indicated below, Ukrainians, organized and unorganized, resisted both powers. The extent and effects of resistance were so complex that one must consult a wide range of reference works to gain an understanding.

Ukraine, the borderland, was the battleground for back-and-forth fighting and a prize each army wanted. In summer 1939, Eastern Ukraine was part of the Soviet Union. Western Ukraine was held by Czechoslovakia, Poland, and Romania. Germany began the war 1 September 1939 with its invasion of Poland. On 17 September, the Soviet Union occupied east Poland, and on 28 September, Germany and the USSR partitioned Poland. Western Ukraine became part of the Soviet Union, which Western Ukrainians generally did not like.

Germany's invasion of Soviet territory began 22 June1941. Three million soldiers in 162 divisions took three major routes of attack, one of them straight through Ukraine's breadbasket on the way to Kyiv. (The other two were to the north, one going toward Moscow and the other toward Leningrad.) Stalin's purges of top military officers—as many as half those on duty—had weakened effectiveness of Soviet forces. German troops went across Ukraine quickly. For more than two years, the Nazis occupied most of Ukraine, but fighting never ceased in the eastern areas.

A selection of events can show the pattern of fighting. On 19 September, Germans entered Kyiv, on 16 October, took Odessa, and on 24 October, took Khar'kov, all in Eastern Ukraine. On 22 November, the Germans took Rostov, Russia; then, on 29 November, the Soviet army took Rostov back and went on the offensive in Ukraine. With Nazi forces outside Moscow, the severe Russian winter stopped the German advance.

In May 1942, Germans went on the offensive in Crimea, and Soviets counterattacked in the Khar'kov area. In July 1942, the Germans again took Rostov and in August were at Stalingrad but were once more slowed by the Russian winter and by Stalin's tactic of replacing thousands of annihilated Soviet soldiers with more thousands from another area. In February 1943, Soviets defeated German forces at Stalingrad. Two weeks later, Soviet forces recaptured Rostov and Khar'kov, but in March, Germans took Khar'kov again. The Red Army, strengthened by Allied aid, began achieving more victories, recapturing Ukrainian cities: Kyiv in November 1943, Kryvvy Rih (Krivoy Rog) in February 1944, Odessa in April, and Sevastopol (in Crimea) in May.

With the internal threat from Germany gone, Soviet forces on a wide front drove through Poland, Hungary, Yugoslavia, Czechoslovakia, Bulgaria, went into Germany in March 1945, and entered Berlin 21 April 1945. On 29 April, Germans in southern Austria surrendered, but the announcement was withheld until 2 May. After surrender of other territories on successive days, Germany surrendered unconditionally 7 May.

Ukrainians saw the 1941 German invasion in conflicting and ambivalent ways. Some Western Ukrainians thought the Nazis were liberating them from the Soviet Union. Some Ukrainians, Eastern and Western, thought Germany offered better chances for Ukrainian survival and independence but did nothing, while some number worked or fought with the Germans. Many Ukrainian civilians and members of the Red Army were dedicated Communists and fought the Nazis with full dedication. Some felt powerless between Germans and Soviets and were resigned to the worst. Some wanted to fight Germans or Russians or both. Some wanted to wait until Germans and Soviets wore each other down.

Western Ukrainians had already built an organized resistance movement against Poles, Czechs, and Romanians, beginning at the end of World War I. In 1929, the Organization of Ukrainian Nationalists (OUN) evolved from an earlier organization and endured across the years. The organization, which included idealists and pragmatists, theorists and activists, had as its primary goal independence and unity for Ukraine. OUN's military arm, the Ukrainian Insurgent Army (UPA), gained significant strength and ran effective campaigns against Soviet forces and later against German forces. There was a split in the OUN, but resistance lasted through World War II and continued thereafter.

Although some Eastern Ukrainians were strong defenders of the USSR, others were active in or supported the OUN, believing passionately that nothing and no one could be worse than the Communist Party and Joseph Stalin. The terrors of the 1930s had, however, left Eastern Ukraine too weak to do much against the USSR. During the war, Eastern Ukrainians were recruited (forced) by the Soviets to commit terrorist acts against the occupying Nazi army, but for each of those acts, the Ukrainian population paid a heavy price in retribution from Nazi forces.

Estimates of Ukrainians killed during World War II are two to two and one-half million military and four to four and one-half million civilians, a total of six to seven million—in addition to those lost to genocide.

As many as 28,000 villages and more than 700 towns were destroyed. Comparable numbers of industries, schools, medical facilities, and libraries were destroyed or seriously damaged.

Over three million young Ukrainians—along with other millions from other countries—were sent to Germany as farm and factory laborers. Technically, the forced laborers, because they were not in military service, were not prisoners of war, but they were prisoners in war. They have also been called slaves. Certainly, they worked the worst of jobs under the worst of conditions and were treated badly in the process.

They were interned in what is generally referred to as "forced-labor camps," sometimes as "concentration camps," sometimes as "slave camps."

One Woman: Five Lives; Five Countries

A *Los Angeles Times* article written by Mary Williams Walsh was titled "Judge Awards Back Pay to W.W.II Slave Laborer" (6 November 1997, p. A12). In the course of explaining the lawsuit and the award, the author referred to the estimated number of people "the Nazis enslaved."

Forced by armed guards to work long hours, allowed inadequate food and rest, and punished brutally, a majority of the laborers died of malnutrition, disease, or physical abuse. Those from USSR who survived the war faced imprisonment or execution when they were sent back to USSR after the war, for Soviet authorities considered anyone who did not resist (which would have meant death) a traitor.

Ukraine 1945–1951: Closed to the West

At the end of World War II, all of Ukraine was war torn, ravaged, depleted, but the spirit of nationalism showed some life. Eastern Ukraine and Western Ukraine, reunited in 1939, were together after centuries of separation, and Ukrainian territory increased with the drawing of boundaries in the west. As soon as the Germans were out of Western Ukraine, the Soviets subjected that region to the same harsh measures as in Eastern Ukraine. In Western Ukraine, OUN and UPA resisted Soviet rule for at least another decade, with certainly some measure of support from Eastern Ukraine. Resistance to collectivization, Russification, and suppression of the church sent hundreds of thousands of Ukrainians to labor camps in the 1940s. Ukrainians had a reputation for being the most difficult prisoners.

At Yalta and Potsdam in 1945, Stalin, obsessed by the need to preclude another invasion from the West, established a Soviet sphere of influence in Eastern Europe. After the war, he solidified control of territories liberated by Soviet forces and extracted heavy penalties from Germany and Italy.

Russification, ignored during the war, was resumed with intensity. Use of the Russian language was required ex-

243

cept in the most ordinary discourse. Integration of Ukrainian SSR into the USSR was a continuing process. The Ukrainian Communist Party disappeared into the CommunistParty of the Soviet Union. Nikita Kruschev and native Ukrainian Leonid Brezhnev held high Party posts in Ukraine, then moved easily from Kyiv to Moscow.

In 1946, another attack on artists, writers, and scientists for being bourgeois nationalists began. Advocates of Ukrainian culture and nationalism had to adhere to the Party line. After about two years, the attack abated, then resumed after two more years. That seemed to have been a pattern in the past and would continue to be.

As already noted, attitudes about nationality and culture, about the nature of Russians and Ukrainians and their relationship were extremely complex. Who needed the other? Who wanted the other? Who identified with the other? Ukrainians who most resented outside control and wanted nothing less than a free and independent Ukraine were prob ably sustained by a belief that the western world would have to move against Soviet totalitarianism.

On 5 March 1946, Sir Winston Churchill used the expression "iron curtain" to describe Stalin's closing of life in the East from the eyes of the West. The Cold War had begun. Ukraine, which had not been free or open, was more tightly closed.

Ukraine 1951–1971: From Stalin to Khrushchev to Brezhnev

The Russian word "soviet," which means "council" in English was used for each of the many workers' committees formed to press the 1905 revolution. Such units became the bases for political structure— a soviet for each set of workers in each place with representatives to a higher level, finally reaching the Supreme Soviet. Eventually, everything official was done by committees; individuals didn't speak on their own. The committee structure and the attitudes and methods that developed led to the bureaucracy that as much as anything else led to the downfall of the USSR.

The system never worked. In *The Harvest of Sorrow* Robert Conquest documented farm and industrial production from the 1920s to the 1980s. Under Soviet collectivization, never did farms produce the grain or meat expected. The food available per person remained low. The only high figure was the number of official Party directives sent to farmers.

Stalin began five-year plans with stated objectives. Soviet propaganda announced the plans at the beginning and proclaimed success no matter the extent of the failure. Bureaucrats who knew nothing of crops or livestock but were responsible for increases gave senseless, counterproductive orders. (To increase meat production, one functionary ordered all dairy cows slaughtered.)

Farm machinery was to have been the key to increased production, but the factories didn't produce enough machines, and the ones that made it to the farms often didn't run. Scientists were selected on basis of ideology, not science, and crop yields did not increase as projected.

Added to the inefficiencies were the intrigues.

Soviet officials were moved from job to job, promoted and demoted, occasionally purged and then redeemed. Such movement resulted from secret committee action, individual power plays, or both. Lenin had wanted to remove Stalin; somehow Stalin was not removed. To follow or understand the passing of power would require detailed study.

When Stalin died 5 March 1953 amid speculation that he was planning another purge, Nikita Khrushchev became first secretary of the Central Committee. After the war,

Khrushchev was charged with restoring agricultural production in Ukraine, then returned to Moscow in 1949 and in 1953 was in position to replace Stalin. In 1956, Khrushchev denounced Stalin and later demoted Stalin's associates.

In the period immediately after Stalin's death, Ukrainians gave more expression to feelings of nationalism and ethnic Ukrainian Communist leaders became more nationalistic against Khrushchev. Concessions of one sort or another were made in response to Ukrainian activism. There was a continuing tug of war within and between Ukraine and the Central Soviet. For Ukrainians, the question was how much to push and how much to accommodate. For the Central Soviet, the question was whether to suppress or to use Ukrainian culture and nationalism to the advantage of USSR. (When repression of nationalism didn't work, nationalism became a tool for manipulation.)

Khrushchev increased power of officials at national levels in all republics and gave Ukraine some international visibility—even if more show than substance. In 1954, to mark 300 years of Ukraine's being part of Russia, Khrushchev made Crimea part of Ukraine.

Communist hard-liners protested Khrushchev's softer line in the USSR and internationally. Khrushchev tried to protect himself by increasing pressures in Eastern Europe, attempting to influence Third World nations, and, in August 1961, erecting the Berlin Wall. None of that was enough. Khrushchev was deposed as premier and Party head in October 1964 and succeeded by Leonid Brezhnev, who had been instrumental in removing Khrushchev. As head of the Party, Brezhnev moved back toward centralization and away from giving authority to the republics.

In the 1960s, at the same time that Khrushchev was giving ground to the hard-liners, Ukrainian writers and artists were pushing against Russification. Underground publications called for reading of history the way historian Mykailo Hrushevsky read it. Activity was widespread. Even Communist leaders protested loss of local control to the Kremlin. Then, thousands of writers, publishers, artists, filmmakers, scholars, teachers, students, and others were arrested, tried, and sent to labor camps or psychiatric prisons.

In the 1970s, Brezhnev relaxed tensions between the USSR and the United States with agreements on scientific cooperation and the first strategic arms limitation treaty (SALT I). Restrictions on emigration were also somewhat relaxed.

In Ukraine, however, the repressions continued. By the end of the 1970s, open challenges to centralization were replaced by underground activity. By then, the composition of the dissenters had changed because a much greater portion of the population was urban and better educated. Discontented workers were more likely to strike or engage in work stoppages.

Brezhnev, reelected Party chief in 1981, died 10 November 1982 and was quickly replaced by Yuri V. Andropov.

Ukraine: A Nation at Last

After the death of Leonid Brezhnev in November 1982, changes in the USSR were fast and frequent. Simply to record them would be daunting, to explain them next to impossible.

Yuri Andropov succeeded Brezhnev as the Communist Party's general secretary, became president in 1983, and died 9 February 1984. Konstantin Chernenko succeeded Andropov as general secretary, became president in April, and died 10 March 1985. Andropov was in office thirteen months, Chernenko eleven.

Mikhail Gorbachev then became general secretary of

the Communist Party and in 1988 became president. Gorbachev set other kinds of change into motion. He saw that secrecy, corruption, control from above, and entrenched bureaucracies were leading to a collapse of the Soviet system. To him, the idea of communism was good and valid, but the system was not operating in terms of the principles of communism, nor was it functioning well enough for the USSR to compete in the world market, so he began a program of reform. He called for *glasnost*—openness—in social and political matters: a free press and open discussion of issues. He called for *perestroika*—restructuring of government from top to bottom: more involvement of elected officials in all the republics and less involvement by the Party.

Ukraine supported Gorbachev's *glasnost* and *perestroika* but went its own way on policies. Under *perestroika*, various dissenting groups formed for particular purposes—implementation of Helsinki Accords, cultural advancement, religious freedom, youth involvement—with names such as Ukrainian Helsinki Union, Ukrainian Popular Movement, Ukrainian Association of Independent Creative Intelligentsia, Ukrainian Democratic Party, Ukrainian Language Society.

In 1989, a popular front for such groups was organized to stand in opposition to the Communist Party. The Ukrainian Popular Movement for Restructuring was referred to as *Rukh*, the Ukrainian word for "movement." *Rukh* called for independence for the nation but also for protection of individuals, tolerance for all groups, and creation of a free market. The Communist Party responded strongly, but in the March 1990 elections to the Ukrainian Supreme Soviet, *Rukh* candidates were quite successful in Kyiv and L'vov (principal cities in Eastern and Western Ukraine) and became a forceful voice in the Supreme Soviet in Moscow.

Rukh was instrumental in gaining passage of a law

guaranteeing Ukrainian as the state language and the primary language in work and education, except in Crimea where Russians were a majority. *Rukh* also helped to force the retirement of a repressive party First Secretary who held power for fifteen years.

Rukh leaders recognized the necessity for accommodating different ethnic and political groups in different parts of the country. The independence movement was strongest in Western Ukraine, where demonstrations of 200,000 people occurred and where there was an independent workers' movement. That movement was moderately strong in central Ukraine and weakest in the eastern area closest to Russia. More Russians lived there; more Ukrainians in that area spoke Russian, identified with Russia, and favored contact with Russia. In Dnepropetrovsk and Donetsk, however, miners went on strike July 1989 and later worked with *Rukh*.

Soviet censorship relaxed after 1985. People began remembering events of the 1910s, 1920s, and 1930s. History was reexamined from a Ukrainian pre-Revolutionary perspective and not as the Stalinists rewrote it. The blue and yellow Ukrainian flag reappeared in the late 1980s, as did the Ukrainian trident.

Nationalist activity accelerated in country after country of the USSR in 1989. It was a volatile year in Ukraine, much more so than this sketch indicates, and is probably what prompted Gorbachev to spend five days in Kyiv in the winter of 1989, trying to convince workers that they needed the USSR.

One earlier event put a literal and figurative cloud over Ukraine. On 26 April 1986, the world's worst nuclear reactor disaster occurred at the Chernobyl power plant. An uncontrolled reaction caused a steam explosion that released a massive amount of radiation into the atmosphere. Fallout was greatest in Ukraine and Belarus but spread across eastern and northern Europe and into Great Britain. Nearby towns were evacuated.

As many as 8,000 died and countless others were made ill. The popular television program *60 Minutes* has been to the site twice, showing the harm to people and animals and the continuing threat of leaking radiation.

The USSR kept the accident secret until radioactivity was measured in Sweden and then did not disclose the extent of the fallout. Five days after the disaster, Soviet television, making things seem normal, broadcast a May Day program from Kyiv (eighty miles, 130 kilometers, south of Chernobyl and under heavy fallout). The program featured Ukrainian folk dancers in Ukrainian costumes with smiling children watching.

Because Ukraine sorely needs sources of electrical power, other reactors at the plant remained in operation.

The power plant disaster heightened awareness of other sources of pollution. The same inefficiency and incompetence that affected the management of industry and agriculture ignored pollution from those sources. For decades, there was no control over what went into the air, water, and soil—or for soil lost to erosion—and the damage was extreme. In the late 1980s, some groups started to work for measures to revive the environment.

The activities of 1989 continued, and in July 1990, the Supreme Soviet granted Ukraine sovereignty but not independence.

In June 1991, Boris Yeltsin, who was aided in his political rise by Gorbachev and then opposed him, became the first popularly elected president of the Russian Republic.

Gorbachev faced pressures from many groups: hard-line Communists, free-market reformers, nationalists, and others. Hard-liners attempted a coup in August 1991. Yeltsin dramatically led the fight that ended the coup. Change occurred more rapidly after that.

On 24 August 1991, the Ukrainian parliament passed a provisional declaration of independence from the Soviet Union and formed a new government. The next day, all political prisoners were freed and property of the Communist Party seized. In September, the Communist Party of the Soviet Union was banned. On 1 December, in a national referendum, Ukrainian voters upheld the declaration of independence.

In that election, Leonid Kravchuk, formerly chairman of Ukraine's Supreme Soviet, became the nation's first popularly elected president. The banned Communist Party converted itself to the Socialist Party, and many members, along with Kravchuk, stayed in power by co-opting *Rukh* positions. *Rukh* provided opposition, but leaders split in terms of the best path for Ukraine to take and formed new political parties.

Yeltsin was leading the fight to dismantle the Party apparatus and to replace the USSR with the Commonwealth of Independent States (CIS). Ukraine and Belarus joined Russia as founding members of CIS. In December 1991, the USSR voted itself out of existence, and Gorbachev resigned as Soviet president.

In that series of unlikely and incredible events, Ukraine became an independent nation—an independent nation with major problems. Collectivization, man-made famine, war, Russification, purges, draining of resources, Chernobyl, pollution, loss of people, loss of villages and towns: those and other harms had left a nation with an extremely shaky base on which to build. Relations with the Russian Federation would also remain a major matter.

Nadia Diuk and Adrian Karatnycky, in *The Hidden Nations,* mentioned earlier, wrote of a poet named Evhen Sverstyuk who saw a more damaging effect: the failure of people in totalitarian states to think through the results of actions and programs because any deviation is too danger ous. Otherwise, books and articles offering analyses and remedies would have appeared.

There was independence, but old ways of thinking would impede progress. From the outset, the president and parliament were in conflict, and failure to achieve economic reform led to early elections in 1994.

Short-term and long-term objectives for the economy conflicted. Immediate solutions would work against building the base for economic growth.

Efforts continued to reform the economy, increase industrial and agricultural production, counter pollution, privatize property, and otherwise build on the Ukrainian base of rich natural resources and industrious people. Indications of openness and effort could be seen in deregulation of prices on food, transportation, and other services, in the functioning of a free press, in development of opposition parties, and in joining international programs.

Foreign aid helped. At a critical point for the economy and for the disarmament process in early 1994, the United States significantly increased the amount of aid being supplied.

The first years of independence did not make conditions significantly better, but Ukraine did become a nation, and some observers contend that the potential is there for a strong nation.

Footnotes

[1] The word *Ukraine* was derived from the Slavic word, *okraina,* meaning "borderland," and the territory that became modern Ukraine has for centuries been an east-west border between Russia and Europe. Russia lay to the east and north, and what became the nations of Poland, Czechoslovakia, and Hungary lay to the west. To the south were the Sea of Azov, the Black Sea, Moldavia, and Rumania. Much of Ukraine is part of the great Eurasian Steppe, flat grasslands covered with rich, black soil, Ukraine's greatest resource.

[2] Grisha tried to track down where exactly our parents were in Central Asia. The NKVD answered his many letters in 1936 with two cryptic documents which stated only that our parents were shipped out by rail toward the Baikal region of Central Asia by order of the Odessa NKVD. Those two torn, yellowed government forms were all that I was left with, and I have since given them to the Historic Museum in Bound Brook, New Jersey.

[3] In any city or village, those wagons could be seen if one was out on the streets early. It is not easy to look at a pile of corpses. Today, television news reports show pictures of the dead from many areas of the world. Maybe television viewers get used to the sight. But it's different to stand on a street in a familiar neighborhood, see a wagon stop and workers lift a body from the street to the wagon, then see that action repeated a short distance away. One does not, I think, get used to that.

[4] Everyone probably assumed children shake off illnesses and recover faster than adults. Today, when I'm sick, I still tend to ignore it. I was conditioned to think of feeling ill

as being normal.

⁵That question of which year I was born arose again. Possibly, Jasha had been using 1926 for the schools in Kyiv, and Grisha told me to use 1925. For some period of time, I probably mixed the two years, which means my memory of what age I was at certain times may be inconsistent, and even if I could locate school records, they would not help. At some time, I'm not sure when, I did begin using 1925 consistently.

⁶It would not be until years later that I became angry that the man was doing with me what he wished. It would be years before I realized that I was his convenient victim for relieving his sexual desire. I had no idea that the human male can become like an animal when he wants to have sex, that some men succeed by force, that when desire becomes strong enough, those men become strong—and dangerous. And it would be years before I realized that a woman could actually have any desire for sex.

⁷I kept my painful, dirty secret. I could not and would not reveal to anyone, anytime, anywhere, what did happen to me—not until I'd written most of this book and finally realized I had to write that, too.

⁸I'm lucky they didn't adopt me. They would've taken me to Russia, and I would have never gotten to the West. Actually, I was lucky that there were no reprisals from that couple or from the factory manager. It was dangerous to be noticed or to say too much. My tendency to wander, to explore, and to start talking with anyone, anywhere could have gotten me into trouble.

⁹To this day, I become nervous when I hear that a peace treaty has been signed. I expect it to lead to war.

[10]The Soviets did have their natural weapons: harsh winters, lice, and mud. Add to that usual list the long distances across the Soviet Union, and the result was that Western invaders could not sustain operations.

[11]Only today, in the 1990s, when child abuse and sexual abuse are openly discussed, can I write about those matters and can, at last, understand why I never revealed anything to anyone, why I had difficulty with relationships. Understanding does not, however, remove the pain and guilt.

[12]People in the USSR lived with the fear, the terror, that any knock on the door, any directive by anyone could mean being ripped out of the life they knew and sent to prison or to their death. The knock or the directive did not have to be from someone who had authority; everyone learned to fear everyone, known or unknown. Anyone who has lived with such fear does not lose it quickly or easily—if ever. That fear was deep within my system and would rise again whenever my instinct for survival returned. In some periods, I simply had no hope, no desire for life. In no period had I thought of a future; I didn't think that I would live to be twenty. Today, many years later, I understand that the fear, the terror, that the Stalinist system instilled became as much a part of life as some incurable disease, one that might be arrested but that could appear at any time. I was not free from that fear for many years—and still, I can feel a trace of panic when my mail contains an official-looking envelope, or when someone starts questioning me.

[13]In those years, I had to wait "a few days" on so many occasions that in later years I could not remember how many days passed on any particular occasion. Everything became "a week or two" or "two or three days." Waiting for the train was two or three days.

[14]For fifteen years, bread had been my primary food, often my only food. When, at last, I began to have some choice about what to eat, I let another fifteen years pass before I chose, once again, to eat bread.

[15]After the war, Soviets considered anyone who worked in German plants a traitor. We teenagers—without any training or equipment or leadership—were supposed to have sabotaged the German war machine. If I had been found and sent back, I would have been classified a traitor and sent to Siberia.

[16]Food had been the central concern of my daily life for the previous fifteen years. I didn't know how unwashed I was or how little attention I gave to my appearance. (I learned something of such matters when I was in the opera in Simferapol, but that experience was a fantasy.) After I reached Fanti's house, cleanliness and appearance replaced food as the central concerns of daily life. Collectivization, planned starvation, and a world war were overwhelming, overriding historical events, and I have struggled to handle my memories of those events, but the memory of that simple change from unwashed to washed always stops me. The big question is: how did I survive? The stubborn little question is: How could I have lived without baths and showers and shampoos and such?

[17]I've been asked what I thought Gabriel's or Grisha's response would have been if they could have seen me on the runway and then joined me for dinner in the hotel dining room. I can say, of course, they would have been pleased, proud, happy, and would have said their little Genia deserved no less. But under that answer is lingering anger and sadness that my brothers, who had such capacity to enjoy and understand life, and who tried to make their country a better place, had their lives drained away from them senselessly and selfishly. They were the ones who deserved more, much more.

[18]Today, it seems vain of me to sit here calling myself beautiful. Even if one hundred fashion critics called me beautiful, it would still be vain for me to do so.

[19]It is necessary to mention here that postwar Ukraine continued for decades to suffer under Communist tyranny. Ukrainians who pushed against Russification were systematically purged. Thousands of writers, publishers, artists, filmmakers, scholars, teachers, students, and others were arrested, tried, and sent to labor camps or psychiatric prisons. Anyone who might have had a thought of his own was out, and only those who followed the Kremlin line were in.

[20]My greatest remorse in life is that I did not leave Gene in the Brentwood school. There he could have been secure and developed his abilities. All my life, I had frequently and abruptly moved from one place to another. It was my conditioning, so I moved Gene—and would continue to move him—thinking it was for the best. It would be many years before I realized fully the damage changing schools caused.

Order Form

Eugenia Dallas
6702 Hillpark Drive
Hollywood, CA 90068
Tel - (323) 876-8294   Fax – (323) 874-0761

One Woman: Five Lives; Five Countries by Eugenia Dallas　　_____ copies at $16.95- - - -_____

Please add $2.50 for shipping and handling for up to 5 books. Add $1.30 for each book over 5

<u>Check or money order only.</u>　-　.　　_____

Total:　　_____

Questions may be addressed to the author at the above address.